Megamedia

Megamedia

How Giant Corporations Dominate
Mass Media, Distort Competition,
and Endanger Democracy

Dean Alger

ROWMAN & LITTLEFIELD PUBLISHERS, INC.
Lanham • Boulder • New York • Oxford

This book is dedicated to the Holloway family, from whence I came.

ROWMAN & LITTLEFIELD PUBLISHERS, INC.

Published in the United States of America
by Rowman & Littlefield Publishers, Inc.
4720 Boston Way, Lanham, Maryland 20706

12 Hid's Copse Road
Cumnor Hill, Oxford OX2 9JJ, England

British Library Cataloguing in Publication Information Available

Library of Congress Cataloging-in-Publication Data

Alger, Dean.
   Megamedia : how giant corporations dominate mass media, distort
competition, and endanger democracy / Dean Alger.
      p. cm.
   Includes bibliographical references and index.
   ISBN 0–8476–8389–3 (alk. paper).
   1. Mass media—Ownership.   2. Democracy.   I. Title.
P90.E25A44   1998
338.8'26130223—DC21   98-21270
                                                                                  CIP

Printed in the United States of America

∞ ™ The paper used in this publication meets the minimum requirements of
American National Standard for Information Sciences—Permanence of Paper for
Printed Library Materials, ANSI Z39.48–1984.

Contents

Preface

This book was born of a deep belief in democracy and many years of efforts to contribute to its enhancement—from teaching basic college courses on government and politics to serving as an analyst for new media to working on election-reform initiatives. Regarding those crucial vehicles of the dialogue of democracy, the mass media, I take very seriously the "we the people" opening to the U.S. Constitution. The mass media are in a profoundly unique category of activity, as is clearly signaled in the First Amendment. If the trends, impacts, and implications reviewed in this book are correct, it should serve as a clarion call for efforts to ensure that those crucibles of common discussion genuinely serve the needs of the general public and the democratic process, rather than being primarily the captive, big-bucks-generating organs of a few private empire builders.

Especially since I have an academic background, it is also important to note that this book is intended for a general intelligent "trade" audience, as well as for people in public affairs and the academic world. Therefore, it has not been written in the more formalistic, jargon-laden manner of many academic books. I certainly hope that academics will nonetheless feel that it makes a contribution to the discussion of this momentous issue. Nor is the book as a whole a pure social science study, although it draws on social science.

This book is not the definitive work on this large and complex subject. Besides the obvious fact that this story continues to unfold, the resources for a truly full-scale investigation were not available. This is, however, a substantial, well-researched description and analysis of the issue. I also hope that this book will be sufficiently compelling to stimulate subsequent support for a larger systematic research and assessment of these developments (research that should include professionals with backgrounds such as my own in political science and media studies, and in economics).

I would like to thank numerous people for their assistance and encouragement in this effort. Perhaps most notably, I have been inspired by Marvin Kalb and his deep commitment to the role that journalism and the media in general must play in a democracy and a civil society. Others who have contributed suggestions, critiques, materials, and other support are Mark Anderson, Ed Baumeister, John Busterna, U.S. Senator Byron Dorgan, Ellen Mickiewicz, Richard Parker, Robert Spitzer, and Robert Trager. As always, however, the responsibility for interpretations rests with the author. For work as research assistants, thanks to Dan "Sherlock" Husman, my intrepid investigative RA, and to Jeff Fox, as well as to my continuing southern California RA, Virginia Porter (who doubles as my aunt). Thanks to my editor at Rowman & Littlefield, Jennifer Knerr, for recognizing the importance of this subject and for various helpful editorial suggestions as the book proceeded. Thanks also go to Brent "Boom Boom" Williams for continuing support and encouragement.

—Dean Alger, Minneapolis, June 1998

A Note on the Reference Style

Since some readers feel distracted by numerous reference note numbers in the text of a book, I have used a method for reference citations that is different from the traditional one. To minimize disturbance in the flow of reading, reference numbers are included in the text only at the end of each formal section or, where the section is long, at the end of the discussion of a particular subject or logical grouping. Simply, then, all the quotes or other matters requiring citation following a given reference number up to the next reference number in the text are collected under the corresponding endnote at the end of the book. Under each reference number, the citations are given in order of their appearance in the text starting after the previous number; in the endnotes, the corresponding passages are identified by key words where the reference is not obvious.

1

The March of Megamedia

....

Media Moguls, the Talk of the (Global) Town, and "the Conversation of Democracy"

"No self-respecting dead fish would want to be wrapped in a Murdoch paper." This was the observation of Mike Royko, syndicated newspaper columnist from Chicago, on the typical sensationalist, sleazy, crime-splashed newspaper produced by News Corp., the multinational multi-media empire of Australian-turned-American Rupert Murdoch.

That statement by Chicago's legendary columnist is a funny line about the showcase example of an issue of tremendous importance—for nothing less than the future of democracy in America and other parts of the world, and for the quality of life in our societies. How so? The most important part of it was well expressed by Bill Moyers (with his unique experience in media and public affairs) when he referred to "news as the conversation of democracy."

The news media are absolutely central to the functioning of democracy today; and entertainment and other features and programs in the mass media, in the aggregate, have powerful effects on society more generally. How news organizations in particular are operated and, ultimately, who owns and controls the main media we all rely on for information, exchange of ideas, and basic images are fundamental in determining whether the democratic process works as intended, or whether it falters or is subverted. This is why the First Amendment to the U.S. Constitution—the prime pillar of the Bill of Rights—has as its centerpiece freedom of the press and speech.

The essence of the First Amendment's central provision is to ensure that the principal sources of information and ideas for "we the people" are genuinely independent and diverse voices for "the conversation of democracy." That's what democracy is: a "marketplace of ideas," where a wide range of people and organizations have a real opportunity to express information and ideas for all of us to ponder. Correspondingly,

1

we should be greatly concerned if much or most of the main media fall increasingly under the control of a small number of giant corporations and extremely wealthy and willful people, especially when such people are inclined to use the powerful media of mass communication for their own political and economic purposes. Thus, consider the following observation made by Ted Turner:

> I worry about how much control this man is getting. . . . Like the former Führer, Murdoch controls the media for his own personal benefit—for money and power. . . . He thinks that his media should be used by him to further his own political goals. He's also a scumbag because he "goes downmarket" so much in his papers. ["Going downmarket" means using scandal, sex, and splashy crime to appeal to the lowest level of human interests.]

Magazines, as well as newspapers, are principal print sources of the material we all use to participate in democracy. Some special newspapers and magazines have built reputations as independent, distinguished, leading voices in our democracy—and in society in other respects. Should we be concerned if many newspapers, traditionally the foundation of the news media, and if some special magazines and newspapers come under the control of media empire builders who seem to have little commitment to making significant contributions to the conversation of democracy—and seem interested only or principally in milking their "media properties" for as much money as possible? Consider the following comment by author Thomas Maier on S. I. Newhouse Jr. and his family-owned Newhouse/Advance Publications multimedia empire:

> A certain duplicity . . . helped ease Si Newhouse's purchase of the magazine [the *New Yorker* with $180 million in the mid-1980s]. . . . More than any other publication in modern times, the *New Yorker* was a success driven by editorial excellence and became a must read for a generation that prized the written word. . . . [But] Newhouse magazines . . . really knew no other world than one of marketing gimmicks, bottom-line economies, and ultimate subservience of the news side to business needs." . . . Ultimately, what can citizens expect of the only newspaper in a major city that reaps a fortune year after year and yet remains mediocre at best? Can America afford to trust publishers like Si Newhouse?

The essence of the First Amendment's free press provision is to have media sources that are genuinely independent and diverse. That independence is to ensure that the news produced from that source is beholden to no one—not government, not interest groups, not corporations with big financial interests in various areas. But what if the TV networks, for example, those powerful media forces that enter tens of millions of Americans' homes each day, are controlled by large corporate conglomerates, with economic interests in a wide variety of market areas? Could the independence of those prime-time news sources be compromised by corporate conflicts of interest? When giant General Electric Corp. took over the NBC-TV network in the mid-1980s, GE Chief Executive Officer Jack Welch installed GE man Bob Wright as head of NBC. Author Ken Auletta recounts:

> Jabbing his finger at [NBC News President Larry] Grossman, Welch reminded him: "You work for GE!" . . . "News is not the core of the asset" [at NBC, said Welch]. This was his financial calculus. . . . Gerry Solomon had been at NBC News for seventeen years . . . but when his contract expired in 1991 he said he might want out. Here's why: "The argument we hear all the time is that quality counts. But the definition of quality has changed at the networks [since their takeover by corporate conglomerates]. They are not talking about the quality of the reporter, they are talking about the 'quality' of the payoff to the network." He meant that Welch and Wright were talking about costs. Yet journalists talked about "ephemeral things" like "credibility" and the "calling" [of being a journalist], and the "quality" of the news product. "GE doesn't know these things because they can't be quantified."

Books, too, are vital elements in the conversation of democracy, and corporate conglomerate control is having an effect here as well. Novelist and literary figure E. L. Doctorow said of the increasing impact of corporate conglomerate control of book publishing:

> Discovering the idealistic and mental impediments to an efficient, profitmaking machinery, the conglomerate management will eliminate them—change taste, simplify what is complex, find the personnel who will give them what they want, and gradually change the nature of books themselves, and create something else—almost-books, non-books, book pods, just as foods today are packaged for quick sale and mass distribution with artificial flavors.[1]

There are many other such comments from similarly astute observers. Are they accurate and fair, and if so, what are the implications for our society? How has control of the main media by such moguls, with their increasingly massive megamedia corporations, affected the central forums of democracy, newspapers and news shows, magazines and books? Another perceptive observer of the media pointed out, in a speech to a convention of TV broadcasters: "The flow of ideas, the capacity to make informed choices, the ability to criticize, all of the assumptions on which political democracy rests, depend largely on communications. And you are the guardians of the most powerful and effective means of communication ever designed." That observer was President John F. Kennedy.[2]

It is vital to take a close look at how the patterns of control and use of the principal means of mass communication are affecting our society—in America, in Europe, and around the world. Control of the mass media is increasingly concentrated in fewer and fewer giant megamedia corporations. Is the magnitude and nature of that control diminishing and degrading the news and other public affairs articles and programs and thereby endangering our democratic process? Are those patterns of ownership and control, along with some related factors, increasingly degrading feature and entertainment fare in the media and thereby having a negative effect on society in general? If current trends and directions continue, are there likely to be even greater such consequences in the future?

Communication and Democracy

From Great Britain to South Africa to the former Soviet Union to the People's Republic of China, the final years of the twentieth century have been highlighted world-wide by events and developments signaling the crucial role of freedom of speech and press—and the inadequacies, in practice, of the public function of a full and meaningful flow of information and ideas from diverse, independent sources.

In the American tradition, the freedoma of speech and press guaranteed in the First Amendment to the U.S. Constitution have been interpreted as providing special protections for the news media. The news media are, in fact, the only type of private economic organizations given such special mention and protection in the U.S. Constitution. But what is the ultimate purpose of such a special protection? The protection is a means to an end, but what is the end itself? Founding Father and key architect of the American system of government James Madison memorably expressed the ultimate purpose of freedom for the news media: "A popular government without popular information, or the means of acquiring it, is but a prologue to a farce or a tragedy—or perhaps both." In its Code of Ethics, the Society of Professional Journalists in the United States spelled out the meaning of that thought: "The primary purpose of gathering and distributing news and opinion is to serve the general welfare by informing the people and enabling them to make judgements on the issues of the time." This responsibility was characterized in the code as "a public trust"—as it has been in the main communications law in the United States.

Through regular entertainment programs as well as through news and public affairs publications and shows, the media's presentations are prime, pervasive presences in people's lives and have profound impacts on their perceptions of the world, images of leaders, notions about appropriate style and behavior, and other basic aspects of our culture. A number of social science studies have shown that the media are powerful agenda-setters for the public and have a significant impact on the political process. And many studies have shown that the media are doing a poor job of providing citizens with information and analysis on policy issues and candidates' qualifications, largely because news operations are increasingly focused on the political game, conflict, and scandal-chasing.

A thoughtful report at midcentury by the distinguished Commission on Freedom of the Press noted that the mass media "can facilitate thoughts and discussion. [Or] they can stifle it. They can advance the progress of civilization or they can thwart it. They can debase and vulgarize mankind. . . . They can play up or down the news and its significance, foster and feed emotions, create complacent fictions and blind spots. . . . Their scope and power are increasing every day as new instruments become available to them." All of that applies much more powerfully as we end the twentieth century and move into the new millennium.

Clearly, then, who owns and controls these powerful means of mass communication and how the media are used to convey—or to distort or fail to convey—information and images is of critical importance to society in general and the democratic process in specific; the dialogue of democracy is especially dependent on these pervasive means of mass communication.[3]

The March of Megamedia

Earlier Developments in the Megamedia Era

1981
Rupert Murdoch and his News Corp., owner of major print and broadcast media in Australia and Great Britain, as well as nonmedia businesses, takes control of the *Times* of London, long one of the world's greatest newspapers and a genuine institution in Britain. In the 1970s, Murdoch and company had bought Britain's two sleaziest tabloid newspapers, the *Sun* and *News of the World*, as well as the *New York Post* and *New York* magazine.

1984

Rupert Murdoch secures effective control of major Hollywood movie studio and film library Twentieth Century Fox.

1984–1985

Capital Cities Corp., a multimedia company, with the assistance of billionaire investor Warren Buffett, takes control of the ABC-TV network.

1985

Lawrence Tisch and his $17.5 billion Loews Corp. takes control of the CBS-TV network. Loews Corp. includes Lorrillard tobacco, CNA insurance, and other subsidiaries and investments.

General Electric, one of the ten largest industrial corporations in America, with tens of billions of dollars in revenues, takes control of the NBC-TV network, along with RCA Corp., which had owned NBC.

Rupert Murdoch and company buy the six Metromedia TV stations, located in the largest U.S. markets, for nearly $2 billion. With his new TV stations, Murdoch forms a new American TV network, Fox Television.

Later 1980s

Giant German multimedia corporation Bertelsmann buys out American book publishers Doubleday, Bantam Books, and Dell.

Simon & Schuster swallows up venerable academic publisher Prentice Hall and then is bought out by industrial and commercial conglomerate Gulf+Western Corp. Later Paramount corporation, whose holdings include major film and TV production facilities and a movie theater chain, buys out Gulf+Western to become the conglomerate Paramount Communications.

Rupert Murdoch and News Corp. buy out the distinguished American publishing house Harper & Row, which then merges with William Collins publishers of Britain, establishing one of the largest English-language publishers, HarperCollins.

Earlier in the 1980s the Newhouse multimedia empire had bought the book publisher Random House, along with Alfred A. Knopf, Ballantine Books, Vintage Books, Crown Books, the Condé Nast group of magazines, and the respected magazine the *New Yorker*.

1988
Sony electronics corporation buys CBS records for $2 billion.

1989
In a $14.1 billion deal, Time Inc. buys the film, television, and recorded-music giant Warner Communications. Time was publisher of books and such leading magazines as *Time, Sports Illustrated,* and *People* and controlling owner of the second biggest cable TV system as well as leading cable TV channel HBO. The new megamedia corporation became Time Warner.

Sony buys a big piece of Hollywood, Columbia Pictures and TriStar movie studios, for $4.9 billion.

1994
Viacom multimedia and industrial corporation takes control of Paramount Communications for $9.6 billion, as well as Blockbuster Entertainment, the huge video store chain, for $8.4 billion.

1995
May–June: **The Telecommunications Competition and Deregulation Act is introduced into the U.S. Congress** and begins moving through the legislative process, with powerful boosts from many of the multibillion-dollar megamedia corporations.

Early July: America's largest newspaper chain, Gannett, which also has broadcasting properties, buys Multimedia Inc., with its series of newspapers and TV and radio stations, for $1.7 billion.

Late July: Entertainment giant Disney buys Capital Cities–ABC for $19 billion, creating the world's largest megamedia corporation.

August: Industrial and broadcasting giant Westinghouse Corp. buys out CBS for $5.4 billion.

September: In a $7.2 billion deal, Time Warner buys out Turner Communications, owner of prime cable TV channels CNN, TBS, and TNT; a major classic American film library; and the Atlanta Braves and Hawks professional sports teams. By some estimates, this surpassed even the Disney–Capital Cities–ABC conglomeration, making it the largest multimedia corporation in the world. Combined 1995 revenues: about $19 billion.[4]

1996

February: **The Telecommunications Act of 1966 is passed by Congress and signed by the president.** The law greatly reduces or completely eliminates various regulations regarding television, radio, and telephone operations, including restrictions on ownership and control of electronic media. The flow of megamedia mergers increases, including consolidating buyouts involving more modest-sized companies in many smaller local markets.

After Passage of the Telecommunications Act

April: SBC Communications (Southwest Bell telephone) buys out San Francisco–based Pacific Telesis regional telephone corporation for $16.5 billion, creating the second largest U.S. telephone corporation, after AT&T.

Later in the month, Northeastern U.S. regional phone company NYNEX is bought out by Bell Atlantic for $22.1 billion, resulting in a giant telephone corporation in the eastern United States. This deal surpasses the SBC–Pacific Telesis merger of just three weeks earlier, creating the second largest telephone giant in America.

(These developments are quite ironic, in light of the fact that the AT&T monopoly was broken up in 1982, after the issue ran for years in the courts.)

June: Westinghouse/CBS buys Infinity Broadcasting's large group of radio stations, making it (at that point) the giant of radio; the deal includes ownership of multiple stations in each of the nation's top ten radio markets.

July: Murdoch and News Corp. acquire ten more TV stations and TV production studies with the $2.5 billion purchase of New World Communications Group.

August: US West regional telephone giant buys Continental Cable TV for $1.8 billion, suddenly becoming the third biggest force in cable TV.

November: British Telecom (BT) enters an agreement to buy MCI long distance company. Later there are renegotiations and alternative offers; the BT offer falters.

December: Viacom buys half of UPN-TV network, adding that to its other holdings, which include eleven TV stations, along with MTV, VH-1, and other cable TV channels and Paramount movie studios.

1997
February: Radio groups Chancellor Media and Evergreen merge and are linked by ownership with Capstar Broadcasting; they also buy ten radio stations from Viacom. By mid-1997, Chancellor/Capstar controls no fewer than 325 radio stations around the United States, with multiple stations in many major and not-so-major media markets.

June: Murdoch and company acquire International Family Entertainment, which includes the Family Channel on cable TV and MTM Entertainment TV production company; they also make a deal with Primestar broadcast satellite operation (operated in partnership with TCI, Time Warner, and other media giants) and get greatly enhanced sports programming and distribution.

TCI, in an investment and cable systems trade deal, becomes one-third owner of another cable TV systems giant—the sixth largest—Cablevision.

Microsoft invests $1 billion in Comcast, the fourth largest cable TV systems owner, and the two companies plan to work together on development of broadband, interactive cable networks.

August: Chancellor/Capstar's controlling ownership group, Hicks Muse Tate & Furst, buys the seventh largest radio group, SFX, adding another seventy-two radio stations, making a total of nearly four hundred stations controlled by this one source.

Microsoft invests $150 million (plus other arrangements) in Apple Computer.

September: Westinghouse-CBS buys out American Radio Systems, the fourth largest radio chain in total audience, which gives Westinghouse-CBS over 170 radio stations with a total audience nearly equal to that of the Chancellor/Capstar group.

October: Giant European-based print and electronic publishing and data base corporations Reed Elsevier and Wolters Kluwer merge. The two companies' combined revenues in 1996 would have been $6.6 billion. Reed Elsevier, the dominant partner and owner of the noted Lexis/Nexis data base, said it wanted to enhance its electronic publishing and data base capacities. The company also said it planned to "aggressively seek [further] acquisitions."

November: The earlier deal with British Telecom having fallen apart, MCI agrees to a buyout by WorldCom for $37 billion—the largest corporate merger in American history—creating MCI WorldCom.[5]

1998

April: Bertelsmann buys the Random House–Alfred A. Knopf–Crown Publishing group of book publishers from Newhouse/Advance Publications, adding to its Bantam-Doubleday-Dell publishing group and giving Bertelsmann by far the largest English-language publishing operations.

May: In a deal estimated at over $56 billion, SBC Communications agrees to purchase Ameritech. If accepted by government regulators, this merger of phone giants would be even larger than that of NYNEX–Bell Atlantic or WorldCom-MCI, and it would be one of the three largest corporate mergers in American history (all of which took place in 1998) .

June: In one of the largest corporate mergers of any sort in American history, AT&T buys cable TV giant Tele-Communications Inc. The deal was reported to be worth over $45 billion.

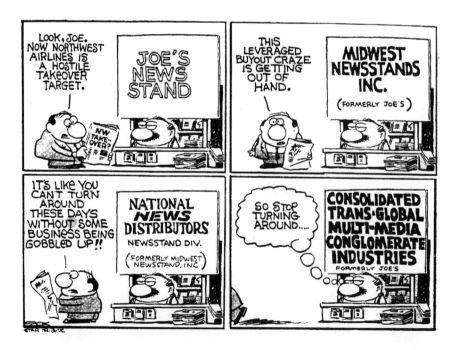

These moves are only the highlights; other megamedia mergers and acquisitions occurred, especially during and after passage of the Telecommunications Act. As economics journalist Allan Sloan remarked in mid-1997, with a dash of sarcasm:

> This new legislation was supposed to usher in a new world in which phone companies, long-distance companies and cable TV companies would all poach on one another's turf. All sorts of new companies would join the fray too. This would give us consumers lower prices and better and more innovative services. Bye-bye big, clunky corporations. Welcome, lean and hungry.
>
> Hello? The new telecommunications world is sure starting to look a lot like the old telecommunications world, full of giant companies about as eager to compete with one another as operators are to refund your quarter when your call gets messed up at a pay phone. Instead of competing, the giants are combining by buying one another.

Indeed. Two summations well express the overall trend. The head of Time Inc. predicted: "There will emerge on a world-wide basis, six, seven, or eight integrated media and entertainment conglomerates" which will dominate mass communications. Even by the early 1990s, as Ken Auletta noted:

> World-wide, five global media giants—Germany's Bertelsmann, Murdoch's News Corporation, France's Hachette, and America's Newhouse Communications and Capital Cities/ABC—already controlled a huge slice of the world's magazines, book publishers, newspapers, book clubs, and record companies, and were now gobbling up broadcast outlets. Group owners now claimed hegemony over 80% of the TV stations in the one hundred largest U.S. markets; chains like Gannett, with its 81 dailies, now monopolized 60% of America's 1,700 daily newspapers; Murdoch owned two-thirds of the newspapers in Australia.

Now, with cable TV and its expansion of the number of channels offered, along with the beginnings of availability of direct broadcast satellite TV service and the advance of the Internet, there are more outlets for information, programs, and images to be communicated to the public. Does that mean there is little reason to worry about megamedia consolidation and conglomeration? The potential for such increased "new media" channels of mass communication to preserve the diversity of voices essential to democracy should be carefully considered; it is considered in this book. But, as Lawrence Grossman, author and former president of the Public Broadcasting System and of NBC News, has observed: "While the number of TV channels and media outlets is burgeoning . . . a few conglomerates, which have no direct responsibility to the American public, wield extraordinary power over the ideas and information the public will receive."

Not all media have equal public impact. Most people have overwhelmingly relied on, and will continue to rely on, the principal mass media for their news, information, and opinion on public affairs—that is, the local and/or regional newspaper, the network and local TV news, major radio stations, the leading national newsmagazines, and books. It is precisely these main media that are controlled by fewer and fewer megamedia corporations. The megamedia corporations also control an increasingly large amount of the feature and entertainment material in print and on the air—from TV shows to movies to books and magazines—that is such a prominent part of society today and that has such an impact on all of us.

Further, the orientation and the state of mind of the heads of those giant media corporations raise troubling questions about the implications for democracy of the march of megamedia. Keeping in mind the unique constitutional role accorded the news media and the public trust reposed in principal news organizations, consider, for example, Rupert Murdoch's statement of orientation: "All newspapers are run to make profits. I don't run anything for respectability."

The orientation and practices of newspaper chain and multimedia giant Gannett are equally telling and troubling. The story is best told in Richard McCord's book *The Chain Gang*. One source summarized Gannett's pattern of seeking newspaper monopolies, what they produce as news, and the impact on communities: "The Gannettoids swallow more communities, . . . spewing out more of their banal newspapers. . . . The Gannett world has little room for criticisms, differences. . . . The problem with Gannett isn't simply its formula or its chairman, but the company's corporate culture." Indeed, another source pointed out: "At Gannett . . . newspapers are often referred to as 'products' or 'units,' and budgets are called 'profit plans.' . . . With no significant competition to worry about, a company like Gannett can—and does—jack up advertising prices almost at will, a practice Gannett openly boasts of when talking to security analysts."

Gannett was sued some years ago in Oregon for antitrust practices in driving out of business a weekly newspaper that was a partial competitor. These practices were shown in glaring detail in the court record—a record that Gannett moved to suppress from public view. Now Gannett, trying to bolster its image, had put out public relations ads saying: "At Gannett, we believe that today, more than ever, journalists must be prepared to move quickly and effectively to defend the public's right to know—the cornerstone of our rights as a free people." But when asked about the inconsistency between that claim and the chain's attempt to suppress the court record in the Oregon case, Gannett chairman Al Neuharth responded: "That's business! I don't think it has anything at all to do with the First Amendment." McCord documents several more recent such cases, as well.

Consider, as well, the mind-set of John Malone, CEO of Tele-Communications Inc. (TCI). TCI is the largest cable TV systems operator in America and owner or part owner of several cable channels, a percentage of Turner Communications, and other media operations. In light of the outpouring of public protest about cable TV systems' skyrocketing prices, poor service, and general monopolistic attitude that followed cable TV's deregulation in 1984, the U.S. Congress in 1992 passed a bill reregulating cable TV, which included provisions to stop the price-gouging. Despite the clear intent of the law, a TCI memo came to light that urged local system managers to raise prices on various services and said: "The best news of all is, we can blame it on re-regulation and the government now. Let's take advantage of it. . . . We cannot be dissuaded from the charges simply because customers object. It will take awhile, but they'll get used to it." If they are that brazen directly in the face of reregulation, what does that promise for their public concern and accountability under much reduced or eliminated regulation and oversight by public authority?[6]

Megamedia's Impact on Democracy and Society

With such states of mind, and with the increasingly monumental control of mass communications by media conglomerates, there are profound concerns about the impact of megamedia in four basic categories: (1) unfair economic competition and distortion of marketplace principles; (2) unfair competition in the realm of information and ideas—the "marketplace of ideas"—through general dominance and elimination of competing media sources, cross-marketing, and other means; (3) deterioration of the news and public affairs materials communicated by the media; and (4) the degradation of features and entertainment shows and the consequent impact on society.

If the public has reason to doubt the independence and integrity of news operations, a vital part of democracy is damaged. It is equally vital for democracy to have a truly diverse set of media sources present in the public arena, a variety of alternative information and perspectives representing a real competition of approaches to news definitions and thoughts on the directions in which our society should head. The continued advance of megamedia and their increasing domination of the prime mass media spell a profound constriction of that diversity and a severe diminution of the marketplace of ideas, and thus a danger to democracy.

When a news organization that is a central institution in public affairs is taken over by a conglomerate corporation that has its primary business in commercial areas quite different from the news process (or media in general), there are two primary concerns: First, will there be an overwhelming, raw bottom-line financial orientation, with little sense of the public trust involved in a news operation? Second, is there imminent danger of conflicts of interest in what the now-captive news operation reports on in the commercial areas in which the parent corporation has business? Additionally, there is the concern that since such a corporation has not had a news operation as a central part of its organization and as a prime part of its image and legitimacy, it will have less—or little—sense of stewardship for such an important institution in the democratic process.

When General Electric bought out NBC and its parent corporation, RCA, in 1985, GE was one of the ten largest corporations of any sort in the United States and produced $50 billion annually in revenues. The top executives of GE seemed to show a tunnel-vision focus on profits and corporate empire-building and little understanding of, or commitment to, their media's public responsibilities. Ken Auletta reported on this in his book on the three networks after their takeover by conglomerates in the mid-1980s. In a talk to a group of NBC staff and representatives of local TV station affiliates, Bob Wright—a GE man hand picked by corporate CEO Jack Welch to head the network—referred to news as "a very expensive product for us" and said that network news was considered "a dinosaur." And, in light of the NBC News budget of $200 million a year, Wright stated that "we shouldn't be out there as your partners spending $200 million on something that you think is nice, but not something that we really think is a *high priority*" (emphasis added). In fact, as Auletta and others have documented, the GE executives, like those outside corporate captains who took over CBS and ABC, proceeded to make major cuts in the news divisions, eliminating numerous correspondents and other news resources. By most accounts, including some given by the news personnel themselves, the network news shows suffered from lesser capacity to cover the news and from corporate pressures to boost ratings and profits by concentrating on low-grade, entertaining stories on topics like celebrities, or on more attention-grabbing fare like crime and scandals. The result has been a reduction in the meaningful coverage of public affairs.[7]

Perspective

When the First Amendment to the U.S. Constitution was written in the late 1700s, the nature and understanding of "the press" was vastly simpler than it is at the end of the 1900s. The feeling in the late 1700s was that if the government could be prevented from interfering with the press, there would be no real problem with press freedom and performance of the democratic role of news organizations. It was relatively easy at the time to have one's thoughts published by a local printer and distribute them. The publication of the simple pamphlet *Common Sense* by Thomas Paine in the 1770s had quite an impact on the American rebellion of 1776, for example. But by the end of the 1900s, there had been a communications revolution, producing mass media of awesome reach and power, along with dramatic developments in the concentration of ownership and control of the media. Those developments and their impacts on, and implications for, societies around the world have not been adequately comprehended. The greatest issue is the implication for democracy and its decision-making process. The impact of powerful and pervasive media stories and images on the nature of our societies more generally is a further issue. These are the concerns of this book, along with an investigation of the nature and impact of the Telecommunications Act.

Noted journalist and press critic A. J. Liebling's classic line, "Freedom of the press is guaranteed only to those who *own* one," expresses the essence of the issue, but it unintentionally illustrates the increased and changed nature of the danger to democracy involved in the ownership developments we have mentioned.

Notice that Liebling said freedom of the press is guaranteed only to those who own *one*. Well, given the megamedia control of numerous print and broadcast media "properties," owning just "one" misses the drastic changes in the structure of control of mass media at the end of the twentieth century, and the actual and potential consequences of those changes.[8]

The Plan of the Book

Chapter 2 is intended to help us think through, in a clear and insightful way, the meaning of democracy and how the dramatic developments in the mass media are affecting, and are likely to affect, the democratic process. To be most effective in that effort, we need a good conceptual framework.

Chapter 3 presents a thorough account of the structure of ownership and control of the media. The focus is on patterns in the United States, but elements of such control worldwide are included. The chapter profiles the "dominant dozen" megamedia corporations—the largest media corporations with the greatest impact in America and the world—and includes notes on key media moguls who rule them. Also included are notes on some significant second-tier megamedia corporations, a review of the "top twelve titans" in each media area in the United States, and a discussion of aggregate control patterns over all media in America and beyond.

Chapter 4 reviews the key elements of the 1996 Telecommunications Act, which significantly changed telephone and mass media law in the United States. Included is a review of the politics and power involved in passage of the Act. The chapter also presents an analysis of how the news media covered the telecommunications bill while it was pending in Congress. What opportunity did media coverage give members of the public to have their say on this issue that would significantly affect them as consumers and citizens? Inadequate review of the nature and likely impacts of the bill might also suggest something about megamedia domination of the main media people rely on.

Chapters 5 and 6 discuss and analyze the consequences of the patterns of ownership and control of the media. Chapter 5 focuses on the increasing concentration of ownership of media and the nature of conglomerates and considers the consequences of that structure of control and corresponding operations for trends in economic competition. Part of the Telecommunications Act's avowed intent was to increase competition, but do the huge sums paid for media properties, the immense financial and other resources of the megamedia corporations, and the nature of their conglomerate operations mean trouble for fair, level-playing-field competition?

Chapter 6 focuses on news operations that are part of conglomerates and other large multimedia corporations. The issue of potential conflicts of interest inherent in a news section of a conglomerate covering matters that relate to industrial and commercial activities of the parent corporation is explored. How are the amount and quality of coverage of matters of public importance affected when a news operation is a mere subsidiary part of a conglomerate? Put simply, does public affairs news deteriorate under such operational conditions, as some allege? What are the consequences for "news as the conversation of democracy"? Also discussed is the impact of such ownership on the nature of books and on creative programming and production in general.

Chapter 7 looks at megamedia patterns in various nations around the world. It starts with three notable and fascinating cases: the Japanese approach to consolidated, cross-media control; the troubling case of Russia, which is struggling to make the transition from state-dominated media to independent media performing a democratic role; and the as yet unsettled case of media control in Eastern Europe in its era of transition. Patterns of media control in Europe and elsewhere are also briefly discussed.

Chapter 8, "Megamedia and the Democratic Prospect," seeks to put in perspective the patterns and trends in the ownership and control of the mass media and their relation to our societies and the democratic process. The chapter also briefly looks at the prospects for the future in the effort to have the mass media make a positive contribution to, and preserve, a diverse, accountable, challenging democratic process.

Chapter 9 discusses ways to assure a real diversity of independent sources of news and opinion. It investigates ways to enhance diversity in existing dominant media organizations and ways to hold such megamedia corporations accountable for their effect on the democratic process. Alternative means to communicate diverse and independent information and opinion to the general public are also explored. Possibilities for a specially enhanced role for public television and radio in the United States are given particular attention.

2

Megamedia and the Meaning of Democracy

••

Conceptions of Democracy and the Role of the Mass Media

Democracy. President Abraham Lincoln's simple definition continues to be the ultimate expression of its meaning: "Government of the people, by the people and for the people." But in large-scale nations, government of the people and by the people is clearly a very demanding notion. A good discussion of the meaning of democracy in the world of today and the role of the media in it is needed to make sense of the megamedia issue and to help provide a framework for analysis.

The distinguished political theorist Robert Dahl, after long study of democratic theory and practice, says that two of the primary criteria for a truly democratic process are "effective participation" and "enlightened understanding." *Effective participation* means "Citizens ought to have an adequate opportunity, and an equal opportunity, for expressing their preferences as to the final outcome [of public decisions on society's issues]. They must have adequate and equal opportunities for placing questions on the agenda and for expressing reasons for endorsing one outcome rather than another." *Enlightened understanding* means that the procedures and mechanisms for making decisions on matters of importance for society must give citizens ample opportunities for acquiring an understanding of means and ends involved in a given issue and an understanding of the likely consequences of policies for their interests, as well as for the interests of all other relevant persons, if we are to try to decide on policies for the general good. That is, if a democracy is to function well, formal procedures and practical mechanisms, especially means of public communication, must ensure that adequate information on public issues is effectively conveyed to the public in general. As Dahl also points out: "Thus the criterion makes it hard to justify procedures that would cut off or suppress information which, were it available, might well cause citizens to arrive at a different decision; or that would give some citizens much easier access than others to information of crucial importance."

19

The "enlightened understanding" criterion for democracy is surely the most fundamental—literally. If "we the people" are to make choices on basic directions for our nation, such decisions must rest on a foundation of acquired information on and genuine understanding of the issues we face and of public leaders to represent us in government to follow through on our choices. As Dahl said in another of his books on democratic theory, in what some would call a bit more down to earth and less idealistic formulation: "But at a minimum . . . democratic theory is concerned with processes by which ordinary citizens exert a relatively high degree of control over leaders."

An expansion on those basic principles leads to the essence of democratic theory and perhaps the most vital element of theory for the megamedia subject. A central principle in democratic theory has been the need for a genuine, open "marketplace of ideas" and information if democracy is to function well. The crucial core of that principle was articulated especially well by Supreme Court Justice Hugo Black in a case some years ago:

> The First Amendment rests on the assumption that the widest possible dissemination of information *from diverse and antagonistic sources* is essential to the welfare of the public. . . . Surely a command that the government itself shall not impede the free flow of ideas does not afford non-governmental combinations a refuge if they impose restraints upon that constitutionally guaranteed freedom. (emphasis added)

If a few megamedia corporations control most of the major print, broadcast, cable, and other media that most of the public relies on as their *main sources* of information, opinion, and creative expression, then this fundamental pillar of democracy is likely to be seriously weakened. Indeed, the Florida Supreme Court concluded: "The right of the public to know all sides of a controversy and from such information to make an enlightened choice is being jeopardized by the growing concentration of ownership of the mass media into fewer and fewer hands, resulting in a form of private censorship" (*Miami Herald v. Tornillo*).

Further, it is important to grasp the realities of how media communications affect the public and public affairs processes. The two key concepts of "public arena" and "public agenda" and the conceptualizations of political scientist E. E. Schattschneider are helpful. The *public agenda* is the set of issues that have become the key issues governmental policymakers and the public are focused on. Typically, those issues have become part of the principal public agenda because they have predominated in the *public arena*, the main arena in which news and ideas on the issues are publicly discussed. This usually means the issues have predominated in the principal mass media most people rely on. As Schattschneider pointed out in his masterpiece, *The Semisovereign People:* "At the nub of politics are, first, the way in which the public participates in the spread of conflict [over a given issue in public affairs] and second, the processes by which the unstable relation of the public to the conflict is controlled. . . . The most important strategy of politics is concerned with the scope of conflict." That is, if a policy issue is not broadly covered by the main newspapers and news shows and widely discussed in the public arena, it is likely that the scope of societal conflict about the issue will be rather narrow and only governmental insiders and well-organized, well-funded special interests will be effectively involved in the debate over what policy option to choose—or not choose.

Schattschneider also notes that competitiveness, visibility (publicity or prominence in the public arena), and instruments and resources for "socializing the conflict" are key factors. But the effective intensity of the competition on an issue is largely a function of the visibility a competitor can generate and the resources it has to operate in the public arena. The magnitude of visibility that can be generated is, as a rule, the amount of media attention that is devoted to the issue, especially by the main media sources with the largest audiences. Regarding the third element, Schattschneider's discussion focuses on government: "The effectiveness of democratic government as an instrument for the socialization of conflict depends on the amplitude of its powers and resources." But clearly, the principal means of carrying discussion of an issue in the public arena is the mass media; and in considering the "dependence of the socialization of conflict on the amplitude of its powers and resources," our attention is best directed to the resources of the megamedia organizations that increasingly control the main media outlets and dominate the public arena.

Some contend, however, that the Internet and other newer technological communications capacities can play a major role in overcoming concentration of control in the main media. There are some rays of hope for enhanced diversity of information and expression, and there certainly is considerable potential. A brief cautionary note is in order here. Research in political science has shown a very limited public capacity and inclination to chase after public affairs information. The local and regional newspaper, the network and local TV news shows, and the main newsmagazines are the media that are readily accessible and that most people are used to relying on; they are the "natural" focus of people's attention. Media channels that require logging on or tuning in and special effort to search out and read will not be main sources of news, information, and opinion (although Internet operations are making progress on lessening the search process). Beyond that, various realities of media concentration, control, and operations in the Internet world seem to hinder the diversity and independence in that realm; these are discussed in subsequent chapters.[1]

Building a Civil Society, the Old-Fashioned Concept of "the Commonweal," and Power

Beyond the presentation of information and varying opinions on explicitly public issues, we need to consider a somewhat more subtle and, in a way, deeper requirement of a functioning democracy. The American Founding Father and sage Benjamin Franklin introduced the ultimate focus of the point in a legendary comment to a citizen who had asked him what kind of government the Constitutional Convention of 1787 had given the new nation. (Translating one term into modern usage) Franklin replied: "A democracy, madam—if you can keep it." That comment suggests the need to pay close attention to how a society educates and cultivates its citizenry and what kind of a general climate is created in the society. The education and cultivation of societal members as citizens can affect their feelings about whether they can effectively participate and have their voice heard in the democratic process. The general environment that is created can affect the nature of people's interactions; their perceptions of, and their respect for, one another; and, in general, the quality of the community experience.

Over the past two centuries various nations have established the basic institutions and official mechanisms of representative democracy. But if democracies are to function well, as contemporary political theorists back through American educator and philosopher John Dewey in the 1920s have pointed out, there needs to be a greater focus on building community and civil society and on developing the conditions and climate that encourage and enable people to act as effective citizens.

The need to build community and a civil society includes the need, through formal education and public communications and interaction processes, to develop in citizens that old-fashioned concept that is seeing a revival in contemporary discussion: character. Nineteenth-century American educator Horace Mann remarked that with rule by the people, "there must be universal elevation of character, intellectual and moral, or there will be universal mismanagement and calamity." Thus, "we the people" are capable of genuine self-government only to the extent that the general public has widely developed good character, good judgment, and a broad view of things and to the extent that the conditions in society enable and encourage meaningful discussion of important issues, based on adequate and accessible information and ideas.

The media—our society's primary public arena—are pervasive, powerful presences in everyone's lives that have profound impacts on styles, behaviors, and perceptions in many realms, not just on public affairs issues. Communications scholar George Gerbner, who has given us some of the most significant analyses of media influence, says in one work:

> The fabric of popular culture that relates elements of existence to each other and structures the common consciousness of what is, what is important, and what is right, is now largely a manufactured product. . . . The ways we reflect on things, act on things and interact with one another are rooted in our ability to compose images, produce messages, and use complex symbol systems. A change in that ability transforms the nature of human affairs. We are in the midst of such a transformation. It stems from the mass production of symbols and messages—a new industrial revolution in the field of culture. New media of communication provide new ways of selecting, composing and sharing perspectives. . . . Along with other dramatic changes, we have altered the symbolic environment that gives meaning and direction to human affairs.

This, then, leads us to explore what patterns of communications predominate in the mass media, thus creating central elements of the climate of society today. Are there changes in the nature of those programs and articles as the media have become increasingly owned and controlled by giant multimedia corporations and conglomerates?

Much recent comment suggests very deteriorated news and entertainment fare presented by the prime media today. So, what kind of impact do these types of communications have on building character in a democratic society? It is fascinating to contemplate that question in light of the ancient Greek philosopher Plato's comments about "rhetoricians"—purveyors of slick, demagogic speech in ancient Athens. For "rhetoricians" substitute "megamedia moguls" and consider whether there is a wisdom of the ages regarding power, money, and corruption of the values of civil society today, especially in the dominant form of public comunication, television. Also, as Plato eloquently articulated it, consider how "true speech is banished, the authentic gold driven out by the tinny dross of what is pleasing and immediately popular." Plato continues:

> Once they have emptied and purged [the good] from the soul of man whom they are seizing . . . they proceed to return insolence, anarchy, wastefullness, and shamelessness from exile, in a blaze of light, crowned and accompanied by a numerous chorus, extolling and flattering them by calling insolence good education, anarchy freedom, wastefullness, magnificence, and shamelessness, courage.

Unfortunately, the dominant political philosophy in the United States (and to an extent, in other Western representative democracies) adds a further problematic dimension, especially in conjunction with the nature of the mass media themselves. Political scientists have called that political philosophy "liberal democratic theory"; a fuller, more descriptive name would be "individualist liberal democratic theory—with a strong laissez-faire strain." "Liberal" refers to the historical development out of aristocracy and feudalism by liberalizing indivdual freedom in economic endeavors and opening political participation to the general public. Liberal democratic theory focuses on individual rights, emphasizes individual choice, and is concerned with freedom *from* governmental restrictions. But as political theorist Benjamin Barber has written: "Liberal democracy is a 'thin' theory of democracy, [which authorizes] means to exclusively individualistic and private ends. From this precarious foundation, no firm theory of citizenship, participation, public goods, or civic virtue can be expected to arise. Liberal democracy, therefore, can never lead too far from Ambrose Bierce's cynical definition of politics as 'the conduct of public affairs for private advantage.'" Several prominent contemporary political theorists and some others back to John Dewey have also pointed out that this basic orientation, especially in a society with a dominant capitalist economy, tends to conceptualize and reinforce a very atomized condition of citizens. People are conceived of, and treated as, separated, individualized, and private people in the midst of large numbers of others, but there is little or no sense of what it takes to constitute a community and to develop common ground and a sense of the general public good—"the commonweal," to use the old-fashioned term.

A related development is well discussed by political theorist John Keane, among others. Increasingly through the twentieth century in the United States the free speech clause of the First Amendment, intended as the keystone of the Bill of Rights for citizens, has been turned to the uses of corporations for protection of, and benefits from, corporate speech. That, along with the ever-growing conglomerate dominance of the mass media, led Keane to conclude: "The language of individualism is used to crush individualism."[2]

All those developments have led to considerable confusion about the distinction between public and private matters and functions, with the trends in media being prime contributors to, and reinforcers of, the loss of basic public processes and community orientations. Correlatively, we are increasingly losing what political theorists have called "public space." This is a distinct public realm where we as citizens can talk over public concerns and interact with one another to achieve better understanding of the issues and of each other. The agora was the open public space where citizens met in ancient Athens; it was a central element in the Greek democratic experience. Public squares in towns across America, where all sorts of public events took place and some still do, are other simple, tangible examples of public space. Newspapers, taking seriously their First Amendment responsibilities, can provide another vital dimension of public space, a public forum. In the 1960s and 1970s, there was a kind of public space in the three TV networks, with the nightly news, regular documentaries, and other public affairs shows, and with the vast majority of Americans having the shared experience of watching those three networks. The BBC in Britain carried on an extraordinary level of quality TV programming in general and of news and public affairs shows in specific, and, as in other nations in Europe, that shared experience in public broadcasting was a profound part of the society. But just as town centers have been eclipsed by, and often abandoned because of, shopping malls, which serve only atomized individual people-as-consumers, not citizens—the "malling of America," as one wit put it—today network documentaries are rare and mass media offerings appeal primarily to the atomized individual and his/her immediate entertainment inclinations. The ultimate consequence for democracy is well stated by Barber: "Even as the audience is broken into splinters, those who control it become fewer and more monopolistic."

It is interesting that there is now a growing movement among conservatives as well as liberals (in the modern political sense of those terms) questioning the unbridled orientation towards capitalist consumption and the consequent loss of human values and community.[3]

Unfortunately, the very nature of broadcast and cable media, at least as they are currently operated, tends to reinforce the atomization, privatization, and loss of public space. As I and others have analyzed elsewhere, the electronic media emphasize the visual and aural image, transitory impressions, and emotional reactions. The written word, on the other hand, a number of scholars have concluded, has a "sequential, propositional character" and tends to foster "the analytic management of knowledge." TV is a mass medium, but it communicates in a very personal way, tending to focus on people as individuals and communicating principally to isolated individuals (or families) in their separate homes. Further, by the late twentieth century, TV viewing has come to consume large amounts of people's nonwork time, causing a significant reduction in social gatherings away from home, reading books, conversation, and other daily activities, especially those involving organizational and social interaction.

Indeed, Harvard's Robert Putnam has detailed the increasing loss of "social capital" during the age of television. *Social capital* means "features of social life—networks, norms, and trust—that enable [people/citizens] to act together more effectively to pursue shared objectives." The key element is community associations and organizations that people join and participate in, which serve to develop "the norms, networks and trust [that help] link substantial sectors of the community and span underlying social cleavages." Putnam's studies, like others, have found that "the performance of government and other social institutions is powerfully influenced by citizen engagement in community affairs." Simply put, democracy works more as intended, and is better preserved, with substantial such social connections, interactions, and citizen engagement. But those connections are reduced if not devastated by television, especially television that increasingly splinters the audience, eliminates public affairs and socially responsible programming, and substitutes low-grade entertainment. The result is a loss of shared community and national experience in developments of public significance. And a product of the increasing bottom-line orientation of media owners and of the expanded channels brought by cable and satellite TV is the scheduling of all sorts of sensational programming opposite major candidate debates, chief executive speeches, and even prime news shows, thus attempting to entice people away from those central vehicles of the democratic dialogue. As communications scholar Neil Postman has so aptly put it, with the megamedia programming patterns of today, we seem to be "amusing ourselves to death."

As early as the late 1920s, when radio had become prominent, John Dewey saw this problem developing:

> We have the physical tools of communication as never before. The thoughts and aspirations congruous with them are not communicated, and hence are not common. Without such communication the public will remain shadowy and formless, seeking spasmodically for itself, but seizing and holding its shadow rather than its substance. . . . Communication alone can create a great community.

The consequences of the loss of social capital, along with the degenerating tendencies in media programs, are profound. An ultimate consequence for democracy was articulated by theorist Jean Bethke Elshtain, drawing on the Czech man of letters, philosopher, and leader Vaclav Havel: "For once a world of personal responsibility with its characteristic virtues and marks of decency (honor, friendship, fidelity, and fairness) is ruptured or emptied, what rushes in to take its place is politics as a 'technology of power.'" The ultimate technology of power is the mass media, especially when controlled by a few giant multinational corporations.

In the 1930s, President Franklin Roosevelt denounced the "economic royalists" of concentrated economic power and expressed concern that they were using their vast power to undermine American democracy; the economic developments "had enabled new tyrants to build kingdoms upon concentration of control over material things." The concern today is the great concentration of control over the mass media, which are so central to democratic societies; that centrality is why this sort of concentration of control is categorically different and of even greater concern. Early in the century there was a vigorous national debate in America about the concentration of economic power and its implications. At that time over 80 percent of newspapers and magazines, the primary news media of the time, were under independent ownership. But at the end of the century, media chains and conglomerates overwhelmingly control the mass media.[4]

That leads to some key questions: If conglomerates control the principal means of communication that carry national discussion and debate, what is the likelihood there will be a vigorous, widespread democratic dialogue in the general public arena about the issues discussed in this book? How likely is it that there will be aggressive investigation by news organizations of those patterns and their consequences for our society? What factors determine the continuing trends in media concentration and how the big media corporations operate?

3

The Dominant Dozen
and the Magnitude of Media Empires

··

Profiles in Press Control Early in the Twentieth Century

There was certainly a marketplace of ideas and news at the turn of the twentieth century in cities around America. In the early 1890s, New York City had fifteen general-circulation, English-language newspapers (morning and afternoon), with twelve different owners. All sizable cities had several vigorously competing daily newspapers, and many not-so-sizable cities had at least two competing dailies. Many of those newspapers had owners and chief editors who were fiercely independent of other news media and of any other business and had a feisty, crusading orientation.

Some newspaper operations, like those of Joseph Pulitzer and especially William Randolph Hearst, were guilty of great sensationalism and other journalistic excess some or much of the time; but Pulitzer and Hearst also tended to champion the causes of average folks and to challenge aggressively the greed, arrogance, and power of the largest corporations, the "trusts" (monopoly industrial corporations) and the rich, as well as corruption in government. Around the turn of the century, several national magazines joined the fray as people's champions and challengers of business and government powers.

Late in his career Pulitzer printed his policy on the editorial page of his *St. Louis Post-Dispatch,* keynotes of which said that the newspaper "will always fight for progress and reform, never tolerate injustice or corruption, always fight demagogues of all parties, . . . always oppose privileged classes and public plunderers, never lack sympathy for the poor, . . . always be drastically independent, never be afraid to attack wrong, whether by predatory plutocracy or predatory poverty." Indeed, the arrogant, greedy industrial titans of the time like John D. Rockefeller and J. P. Morgan (the "robber barons") were regular targets of Pulitzer's editorial arrows. Pulitzer capped those concerns by leaving a large sum for the establishment of the prizes for journalistic excellence that carry his name.

Other notable newspaper owners or owner-editors consciously served as champions of average people and sought to hold powerful governments and powerful corporations accountable. Being both owner and editor working within the newspaper's headquarters and universally identified with the paper, as well as with the local community, encouraged a strong sense of stewardship of the paper and its responsibilities in society. A particularly notable owner-editor who embraced the role of people's champion was E. W. Scripps. He saw his newspaper as the advocate of the large majority who were not wealthy or highly educated and needed a strong champion and a newspaper that could be "the only [continuing] schoolroom the working person had." Scripps came to establish one of the early newspaper chains, with papers throughout much of the Midwest, but the principles remained the same while he lived.

William Allen White was quite different from Scripps, and certainly different from Hearst and Pulitzer, in personal style and political orientation, and his approach was different from the muckraking magazines. But he shared their suspicion of the big industrial trusts, including the trusts' impact on community life; he also had grave doubts about large newspaper chains and the precursors of the general megamedia trend. White was long-serving owner-editor of the *Emporia Gazette* of Kansas. His integrity and wise observations on American politics and life brought him national note in the first decades of the twentieth century. He became the epitome of the owner-editor who is an integral part of the local community and is profoundly committed to journalism that chronicles the community's times but also provides serious news and opinion about the region and the world.

In an obituary on early newspaper chain and magazine owner Frank Munsey, William Allen White gave us an eloquent—and biting—early articulation of doubts about the intense corporatization of the news process and the chain-ownership trend:

> Frank Munsey, the great publisher, is dead.
> Frank Munsey contributed to the journalism of his day the talent of a meatpacker, the morals of a money changer, and the manners of an undertaker. He and his kind have about succeeded in transforming a once-noble profession into an eight percent security.
> May he rest in trust.

The first hints of the trends we see today appeared early in the twentieth century. But later on, under megamedia control, that "eight percent security" would become a 10–40 percent security for media moguls and a Wall Street weight on the news process.[1]

In 1900, newspapers were the source of news and public affairs; they are the prime news source that has continued through the century. In 1900, 559 cities in America—over 60 percent of cities with daily newspapers—had competing papers. But by the mid-1990s, fewer than 30 cities had competing dailies—0.2 percent of cities with daily newspapers. Some analysts say that, realistically, the total is even lower owing to joint operating agreements and other arrangements that call into question how seriously competitive are some of the pairs of papers in some cities. At its height in the 1930s, Hearst's chain actually had the highest percentage of daily circulation ever, and there was much concern about Hearst's power. The chain did not last long at that size and was an anomaly, however; indeed, through the first three decades of the century, 80 percent or more of the newspapers in the United States were independently owned. By the 1990s, over 80 percent of newspapers were under chain or conglomerate control. Growth in the last third of the twentieth century has been steadily in the direction of greater concentration—a pattern that accelerated in the 1980s and 1990s.

The largest newspaper chains are Gannett and Knight-Ridder. By 1997, Gannett's 92 daily newspapers, with total daily circulation of about 6 million, and Knight-Ridder's 35 dailies with total circulation of 4.3 million, meant just two chains reached roughly 25 million in actual daily *readership*, since each paper is read by about 2.5 people, on average. The top twelve newspaper chains (see table, page 90) controlled over 400 dailies with circulation of about 35 million and total readership of over 80 million people—which comes close to the total number of votes cast in the 1996 presidential election.[2]

Megamedia Control at the End of the Twentieth Century

The traditional mass medium of newspapers is only the beginning of the tale of concentration in ownership. Increasingly, the megamedia giants have become multimedia owners—owners of various combinations of broadcast and cable TV networks, TV and radio stations, cable TV distribution systems, satellite TV systems, movie and TV entertainment program production companies, book and magazine publishing, and Internet operations, as well as newspapers.

Of even greater consequence, mass media have increasingly become the property of huge corporate conglomerates. A *conglomerate* is a corporation that owns businesses in a variety of commercial markets. In earlier times, a business was in cereals or machinery or office supplies—and a newspaper business was just that. But now, many of the mass media outlets have become merely parts of corporate conglomerates. The most notable example is General Electric's ownership of the NBC TV network. General Electric has vast operations in consumer electronics, military contracting, nuclear and electrical power generation, financial services, aircraft engines, along with NBC.

Such conglomerate control raises serious questions about the consequences for news coverage, economic competition on a level playing field, and other economic and sociopolitical functions. For example, conflict of interest issues arise when matters relating to various commercial areas of the parent conglomerate become public issues—military contracting and cost overruns or faulty products, for instance—and are thus potential news items. Is there a danger that the NBC news division, for example, will pull its punches when reporting on developments involving its parent corporation—or not go after a story in the first place?

The pioneer in the study of concentration of media ownership has been former journalist and journalism professor Ben Bagdikian. In the 1983 first edition of his book *The Media Monopoly*, Bagdikian concluded that fifty corporations dominated the media in general—newspapers, TV, radio, books, magazines, movies, and so on. By 1996, in the fifth edition of the book, Bagdikian concluded that "the number of media corporations with dominant power in society is closer to ten."

The judgment here is that twelve megamedia corporations dominate mass media in the world today—the "Dominant Dozen." These twelve, along with the principal megamedia moguls leading them, are profiled here A few other noteworthy megamedia corporations that are not quite at the level of the Dominant Dozen are also briefly reviewed, along with a brief note on the special category of the giant telephone corporations.

The megamedia corporations are taken up in order of size and importance. There is not a precise, scientific formula used to decide the specific rank order. The decisions on rankings were informed judgments based on the breadth of media reach, the prominence and importance of the respective media organizations, especially for news and public affairs, and the sheer overall corporate size and economic might of the general corporation. The emphasis is on the scope and importance of the media operations. Dominance in the United States is more heavily weighted since the United States is now the only political and military superpower, has the largest market, and is most influential in entertainment and cultural production.

Some readers may disagree with the rankings of the Dominant Dozen or think some other megamedia corporation should be in that elite group. If this ranking and review stimulates some debate about those giants in media and their impact, that is part of what this book is designed to do.[3]

THE DOMINANT DOZEN

1. (tie)   **Disney–Capital Cities–ABC**
the ultimate multimedia empire

1. (tie)   **Time Warner–Turner**
the other ultimate multimedia empire

3.   **News Corporation**
Rupert Murdoch's multicontinent, multimedia empire

4.   **Bertelsmann**
the German-based international multimedia giant

5.   **General Electric–NBC**
the ultimate conglomerate that swallowed media

6.   **CBS Inc. (until 1998, Westinghouse-CBS)**
conglomerate tribulations and "the Tiffany Network"

7.   **Newhouse/Advance Publications**
the Newhouse multimedia empire

8.   **Viacom**
industrial and media giant with MTV, VH-1, Paramount Pictures

9.   **Microsoft**
software supercorporation, expanding into other media realms (and not number 9 for long)

10.   **Matra-Hachette-Filipacchi**
industrial-megamedia conglomerate in the French fashion

11.   **Gannett**
from giant newspaper chain to multimedia empire

12.   **Tele-Communications Inc. (TCI)**
cable TV colossus

Note: While this book was in production, AT&T acquired TCI. An initial assessment suggests that the newly combined telephone, cable TV, and Internet behemoth should be ranked as high as number 5 in the Dominant Dozen.

1. (tie) Disney–Cap Cities–ABC and the Origins of American Broadcasting

To understand the origins of the ABC broadcasting network and some important related matters, we need to go back to the beginnings of radio. After 1910, there was considerable battling among corporations that held the patents for various elements of early radio technology, including General Electric, American Marconi, Westinghouse, and United Fruit Co. An agreement between the U.S. government and those corporations established the Radio Corp. of America (RCA), primarily to sell radio sets, at first; those corporations were designated "the Radio Group." Then, after Westinghouse started the first full-scale broadcast station in Pittsburgh in 1920, there was much battling about who could operate radio stations; among those in the contest was AT&T.

Through the 1920s, radio stations were established in various areas. The leading original ideas for radio were not commercial and did not include advertising. Most notably, RCA executive David Sarnoff's early plan for a national broadcasting company suggested using a percentage of RCA's radio manufacturing revenues to pay for a nonprofit radio operation—a public service mode of broadcasting "to be kept free of the taint of money-making."

An agreement between the government, the Radio Group, and AT&T led to the withdrawal of AT&T from broadcasting and led RCA to form a broadcasting subsidiary, the National Broadcasting Co. (NBC) in 1926. The Radio Act of 1927 established a government commission to license radio stations. It is revealing that "conservative congressmen, . . . supported by their broadcast allies, succeeded in defeating nearly every amendment that sought to strengthen the provisions of the act relating to issues of corporate control and monopoly." The act also somewhat paradoxically stated that the airwaves were a *public resource.* Beginning in the late 1920s, NBC operated two national radio networks, the "red" network and the "blue" network. In 1929, the Columbia Broadcasting System (CBS) became operational.

By the late 1930s, the dominance of radio by NBC (especially) and CBS caused much complaint about a virtual monopoly—"the radio trust." The Federal Communications Commission (FCC), with President Roosevelt's nominees in control, investigated this, producing in 1940 the *Report on Chain Broadcasting.* That report included the following signal observation—a rarity of candor on the concentration of ownership issue in the history of the FCC:

> National and Columbia, directed by a few men, hold a powerful influence over the public domain of the air. . . . If freedom of communication

is one of the precious possessions of the American people, such a condition is not thought by the committee [of three commissioners] to be
in the public interest and presents inherent dangers to the welfare of a
country where democratic processes prevail. . . . To the extent that the
ownership and control of radio-broadcast stations falls into fewer and
fewer hands, whether they be network organizations or other private
interests, the free dissemination of ideas and information, upon which
our democracy depends, is threatened.

As a consequence of the report and other pressures, in the mid-1940s NBC
sold its blue network to wealthy businessman Edward Noble, who then
changed its name to the American Broadcasting Co. (ABC).

In the early 1950s, after financial troubles, Noble sold ABC to
Leonard Goldensohn, who was head of United Paramount Theatres;
Goldensohn also had a sizable stake in the other, weaker TV network of
the time, the now-forgotten DuMont network. This new ownership raised
further concentration-of-control issues, but the FCC eventually voted 5-2
for the ABC–United Paramount merger. The two dissenting commissioners said that this would create "'a monopolistic multimedia economic
power' that would not serve the public interest."

Aside from the issue of the structure of ownership, Goldensohn over
the next three decades developed a fairly strong sense of stewardship for
this major media organization and its feature network news show.[4]

By 1984, ABC was a very successful network that also had other
media properties. In stock market terms, however, it was judged as
undervalued. Consequently, ABC was economically "in play."

This was the Reagan era, and President Reagan had placed in a
majority of the seats on the FCC commissioners who were intensely laissez-faire in orientation and had little commitment to the public service
function of broadcasting. Indeed, Chairman Mark Fowler said TV was
basically like any other business, simply "a toaster with pictures." Nor
was there much concern about concentration of ownership; in fact, in the
mid-1980s the FCC relaxed the limit of seven stations that one corporation
was allowed to own, raising the limit to twelve.

In 1985, Capital Cities multimedia corporation, with the assistance of
billionaire investor Warren Buffett, a member of its board of directors,
bought out ABC to create Cap Cities–ABC. Talks for the buyout were
prompted by the relaxation of federal strictures on station ownership.
Cap Cities owned seven TV stations, twelve radio stations, ten daily
newspapers, and other media properties, including cable systems. Local
TV had been spectacularly profitable from the 1960s into the 1980s, and
Cap Cities was at the extreme end of the profitability spectrum, its stations earning about 55 percent profit rates, in part because its two top

executives, Tom Murphy and James Burke, "managed costs ruthlessly." Cap Cities executives brought that orientation to the network when they took over. By the end of 1986, they had cut $20 million from the ABC News budget and eliminated three hundred jobs in the news division. The further bad news for ABC was the Cap Cities orientation to newscasts: crime-saturated and sensationalist. Murphy said unapologetically: "We are giving the American people what they want. If you want to give people what you think they need, go into public broadcasting."

With rumblings among media interests about the likely passage of the Telecommunications Act, in August 1995 the Disney multimedia powerhouse in entertainment bought out Cap Cities–ABC for $19 billion. The compensation package for Disney CEO Michael Eisner was a staggering $203 million for 1994; in late 1997, Eisner exercised stock options he had been given and realized a pretax profit of no less than $374 million.[5]

The scope and resources of the new Disney–Cap Cities–ABC conglomerate are breathtaking. Total revenues for 1997 were $22.5 billion, with nearly $2 billion in profits. The large array of mass communication vehicles, programming, and related products and services is awesome and increasingly international. The holdings of this megamedia conglomerate are shown below.[6]

Disney–Cap Cities–ABC

Broadcasting
ABC TV Network, broadcasting ABC News shows, *Good Morning America*, *Prime Time Live*, *Nightline*, etc., ABC Sports programming, ABC entertainment programming, etc.; with 223 affiliated TV stations covering the entire U.S.
ABC Radio Network, with 2,900 affiliated stations throughout the U.S. "serving more than 122 million people weekly through seven different program services"
Owners of 9 VHF TV stations, with 5 in the top 10 markets in the U.S., and 1 UHF TV station
Owners of 11 AM and 10 FM radio stations, including 3 stations each in Los Angeles, Atlanta, and Minneapolis
14% stake in Young Broadcasting, with 8 TV stations in the U.S.

Cable TV Systems and Channels/Networks
Disney Channel
80% of ESPN cable TV channel and ESPN International, which

reaches 70 million cable subscribers in the U.S. and 105 million subscribers in over 160 nations, plus ESPN 2

50% of Lifetime cable TV channel

37.5% of Arts & Entertainment cable TV channel

Disney Interactive—entertainment and educational computer software and video games, plus development of content for on-line services

Partnership with 3 phone companies to provide video programming and interactive services

Internet
ABC Online

TV Production, Movies, Video, Music
Disney Television Production studios and Walt Disney Pictures movie studio

Buena Vista Television production company

Buena Vista Home Video, maker of videotapes

Miramax and Touchstone movie production companies

Buena Vista Pictures Distribution and Buena Vista International, distributors for Disney and Touchstone movies

Walt Disney Records, and Hollywood Records

Publishing
6 (smallish) daily newspapers (another 2 large and 2 modest-sized papers sold to Knight-Ridder in 1997).

About 40 weekly newspapers

Magazines: *Discover, Women's Wear Daily, Los Angeles* magazine, *Institutional Investor;* plus Disney Publishing, including *Family Fun,* etc., and new *ESPN Magazine* (1998)

Chilton Publications—auto, steel, food, and other trade periodical and book publications

Guilford Publishing Co.

Hitchcock Publishing Co., and several small publishing companies, plus a series of medical periodicals

Theme Parks, Resorts, and Travel
Disneyland

Disney World and Disney World Resort

Part owner of Disneyland-Paris and Tokyo Disneyland

12 resort hotels

Disney Vacation Club

Expanding into cruise line business in 1997

International TV, Film, and Broadcasting
50% owner of Tele-München Fernseh GmbH & Co., a television and
film production and distribution company based in Munich
50% owner of RTL Disney Fernseh GmbH & Co., a German entertainment commercial broadcasting company based in Munich
(shared with Bertelsmann)
23% owner of RTL 2 Fernseh GmbH & Co., a German commercial
broadcasting company based in Munich
37.5% owner of TM3 Fernseh GmbH & Co., a women-oriented commercial broadcasting company based in Munich
20–33% stake in Eurosport network (throughout Europe), Spanish
Tesauro SA TV company, and Scandinavian Broadcasting System
SA, "which capitalizes upon the commercial broadcasting boom
across Northern and Central Europe, launching new channels in
Austria, Hungary, and Finland"
20% owner of TVA, a Brazilian pay-TV company

Other
Over 500 Disney Stores, and licensing of Disney products.
The Mighty Ducks professional hockey team.
25% ownership of California Angels major league baseball team

Business Connections with Other Megamedia Corporations
Joint ventures, equity interests, or major arrangements with Bertelsmann, TCI, Hearst Corp., Kirch (other German megamedia company), and various other media and telephone companies

1. (tie) Time Warner–Turner

Time Warner

Time magazine, America's first weekly newsmagazine, was started in
1923 by Henry Luce and Britton Haddon (who died in the 1920s). *Time's*
increasing success by the end of the 1920s helped lead Luce to start *Fortune* business magazine in 1930. The pioneer photojournalism magazine,
Life, was added in 1936. In 1954 the nation's first general sports magazine,
Sports Illustrated, was launched by Time-Life. By 1960, Time-Life was generating $270 million in annual revenues, and the company moved into its
new forty-eight-story building in Rockefeller Center in New York City.

People magazine was added to the list in 1974 and quickly achieved a large circulation. *Time* gained increasing prominence and distinction through the 1960s, 1970s, and 1980s. Henry Luce was a major figure in media. But in the 1940s and 1950s, *Time* magazine was not a politically neutral news organ; Luce had it regularly supporting Republican presidential candidates. Later, as the magazine grew and more distinguished journalists joined its ranks and the Luce influence waned, *Time* became more neutral.

By the mid-1980s, Time Inc. had added other magazines and book publishing, substantial cable TV distribution systems, HBO and Cinemax cable TV channels, and other media properties. In 1989 came the dramatic announcement: Time was acquiring Warner Communications, the pioneering American film company. The new conglomerate would be Time Warner. Six years later came another dramatic announcement: Time Warner was acquiring Turner Broadcasting, Ted Turner's pioneering cable TV company, with TBS Superstation, CNN, and other holdings. Total Time Warner revenues for 1997 were well over $13 billion.

Warner Bros., founded by brothers Harry and Jack Warner, was one of the original Hollywood movie studios. The brothers produced the first talking picture, *The Jazz Singer* with Al Jolson. The film's great success led them out of financial difficulties and into a stream of bigger and bigger movie- and money-making. In the 1960s the company got into recorded music and eventually became one of the giants in that area; Warner also became more and more involved in book publishing.[7]

Ted Turner and Turner Broadcasting

In some signifcant ways Ted Turner's story is an exception to the patterns seen in most other megamedia corporations, with their increasing lack of concern for the public good—at least after his early years and until he sold out to Time Warner in 1995.

Robert Edward Turner III grew up in the family of a very successful billboard business owner. But Ted's father, Ed, was a troubled man who treated his namesake son harshly and eventually took his own life. Those circumstances and the lack of fatherly approval, along with his own natural energy and boldness, apparently drove Ted in the business world for years. That and an overdose of boisterousness also led Ted for many years through a wild and colorful personal life, which included world-class sailing accomplishments—and world-class womanizing and drinking. He showed business ability in the billboard company. But it was in 1970 that Turner first got into the electronic media realm and began to show the remarkable vision that helped transform television and made him a notable and rich man. That year his company acquired a pitiful, money-losing UHF TV station in Atlanta. As his financial advisers put it at the time: "We were certain Ted had gone crazy this time." It turned out to be crazy like a fox.

Through various means, including acquiring broadcast rights to Atlanta sports teams, Turner built up his UHF station. A 1972 FCC ruling allowed the emerging cable TV operators to import TV signals from independent stations out of the immediate media market that did not compete with the areas's network affiliates. With that ruling, the development of cable TV, the introduction of communications satellites, and the vision to see the possibilities and to secure a place on an early satellite, Ted turned his little UHF station in Atlanta into the first superstation in America, which later became TBS.

In the early years, the programming on Turner's UHF TV station was largely cheap TV show reruns and old movies—along with that unique "sport," professional wrestling. At first, Turner showed little interest in meaningful news. But as a result of interactions with certain key individuals and of his own development driven by a restless, unconventional mind, in the late 1970s Turner began the process of establishing something extraordinary on cable TV: an all-news channel/network. Many thought this was another of Ted's crazy ideas that would bankrupt him. A couple of attempts by others in the 1970s to put on a similar all-news channel had not gotten off the ground. But on 1 June 1980, Cable News Network, the now-famous CNN, signed on for the first time. With typical hyperbole, Turner pronounced: "I think the people of America need this in-depth news service, and I'm willing to risk everything I have to provide that service. . . . We won't sign off until the end of the world—and we'll cover that live!"

The CNN operation kept costs low by such means as hiring young people fresh out of journalism school and not paying huge salaries for TV news stars. In the early years, there were criticisms that CNN's production was good on breaking news stories but lacked depth and analysis. But increasingly they enhanced CNN's capacities, and CNN got better. CNN expanded around the world through the 1980s and early 1990s, adding foreign bureaus at a time when conglomerate-dominated ABC, CBS, and NBC were cutting back on foreign bureaus and coverage. Later CNN added a segment in which parts of news shows from other nations were broadcast in the weekly *World Report*, along with other international material. By its tenth year CNN had developed coverage and signal availability on six continents, becoming the first truly global TV network. It had also become quite profitable, generating $150 million in profits by 1991.

Ted Turner increased his interaction with significant figures, such as

Jacques Cousteau, and further developed his perspective on the world. He wanted to think big and became more committed to contributing to national and world discussion of major issues. He established the Better World Society, with an annual budget of $2 million, to produce issue-oriented TV programs. From 1985 through the end of the decade, the society funded over forty documentaries, most broadcast on TBS, some on other cable channels. In the late 1970s, Turner also established and broadcast the Goodwill Games between the United States and the Soviet Union, held halfway between the Olympics. "He's been very good for television," said Grant Tinker, who headed NBC for years.

In 1986 Turner acquired the MGM and United Artists film libraries, perhaps the best in the world. This gave him extraordinary material for showing on his TBS and TNT cable networks, but it also saddled him with a mountain of debt. He was bailed out by TCI, the biggest cable systems operator; Time, the second largest cable systems operator; and other cable companies—but at the cost of their presence on the Turner Broadcasting Board of Directors and the loss of some freedom of action. The blustery head of TCI, John Malone, commented: "If we hadn't rescued Ted Turner, TBS would have been bought out by Rupert Murdoch and CNN now would be running 'Murder of the Week.'" Turner continued as leader of the company. By the 1990s, however, Turner saw how dominant the megamedia trend was and decided to be a key part of a giant. In 1995, he sold Turner Broadcasting to Time Warner and became vice chairman of Time Warner. Turner's media success had made him a very rich man: in mid-1997, Forbes magazine estimated his personal wealth at $2.1 billion. In a bold gesture, in fall 1997 he pledged $1 billion in stock ownership to bolster United Nations programs—and challenged other ultra-rich people to do something socially responsible with their wealth.

The U.S. Federal Trade Commission (FTC) was established in part to scrutinize mergers to see whether they are likely to have a negative impact on free and fair trade, including developing monopoly power in the marketplace. FTC's staff raised objections to the Time Warner merger with Turner. The FTC eventually accepted the merger with some modest revisions and some restrictions on operations. Regarding the TCI–Time Warner–Turner connection in cable TV systems, the TCI stake in the new, merged corporation was set at 7.5 percent, and the stock had to be placed in a separate company. Time Warner local cable TV systems were also required eventually to carry an independent all-news channel to compete with CNN. The head of telecommunications policy for the Consumer Federation of America complained that these modest restrictions were inadequate: "We are still disappointed they didn't take more aggressive action against the merger." And, he said, even though TCI was required to put its TimeWarner-Turner stock in a different company, the two cable operations "still have an incentive to work toward the same goals."[8]

The wide-ranging media and nonmedia holdings of Time Warner are shown below. As Herman and McChesney point out: "Time Warner is a major force in virtually every medium and on every continent."[9]

Time Warner–Turner

Magazines
Time
Life
Sports Illustrated
Fortune
People
Money
Parenting
In Style
Sunset
Health
Martha Stewart Living
Entertainment Weekly
83.25% of *American Lawyer*
50% of D.C. Comics
Over a dozen other magazines, including new *Teen People*, begun in
  early 1998

Broadcast Television Network
Warner Bros. (WB) TV network, America's 5th broadcast TV network

U.S. Cable TV Systems and Channels/Networks
Time Warner Cable, 2nd-largest local cable TV systems owner in the
  U.S., with over 12 million subscribers as of late 1996
Cable TV channels/networks (some part-owned): CNN, CNN Inter-
  national, TBS, TNT, Headline News, Turner Classic Movies, Car-
  toon Network, HBO, Cinemax, plus stakes in Comedy Central, E!
  Entertainment TV, Courtroom Television Network, Black Enter-
  tainment Network, Sega Channel
Time Warner Sports programming

International Broadcasting and Cable
Significant interests in Germany's N-TV, New Zealand's Sky Network Television, the European cable music channel VIVA, and Asian music channel Classic V

Movies, TV, Video Production, and Movie Theaters
Warner Bros. film studio
Warner Bros. Television production studios
Warner Bros. Home Video
Turner worldwide Home video
Turner Pictures
Castle Rock Entertainment movie production company
New Line Cinema movie production company
Warner Bros. film library
Turner Film Library (including over 3,000 classic movies from former MGM and RKO movie studios)
Hanna Barbera Cartoons
Owns many movie houses, with over 1,000 screens, around the world

Book Publishing
Time-Life Books
Little, Brown & Co.
Warner Books
Oxmoor Books; Sunset Books
Book-of-the-Month Club

Recorded Music
Warner Music Group is one of the world's 4 largest recorded music companies; it includes:
Warner Bros. Records
Atlantic Recording/The Atlantic Group
Elektra Records/Elektra Entertainment Group
Warner/Chappell Music; WEA Inc.

Internet and New Media
CNN Interactive WWWebsite
Turner New Media (CD-ROMs, etc.)

Pro Sports Teams and Promotions
Atlanta Braves major league baseball team
Atlanta Hawks NBA basketball team

World Championship Wrestling
Goodwill Games

Other

Six Flags entertainment/excursion parks; plus Warner Bros. Movie
World theme park in Germany

Over 150 Warner Bros. stores, plus Turner Retail Group

25% stake in Atari; 14% stake in Hasbro

Business Connections with Other Megamedia Corporations

Tele-Communications Inc. (TCI), America's largest cable TV systems
owner, owned 21% of Turner Broadcasting before the merger.
Time Warner is the second largest cable TV sytsems owner in the
U.S. Thus, as of mid-1996 the two now-connected corporations
had 46% of the nation's 62 million cable TV subscribers.

Other joint ventures, equity interests or major arrangements with
Viacom, Sony, Bertelsmann, News Corp., Kirch (German megamedia co.), EMI, Tribune Co. (carrying WB TV network on its 16 TV
stations around the U.S.), and others

3. Rupert Murdoch and News Corp.

Rupert Murdoch is the most notorious of the media moguls, and his
News Corp. probably has the greatest worldwide reach. Murdoch was
born into the media world. His father, Keith Murdoch, was editor of Australia's *Melbourne Herald.* As the *Herald* gained circulation and acquired
and developed magazines and another newspaper under his leadership,
Keith Murdoch was made managing director of the company. The company and Keith were successful, his influence in Australia grew, and in
1933, two years after son Rupert was born, Keith was knighted. Sir Keith
was a significant figure in Australia by the time Rupert came of age. Thus,
Rupert Murdoch grew up in a wealthy, influential, and privileged environment.

Rupert went off to England to study at Oxford University. While
there, he dabbled in leftist philosophy and delighted in quoting Lenin,
much to his father's displeasure; that probably was part of the idea, something of a rebellion against his dominant and at times domineering father.
Before returning to Australia, Rupert did an apprenticeship in London
with Lord Beaverbrook's rather sensationalist newspaper, the *Daily
Express.* This was a key influence in Murdoch's development; he began to
embrace the idea that "newspapers were meant to entertain, not educate."

Upon the death of Sir Keith, Rupert returned to Australia in 1953 and went to work as publisher on the one newspaper his father had owned (rather than managed), the *Adelaide News* and *Sunday Mail* in northeastern Australia. He was called "the boy publisher." The Murdoch family felt that Sir Keith had made the *Melbourne Herald* media group grow and become rich but that the company had not rewarded him adequately. And they felt the principals of that company, with the connivance of various members of the Australian "establishment," had tried to take advantage of young Rupert and his mother after Sir Keith's death. This is probably part of what has driven Rupert Murdoch to ownership and dominance ever since.

In the late 1950s, with the *Adelaide News* making good money, Murdoch started buying other media properties. First came a magazine, then the *Sunday Times* of Perth. The Murdoch pattern of newspapering was established here. As one critic observed: "The exaggerated story filled with invented quotes; the rewriting of . . . laconic news-service copy into lavish sensationalized yarns; the eye-shattering, usually ungrammatical, irrelevant and gratuitously blood-curdling headline ('Leper Rapes Virgin, Gives Birth to Monster Baby' read a typical early front page)." The *Times* was apparently rather tawdry before Murdoch took control, but it became much more so (and more lively) and was promoted in louder and more gimmicky fashion under Murdoch. With help from cuts in news staff, including firing those who did not operate in the Murdoch mode, the paper became quite profitable.

In the following years, Murdoch's News Corp. moved into other media and other countries. Through his increasingly complex News Corp. organization, Murdoch acquired more and more properties around Australia, then in England, then in America, then in Asia and elsewhere. In 1985, he bought effective control of the major American film and TV studio Twentieth Century Fox, with its great film library. Then he bought Metromedia's TV stations in the largest American markets, forming Fox Television Inc. for the purchase.

He was able to buy those stations despite a U.S. law forbidding foreigners to control American TV stations. He overcame that obstacle to this crucial acquisition in part by renouncing his Australian citizenship and becoming an American citizen. A sympathetic Federal Communications Commission dominated by Reagan appointees in the 1980s (FCC Chair Mark Fowler had worked in Reagan's 1980 campaign) took a hands-off approach to megamedia moves and did not contest the acquisition. (It couldn't have hurt that Murdoch had used his newspapers to support Reagan and Republicans in general.)

From mid-1993 to spring 1995, however, the FCC investigated the issue, finally responding to a challenge of the Murdoch TV acquisitions. While that challenge was pending, and in the immediate aftermath of the 1994 elections in which the Republican Party won control of Congress, Murdoch's HarperCollins publishing company offered a $4.5 million advance for a book from incoming Republican Speaker of the House Newt Gingrich. Around that time, Murdoch and his lobbyist visited Gingrich. A general outcry arose when this came out; eventually, Gingrich felt compelled to give back the advance. (As it turned out, the Gingrich book did not sell nearly enough copies to recoup the big advance.) Also, during and after the 1994 election Murdoch contributed substantial sums to the Republican Party. In May 1995, the FCC allowed the Murdoch TV stations deal to go through, ruling that technically he did violate the foreign-owner rule but giving News Corp. a waiver because the Fox TV Network "served the public interest" since it added a new TV network. Given considerable criticism of the tawdry, low-grade fare on Fox TV and the absence of meaningful news on the network at the time, some questioned that rationale.

Chicago's syndicated columnist Mike Royko expressed the outrage many felt at the way Murdoch got around the foreign ownership restriction. Relating Murdoch's sudden citizenship conversion to general immigration restrictions, Royko noted that Murdoch was not fleeing some political tyranny and questioned the special allowance. Royko went on to say: "Nor does he have a skill that is in short supply in America. By profession, Murdoch is a greedy, money-grubbing, power-seeking, status-climbing cad. Since when is that skill in short supply?" In any case, Murdoch's new TV stations and the Twentieth Century Fox film library and studios gave him the foundation for a new American TV network. It also gave him key resources to be a major force in global mass communications. He "now controlled 93 publishing, broadcasting and other operations. . . . He would reach a quarter of the world's English-speaking population."

By the early 1990s, Murdoch controlled two-thirds of the newspapers in Australia and 40 percent of the circulation of the popular press in Britain, as well as that nation's prime press institution, the *Times* of London. By 1996, after his purchase of New World media, Murdoch's American TV stations reached over 40 percent of the public, the greatest reach of any corporation in the United States; his Fox TV network reached many more. He has been called by many a modern-day media buccaneer, ruthless, power-hungry, with no compunction about using his great media reach and power to favor politicians of his (conservative) ideology—and to take favors from them. Others have characterized him as a great businessman, a remarkable risk-taker, and a visionary. A risk-taker he has certainly been, as he acquired or developed media property after media property, including starting a new satellite TV service over Europe. That risk-taking has also entailed taking on enormous debt, however—over $2.3 billion by the end of 1985, and it got worse over the next five years. In 1990, owing 146 different lenders from a few million to hundreds of millions of dollars each, Murdoch's News Corp. came close to bankruptcy when bank loans were due and some creditors would not accept any more promises of payment. But with help from his legendary persuasiveness, he narrowly avoided the collapse of his financial house of cards.

Murdoch survived and continued to reign supreme over an increasingly worldwide media empire. News Corp. had media operations in Australia, the United States, Britain, Europe, Latin America, eastern Asia, and India. Author William Shawcross noted that News Corp. had become "the first vertically integrated entertainment-and-communications company of truly global reach." As Britain's respected economics and public affairs magazine the *Economist* said, News Corp.'s "global reach, its sweeping ambition, and the extent to which it is the creature of one man" makes it an extraordinary player in the international megamedia game.[10]

The empire continued to grow through the 1990s, despite the failure of an effort to link up with Echostar direct broadcast TV service and produce American Sky Broadcasting. In June 1997, Murdoch struck a deal with the second-largest direct broadcast satellite operation, Primestar. News Corp.'s cable networks, Fox Sports Net and Fox News Channel receive full distribution on Primestar as a result. In mid-1997, Murdoch's operation, in collaboration with the giant of cable TV systems, TCI, bought 40 percent of Rainbow Media, the programming wing of major cable TV systems operator Cablevision, and thereby they launched a national sports network as something of a competitor to ESPN. The new operation, Fox Sports Net, includes a network of seventeen regional cable sports channels, which allows the network to emphasize home-team broadcasts in the respective areas. Fox Sports Net also has a substantial lineup of major league sports event contracts. The other half of Fox Sports Net is owned by Cablevision's Rainbow Media. And, illustrating the myriad megamedia interconnections, NBC owns 25 percent of Rainbow Media. Further deepening Murdoch's dominance in the sports world, in spring 1998 he bought control of the Los Angeles Dodgers baseball team. He also controls elements of professional rugby in Australia. In June 1997, News Corp. acquired International Family Entertainment, which included, among others, the Family Channel and MTM Entertainment. By 1997 News Corp. had become a behemoth, with revenues of over $11 billion. The complex, multination structure of the corporation also enabled Murdoch and his chief accountants to shift profits and liabilities around the world, resulting in News Corp. paying far lower taxes in the United States, Britain, and Australia than most comparable corporations; in fact, News Corp., as of the mid-1990s, paid a worldwide tax bill of a mere 7 percent. In 1997, *Forbes* magazine estimated Murdoch's personal wealth at $2.8 billion. Murdoch's media empire is outlined below.[11]

Murdoch's News Corp.

Newspapers
Australia and the Pacific Basin: 127 daily and weekly papers, roughly two-thirds of all newspapers in Australia, including Australia's only national paper, the *Australian*, and the prime Hong Kong paper, the *South China Morning Post*

Great Britain: the *Times* and the *Sunday Times*, the *Sun, News of the World, Today*

U.S.: *New York Post, Boston Herald, San Antonio Express-News*

Other parts of the world: Budapest papers *Mai Nap* and *Reform*

Magazines (worldwide)
TV Guide (U.S.)

New York

Daily Racing Form

Seventeen

Elle women's fashion magazine, U.S. edition, a joint venture with Hachette.

Other magazines and newspaper inserts in Australia, North America, and Europe

Broadcast Television Network
Fox TV Network, U.S.

TV Stations
22 TV stations in the U.S. with 9 of them in the top 10 media markets in the nation (some are UHF stations), including prime VHF stations in New York, Los Angeles, Washington, D.C., Detroit, and elsewhere

3 TV stations in Australia, 2 in major cities

32.6% of Blackstar Communications (3 TV stations); 25% of SF Communications (4 TV stations); 15% of Seven Network of Australia

Satellite TV and Radio
40% of BSkyB, dominant satellite TV service of Britain, which has a
40% interest in Granada Sky Television satellite channel group of
Britain
49.9% of VOX of Germany
50% of Foxtel of Australia
STAR TV in Asia
49.9% of Zee TV of India
Canal Fox and 30% of Sky Latin America (primarily in Mexico and
Brazil)
50% stake in channel V, Asian music video channel
45% stake in Phoenix Satellite TV Co. of Hong Kong
Mid-1997 agreement with Primestar for minority ownership and
joint operations
Developing in 1997–1998: JSky, satellite TV service for Japan
Sky Radio of Great Britain

Movie, TV, and Video Production and Cable Channels
Twentieth Century Fox Movies and TV production
Fox 2000; Fox Searchlight; Fox Family Films; Fox Animation studios;
Fox Studios, Australia.
fx and fxm cable channels.
Cannell Entertainment
MTM Entertainment TV production and distribution
37.5% of Guthy/Renker
Fox News Channel
The Family Channel cable TV network
Fit TV cable channel
Fox Video operations in France, Germany, Great Britain, New
Zealand, Spain, and the Far East
50% of joint Fox/Liberty Media (with TCI)
Through Fox/Liberty Media, owns 50% of Fox Sports Net

Book Publishers
HarperCollins, U.S., Britain, and Australia
Ballinger Publishing Co.
Barnes & Noble Books
CineBooks Inc.
Zondervan Corp., religious books and music
Geographia Ltd., publishers of maps and guides (Britain)
Marshall Pickering Holdings, publishing and printing (Britain)

Other Media
News Electronic Data
71% of Sky Radio, Britain
News Datacom Ltd., News Multimedia Ltd., and Broadsystem Ltd.
  of Britain
50% of Beijing PDN Zinren information technology
New World Sales and Marketing
New World International/Genesis Entertainment
As owner of the *Times* (London), has a piece of Reuters News Service

Nonmedia Holdings
Owns 50% of Ansett Transport Industries, including Ansett Airlines,
  one of 2 domestic airlines in Australia, and air cargo carrier
Los Angeles Dodgers
Rugby league in Australia

Business Connections with Other Megamedia Corporations
In spring 1995, MCI Communications Corp., the second-largest long
  distance telephone company in the U.S., agreed to invest as much
  as $2 billion in Murdoch's holding company, News Corp. The
  intent was to develop major new elements in the "information
  superhighway."
Other joint ventures, equity interests, and major arrangements with
  Time Warner, Viacom, Universal, PolyGram, Sony, Bertelsmann,
  and others

4. Bertelsmann, the German Giant

Bertelsmann AG was founded in Gutersloh, Germany, by Carl Bertelsmann in 1835, beginning with a printing press for religious scriptures and
related publications. As of 1995, this giant was nearly 90 percent owned
by the Mohn family; like Murdoch's News Corp. and Newhouse's
Advance Publications, Bertelsmann is privately owned, which also makes
obtaining information—and maintaining accountability—much more difficult.

For most of the post–World War II period, Bertelsmann was led by
Reinhard Mohn. Mohn had been drafted into the Luftwaffe during World
War II, was captured by the American army, and spent the rest of the war
in a POW camp in Kansas, where he learned English and studied business
administration. He was quite unlike the intense empire-building, power-
hungry, egotistical media moguls like Murdoch, or the flamboyant, ego-

dominant, publicity-seeking media moguls like Ted Turner. Rather, Mohn was a very Calvinist, work-ethic-oriented head of the family who stayed pretty much in the background while methodically building up the company. Even late in his career in the 1990s, Mohn worked out of a very plain, unpretentious office, and he went to lunch in the employee cafeteria and stood in line like everyone else—in stark contrast to the imperial office and opulent executive perks of the typical megamedia baron.

In the economic realm as well, Mohn and his company have been different from those prototypical media moguls. Instead of scurrying about engaging in frenzied mergers and acquisitions—and running up lots of debt—Mohn's Bertelsmann has concentrated on buying relatively modest-sized companies and developing their capacities, enabling Bertelsmann's components to grow. In one way Mohn is somewhat similar to Ted Turner: he has established the nonprofit Bertelsmann Foundation, which funds medical research, literacy promotion, and other constructive projects; it also funds research on the best ways to run a corporation. Bertelsmann's top executives have not tended to push political orientations on and through their media properties.

In the postwar years, Bertelsmann began to spread beyond publishing religious books, technical books, and some fiction. The company first went into book and record clubs, then into magazines and newspapers, and more recently into electronic media. By the 1990s, it had become one of the largest megamedia corporations in the world, with revenues of about $14 billion in fiscal year 1997. In January 1997 Bertelsmann took a big step when the Ufa TV division of the company merged with CLT, one of Europe's largest chains of TV and radio stations.

> The new entity instantly becomes Europe's largest, most lucrative media company, with estimated annual revenue of $3.2 billion [in European broadcast media alone]. It has stakes in more than 19 TV and 26 radio networks in 10 countries, as well as some of Europe's biggest [film and video] libraries and production houses.

This merger was enabled by a change in German media law that loosened ownership restrictions. The new merged corporation also owns part of the new Channel 5 in Britain, all of the new RTL7 TV station/network in Poland, and the leading radio station in Romania, among other initiatives in Eastern Europe. And in March 1998 Bertelsmann added dramatically to its already strong position in publishing by acquiring the Random House–Knopf–Pantheon group of publishing houses from Newhouse's Advance Publications. Random House was America's largest commercial book publisher. The purchase made Bertelsmann the number one giant in book publishing by far.[12] The following details Bertelsmann's holdings.[13]

Bertelsmann AG

Book Publishing
In Germany, owns 20 book publishing companies and has interests
in 4 others
In the U.S. (and elsewhere): Bantam Books (world's largest paper-
back book publisher); Doubleday Books Group, including Dell
Books; Random House, Alfred A. Knopf, Pantheon, Crown Pub-
lishing, Times Books, Ballantine Books, Fawett Books, Schocken
Books, some other smaller presses, and Fodor Travel Books
Doubleday Book Club and BMG Music Club
Book clubs in Latin America

Magazine Publishing
75% owner of Gruner & Jahr (with well over a billion dollars in revenue per year), one of Germany's leading magazine publishers,
which publishes *Der Stern, Geo,* and many special-interest titles like
the women's magazine *Best* and the business magazine *Capital*
In U.S.: *Parents, Family Circle, McCall's, Fitness, Child, YM, American
Homestyle*
Over 100 magazines around the world

Newspaper
Hamburger Morgenpost

Recorded Music and Music Publishing
Owner of RCA Music, one of the largest in the world
Also in the U.S.: Arista Records; 4BMG classics/RCA Victor; BMG
direct; BMG Music; BMG Latin; Killer Tracks; Private Music; Zoo
Entertainment; 50% of Reunion Records; 50% of Windham Hill
recordings; 20% of Image Recording Co.; BMG Music Publishing;
BMG Songs; Careers-BMG
3 recorded music companies in Germany

Broadcast and Cable TV and Radio
Controls CLT/RTL, Europe's largest commercial TV broadcaster
BMG Video
50% of Kabel-Marketing-Gesellschaft (KMG), Germany's largest
cable TV company
50% of ION Multimedia
50% of NiceMan
Joint ventures with prime French commercial TV station, French

Canal Plus; also operates leading German pay-TV channel Premier with a German partner

Interests in Dutch TV channels RTL4 and RTL5 and in French channels M6 and TMC

Major interests in 18 radio stations around Europe

29% of new Channel 5 in Great Britain

New RTL7 TV station/network in Poland

Radio Contact, market leader in Romania

90% of RUFA, a news agency that produces radio newscasts for local radio stations in Germany

Film, Video, and TV Production
Stern-TV
Geo-Film
Ufa-Film

Printing, U.S.
Berryville Graphics
Delta Lithograph
Dynamic Graphic Finishing
Offset Paperback Manufacturers

Online Computer Service
Joint venture with America Online offering on-line service in Europe

5. General Electric–NBC

The National Broadcasting Co. radio network was founded in the 1920s and was an early leader in radio. For most of their history, RCA and NBC were headed by David Sarnoff, one of the main pioneers of broadcast media in America. Sarnoff was born in Minsk, Russia, and his family immigrated to the United States in 1900. He began his career as a radio transmission operator for the Marconi Wireless Telegraph Co. (In 1912, young Sarnoff was the first to pick up the distress signal from the sinking *Titanic*, which he passed on to the authorities and the world.) It was Sarnoff, in a higher position three years later with the Marconi company, who first proposed producing for the general public a "radio music box"—a commercial radio receiver. When the Radio Corp. of America was set up in 1921 to make and sell such consumer radios, Sarnoff became its general manager, and he directed NBC from its inception in 1926. Sarnoff was originally a proponent of the "public service" model of broadcasting and thought radio should not be stained by raw money-making. While moving into the for-profit mode of operation for NBC in the years thereafter, Sarnoff retained a strong sense of stewardship for the broadcast and news institution of NBC and the public trust involved.

When television began its ascent following World War II, NBC quickly attained prominence in the new medium. In terms of broadcast news and the image of the network, NBC was at its height in the late 1950s and early 1960s when the Huntley-Brinkley anchor team on *NBC Nightly News* dominated the airwaves. David Sarnoff retired from RCA and NBC as chairman of the board of RCA in 1970. He was succeeded by corporate executives increasingly focused on the bottom line who had not had the pioneering experience in, and sense of stewardship for, the American institution of broadcast news. Former NBC News president Reuven Frank pointed out the realities of the orientation of RCA's post-Sarnoff board chairman Edgar Griffiths and fellow RCA executives: "One source of problems [for NBC News] was . . . RCA, to whom NBC was a cash cow. NBC always made money . . . which RCA always seemed to need . . . Sometimes RCA demanded and got enough money to damage NBC." Griffiths was the "prototypical money man, meistersinger of the bottom line whose pure tones were undistorted by the sentimental slurring of tradition or obligation."

In 1985, industrial giant General Electric bought out RCA-NBC and subsequently sold off many of the other RCA holdings; the RCA recorded music operation, a veritable American icon, was sold to Bertelsmann. By 1997, the General Electric industrial conglomerate was ranked as the fifth largest corporation in the United States. GE's financial numbers are mind-boggling: the corporation generated over $90 billion in revenues and over $7 billion in profits in 1997. Further, under the hard-driving leadership of CEO Jack Welch, the market value of GE increased from $13.5 billion in early 1982 to $169.4 billion in early 1997—an increase of 1,155 percent. GE's industrial products produced revenues of over $10 billion in 1997; four other general areas of GE business produced over $6 billion each. The broadcast area, principally NBC, produced over $5 billion in revenues in 1997. In profits, NBC ranked eighth, behind most of the industrial and commercial product and service areas, financing, and insurance in GE.

It is in this corporate conglomerate context that NBC must operate. GE demanded big cuts in NBC personnel and put great pressure on NBC News to be another GE profit center. Network employee totals were cut by almost 1,500 in 1986 and 1987. CEO Jack Welch frequently talked of "downsizing" and "restructuring" as he chopped away at costs and jobs in GE divisions and subsidiaries. Critics called him "neutron Jack," since, like the projected neutron bomb, he made people disappear, but the buildings remained. Welch's 1997 compensation package: $30 million.[14]

GE is ranked fifth here, despite the fact that the corporation as a whole is a much larger business enterprise than the first four, because its media business is not nearly as large as Disney-ABC, Time Warner, News Corp., or Bertelsmann. It has, however, engaged in strong expansion in Europe and elsewhere in recent years. For example, NBC Europe is seen, via its ownership of Super Channel, in about 70 million European homes.[15] The holdings of General Electric are detailed below. (Not every single piece of the conglomerate is listed here, it is too elaborate; but all significant areas are listed.)

General Electric–NBC

MEDIA HOLDINGS

Broadcasting
NBC Television network, broadcasting *NBC Nightly News*, the *Today Show, Dateline NBC, Meet the Press,* and other quasi–public affairs and entertainment shows; with over 200 affiliated local TV stations
Owns 11 local TV stations in 8 of the largest markets and 3 lesser markets, reaching 25% of American households (All but the smallest one are VHF stations.)

Cable TV and Internet-Interactive and Related Media
CNBC business, news, and talk show cable channel
Equity investments in cable TV channels/networks American Movie Classics, Arts & Entertainment, Bravo, Court TV, Prime Network, and regional sports channels around the U.S.
Partner in MSNBC Cable news and features channel, and MSNBC Interactive on-line news and information service
NBC Digital Publishing (CD-ROMs)
NBC Online Ventures (establishes news, sports, and entertainment sites on the World Wide Web and Microsoft Network)
NBC Europe and CNBC Europe; NBC Asia and CNBC Asia; MSNBC operating in Europe as of 1998
Agreement with French Canal Plus allows NBC's cable channels to be "the first U.S. networks to be carried over French digital television"
CNBC Asia, "first 24-hour business news channel to be broadcast live from 3 continents"

INDUSTRIAL AND COMMERCIAL HOLDINGS (NONMEDIA)

Aircraft Engines
GE Aircraft Engines, makers of jet engines for airplanes
Subsidiary: Marines & Industrial Engines Service Division

Appliances
GE Appliances—manufactures and markets refrigerators, electric
and gas stoves, microwave ovens, freezers, dishwashers, clothes
washers and dryers, room air conditioners, disposals, trash com-
pacters
Subsidiary: Roper Corp., maker of electric and gas ranges

Aviation
General Electric Capital Aviation Services—leasing and financing of
commercial jet aircraft

Car and Truck Fleet Management and Leasing
GE Capital Fleet Services—management and servicing of fleets of
cars and trucks; distribution services; equipment leasing; Corpo-
rate Payment Systems and Travel Service; Marine and Air Cargo
Container Leasing; Ground and Air Courier Service
Gelco CTI Container Services
Gelco Travel Services Inc. travel agencies
Other Gelco companies

Financial, Insurance, and Related Businesses
General Electric Capital Services, commercial lending, retail financial
services, equipment financing, etc.
GE Capital Mortgage Services mortgage company
Employers Reinsurance Corp., property and casualty reinsurance
GE Capital Commercial Real Estate, commercial lending company,
business and industrial loans
GE Modular Space, maker and seller of mobile office units, trailers
and construction field offices, etc.
General Electric Investment Corp., investments and trusts manage-
ment
GE Capital Assurance, sells annuities and insurance through broker-
age agencies
Amex Life Assurance; Federal Home Life Insurance Co.; Harvest
Insurance Co., Harvest Life Insurance Agency—life insurance
GNA; HGI Inc. and other financial and insurance companies

Hotels and Food Service
Doubletree Hotels and Motels
Service America Corp. and various subsidiaries—food and refreshment services, vending machine operations, etc.

Lighting Products and Industrial Products and Systems
GE Lighting Division, residential and commercial light bulbs and fixtures, electric lamps, vehicle lighting equipment, etc.
Joint venture: GE–Toshiba Lighting Corp.
GE Distribution & Control Manufacturing, electrical distribution and control equipment
GE Transportation Systems, locomotives and transit equipment
GE/Fanuc Automation North America, industrial automation and robotics products
GE Supply (a network of electrical supply houses in the U.S.) and GE Supply Mexico
General Electric Railcar Repair Services Corp.
Global Compression Services Inc.—fabricate compressors, air and gas compressors
GE Environmental Systems—electrostatic precipitators, fabric filters

Materials and Chemicals
GE Plastics, plastics and resins
GE Silicones
GE Superabrasives

Power Generation and Power Systems
GE Industrial & Power Systems—builds and services electrical and nuclear power generation plants and equipment ("serving utility, industrial and governmental customers worldwide")
Joint venture: GE-Hitachi VHB Inc., maker of gas circuit breakers

Technical Products and Services
GE Medical Systems, including magnetic resonance scanners, computed tomography scanners, x-ray, nuclear imaging, ultrasound, and other diagnostic and therapy equipment and supporting services. Agreement with Columbia/HCA (largest for-profit multi-hospital system in the U.S.) to manage all of its diagnostic imaging equipment service and biomedical equipment service.

Note: GE has significant operations in various of these business areas in Europe and Asia.

6. CBS Inc. (Westinghouse-CBS, 1995–1998)

Although he did not bring CBS radio into existence, in every important sense, William S. Paley was the founding father and guiding force behind the Columbia Broadcasting System from early on into the 1980s. Like David Sarnoff's, Bill Paley's origins were in Russia; his grandfather Isaac Paley, a successful businessman, immigrated with his family to America in the late 1880s. Isaac's son Sam became a successful cigar manufacturer, which enabled Bill Paley to grow up in a wealthy background and gave the family the financial resources to make a fateful investment in the late 1920s.

Bill Paley started out in the family cigar business, Congress Cigar Co. But, as Paley told the story, when he first heard radio on a crystal set—"the wireless"—at a friend's house in 1925, he at first couldn't believe the music was actually "coming out of the air"; he was hooked. CBS started life in 1927 as the United Independent Broadcasters, an alternative to the already dominant NBC radio networks. The Columbia Phonograph Co. provided a much-needed investment a little later, and the company became Columbia Broadcasting System. But the network was shaky, and, after Paley cigar ads on the fledgling network paid off well, in 1928 Bill Paley and his father bought control of CBS. At the age of twenty-seven, Bill Paley took over as head of CBS radio.

Although he faced daunting odds in competing against the NBC radio networks, Paley used a classic American flair for salesmanship and promotion, a good feel for programming and entertainment talent, along with much audacity, to build CBS into a success first in radio and then in television. Now, in truth, much of the time Paley focused principally on entertainment programs, not news and public affairs. And even at the height of CBS's image as "the Tiffany network" from the 1950s through the 1970s, Paley was profit oriented and focused on entertainment; he was not a pure public-service angel, as author Sally Bedell Smith has documented. But in radio in the late 1930s he started something truly significant with Edward R. Murrow, Charles Collingwood, William R. Shirer, and other now legendary broadcast journalists; and he transferred that news and public affairs commitment to TV at CBS News beginning in the 1950s.

Beginning with the hiring of Murrow, Paley demonstrated a strong sense of stewardship for CBS and its public affairs responsibilities; he often referred to "the public trust that we have at CBS." The Murrow hiring, the dramatic success of his radio reports in World War II from London, and the subsequent role Murrow played, with strong backing from

Paley, were the signal developments in that orientation. The backing extended to a major piece of American history when, in 1954, Murrow and producer Fred Friendly of the CBS show *See It Now* challenged Senator Joseph McCarthy and his campaign of fear. McCarthyism, which damaged people's reputations by wantonly labeling people "communists" or "communist sympathizers," was rampant in America. But using McCarthy's own words on film—an early demonstration of the power of TV image and sound—Murrow directly took on McCarthy and his methods. In the 1990s, it is hard to remember how overwhelming was the climate of fear, but this showed genuine courage. And Paley backed him up. After hearing Murrow's description of the program he and Friendly intended to do, Paley just asked if Murrow was sure it was accurate. Then he asked, "Will it cause a big stink?" Murrow said, "Yes." Just before airtime that fateful evening, Paley called Murrow and said: "I'm with you today, and I'll be with you tomorrow"; and he was.

Journalist David Halberstam said: "Murrow was one of those rare legendary figures who was as good as his myth; whose presence is so strong that it still lives. . . . [He was] brilliant as a communicator, a man who spanned the oceans and who more than anyone else made broadcasting respectable for a generation of other talented broadcast [journalists]." Murrow then took that respectability into television and "made it journalistically legitimate and honorable." Murrow was

> a man who was in a way more an educator than a journalist and whose career and the technology which he was part of were one of the conduits of America's transformation from a sleepy post-Depression isolationist nation to a major international superpower. . . . His legacy was a tradition of reporting from which the corporate officials, whatever their private feelings, simply could not back down.
>
> No other broadcast journalist would ever again accumulate the prestige both inside and outside the company that Murrow had. . . . As his comet ascended, so too did that of CBS.

Of course one broadcast journalist did come close to Murrow's level of prestige: Walter Cronkite, of CBS News. Paley's sense of stewardship is also well illustrated by a tale told to me by the distinguished former CBS News chief diplomatic correspondent Marvin Kalb, now director of the Shorenstein Center on Press and Politics in Harvard's Kennedy School of Government:

> At the end of 1962 during a dinner in Paris, Bill Paley told his foreign correspondents what his plans were for CBS in 1963. Charley Colling-

wood said: "Bill, that's going to cost you a lot of money." And Paley-said: "You guys cover the news; I've got Jack Benny to make money for me."

But, alas, matters got messier in the 1980s. CBS started fighting off attempts to take it over in 1984, but some of its actions significantly increased its debt. In 1985, in some fear and confusion, the CBS board became more receptive to merging with a "white knight" corporation. Along came Lawrence Tisch and his Loews Corp.

The Loews Corp. conglomerate included Lorillard Tobacco, Loews Hotels and cinemas, CNA Insurance, Bulova watches, and other investments. CEO Tisch's favorite activity was sitting in his office intensely following his Quotron machine, which spewed out stock-price developments. Through 1985 and 1986, Tisch was not entirely honest about his intentions in gaining control of CBS through stock purchases, and then about becoming the chief executive of CBS, nor about how he would operate once he had control of the network. Speaking frankly, Tisch could be called the poster boy for the damaging of the network news operations by corporate bean counters. By the end of 1986, 1,000 positions had been eliminated from CBS as a whole. At one point Tisch threatened to cut in half the CBS News budget of about $300 million, but he eventually settled for a $36 million cut and the elimination of 215 positions in the news division. Author Ken Auletta has provided one of the best accounts of how Tisch went about things:

> Tisch was a man with an almost religious fervor for cost cutting. . . . [His management consultant Thomas] Flanagan saw things simply as well. "Entertainment [referring to CBS as a whole] is just another business," he said. . . .
>
> Another budget whack with future implications was Tisch's decision, taken alone, to close the CBS Technology Center. . . . This was the laboratory where a passionate and brilliant young scientist, Peter Goldmark, pioneered the LP record and color TV, where CBS engineers blazed the development of one-inch tape and electronic news gathering, . . . in the long run, CBS was ceding its technological self-sufficiency.
>
> Larry Tisch's definition of a well-managed company was something quantifiable in dollars and cents, not ephemeral things like morale or trust or quality or investing in the future.

Former CBS president Frank Stanton, who was second only to Paley in building CBS to "Tiffany" status, said of Tisch: "If you look at him in terms of morale, he's wrecked it."

And so it went, until 1995, when industrial and broadcasting conglomerate Westinghouse Electric Corp. bought out CBS—and Larry Tisch. With the largest bloc of CBS stock, Tisch, after largely trashing the Tiffany network, apparently made off with about $900 million in personal profit.

Westinghouse, founded in 1886, had long experience in broadcasting (unlike GE) and actually began the first general-audience radio station back in 1920 in its corporate hometown of Pittsburgh. By 1995, Westinghouse was a major conglomerate. Besides the new CBS properties, it had a significant broadcast division, Group W, which included seven TV stations and eighteen radio stations, among other operations. Westinghouse also included a number of industrial areas—electronics systems, turbine and nuclear power systems, refrigeration and heating systems, military contracting in electronics, office furniture, finance—with divisions elsewhere in the world. But through 1996 and 1997, Westinghouse-CBS transformed itself. The corporation gradually sold off all its industrial businesses. As of the end of 1997, the corporation became simply CBS Inc. For the issue of conflicts of interest in CBS News operations, this was good news.

Meanwhile, the corporation acquired Infinity Broadcasting, one of the largest radio station chains. This made Westinghouse-CBS one of the two giants of radio and gave it multiple stations in all of the top ten media markets in America. CBS and Westinghouse's Group W already owned TV stations in various of those markets. This raised issues of cross-ownership under federal regulations. The FCC in 1995 granted the merged companies waivers from rules against cross-ownership in a series of media markets where they now owned radio stations and a TV station, such as New York, Los Angeles, and Chicago. As of March 1998 those "temporary" waivers were still in place pending an FCC rule decision on duopoly ownership of TV and radio in the same market.

Westinghouse-CBS sold radio stations in Dallas and Chicago to comply with the newly expanded limit of eight radio stations in a single major area; and to grease the wheels at the Justice Department, they agreed to sell two other stations elsewhere. In late 1997, the concentration increased further when CBS bought American Radio Systems, the fourth largest radio chain, with ninety-eight stations. (The purchase was awaiting formal FCC approval as of March 1998.)

With the acquisition of Infinity Broadcasting came the radio show of sleaze and shock radio jockey Howard Stern and the Don Imus show. It's a long way from Edward R. Murrow to Howard Stern—or Don Imus.[16]

The following details the holdings of CBS. For 1997, the consolidated revenues of all Westinghouse-CBS holdings were well over $9 billion.[17]

CBS Inc.

Broadcasting
CBS TV Network, broadcasting *CBS Evening News, 60 Minutes, CBS Morning News,* and other quasi–public affairs and entertainment shows; with over 200 affiliated local TV stations
Owns 14 TV stations, whose broadcast reaches 32% of the American public
Owns over 170 radio stations, with largest total audience of any radio chain
Partly owns Westwood One, major radio show distribution company
Note: These TV and radio station totals make CBS the largest combined television and radio broadcaster in the U.S.

Cable TV
In early 1997, acquired the Nashville Network (TNN) and Country Music Television (CMT) cable TV channels

Non-U.S. Media Holdings and Ventures
In 1996, bought TeleNoticias, Spanish-language news channel broadcast to 22 Latin American countries. Now called CBS/TeleNoticias. Developing Spanish-language news channel for Hispanic population in the U.S.
In 1997, started a Portuguese-language network for Brazil

7. The Newhouse/Advance Publications Media Empire

The Newhouse media empire was begun by Sam Newhouse, whose father, Meier, had immigrated to the United States from Czarist Russia in the 1890s. Throughout his youth, Sam Newhouse lived in poverty. In 1922, after successfully running a small newspaper in the New York area owned by a lawyer who had befriended him, young Sam Newhouse scraped together some money of his own, got some help from the lawyer, and bought a small, struggling New York newspaper, the *Staten Island Advance.* The name of that paper would serve as the corporate name for the subsequent growing media empire, Advance Publications. And advance is what Newhouse did, steadily developing a megamedia corporation. As author Thomas Maier has written, Sam Newhouse was the classic American success story:

> The single-minded struggle of an enterprising young man who rises from a life of poverty to achieve untold wealth and power. Somehow, it

seemed fitting that one of Newhouse's [later] acquisitions would include Street & Smith, the pulp publisher of Horatio Alger stories.

(Horatio Alger is no relation to the author of *Megamedia and Democracy*.)

From the 1930s through the early 1950s, Sam Newhouse bought eight more newspapers in New York, New Jersey, and Pennsylvania; and in the 1950s and 1960s, he bought papers elsewhere in the nation, including major newspapers like the *Portland Oregonian*, the *Cleveland Plain Dealer*, and the *New Orleans Times-Picayune*. Newhouse would often go after newspapers following the death of the founding owner of a family-owned paper, when heirs might be receptive to sizable money offers. He maximized profits and minimized the need to borrow money by cutting costs intensely, expanding advertising by a variety of means, and focusing on local news; this allowed him to keep the company private, in the family, and to avoid being subject to stockholder demands.

The journalistic results of the Newhouse newspaper control and methods were not generally admired. *Time* magazine said of Sam Newhouse: "If he has not debased the quality of U.S. journalism, he has not notably improved it either." Others were more critical. The Newhouse operation tended to seek monopoly newspaper positions in cities—and to use almost any means it could get away with to attain that position. Author Thomas Maier did an extensive investigation of the Newhouse empire. He found:

> [Newhouse's] actions—which often skirted on the precipice of antitrust violations and reduced major cities to a single daily newspaper—were rarely scrutinized by other media. This was especially so in five cities— St. Louis, Portland, Birmingham, Syracuse, and Harrisburg, Pennsylvania—where Newhouse owned not only the daily newspaper but also a television and radio station or a cable-television franchise, as well.

As Maier mentions, from the 1960s on, the Newhouse empire acquired properties in other mass media: magazines, TV and radio stations, cable TV systems, and book publishing. In the later 1970s, Sam Newhouse's sons, S. I. ("Si") and Donald, began to take the reins of Advance Publications, with Si Newhouse being the prime leader. By the time of Sam's death in 1979, the Newhouse media empire included thirty-one newspapers, seven magazines (including the legendary literary and public affairs magazine, the *New Yorker*), six TV stations, five radio stations, and several cable TV systems. In 1980, Advance Publications added the respected Random House group of book publishers and continued to make acquisitions. By the 1990s, the Newhouse newspaper chain was the third largest in the United States in total circulation. The Newhouse empire, under its Newhouse Broadcasting division, through September 1994 held cable TV systems in seventeen states with a total of 1.4 million subscribers; this made them the seventh-largest cable systems company at that time. In the 1980s, the corporation sold the five Newhouse Broadcasting TV stations and its several radio stations. In September 1994 the Newhouses entered into a joint venture with Time Warner in which Time Warner placed two-thirds of its cable systems, totaling 2.8 million subscribers, together with the Newhouse systems and created Time Warner Entertainment–Advance/Newhouse Cable. Time Warner took over basic management of the venture. Thus, Newhouse/Advance got Time Warner's superior expertise in cable and its marketing power. And America got still another interconnection between the megamedia giants.

"By the mid-1990s, the family's . . . newspapers produced an estimated $2 billion in annual revenues and were worth close to $7 billion. The Newhouse Broadcasting cable franchises . . . were valued at close to $3 billion." In 1998, the Newhouses sold their publishing houses "to concentrate on their core businesses."

All that development and personal ownership has made the two Newhouse brothers fabulously wealthy: in mid-1997, *Forbes* estimated the personal wealth of Si and Donald Newhouse at $4.5 billion each. Retaining private family control and the money for all those acquisitions was greatly facilitated by extraordinary levels of tax avoidance, including inheritance taxes upon the death of Sam Newhouse. Because the corporation is privately held, it is also more difficult for researchers and the public to obtain information on corporate holdings and activities. As Maier notes:

> Si Newhouse has thrived as a silent potentate of the American communications industry, allowing his family enterprise to accumulate billions of dollars in revenues with little public scrutiny or sense of accountability to the commonweal. His defiance is part of a long Newhouse family history of stonewalling or threatening retribution on those who make unwanted inquiries.[18]

The following details the Newhouse multimedia empire.[19]

Newhouse/Advance Publications

Newspapers
Birmingham (Ala.) News
Cleveland Plain-Dealer

Newark Star-Ledger
New Orleans Times-Picayune
Portland Oregonian
Staten Island Advance
Syracuse Post-Standard
Trenton (N.J.) Times
As of late 1997, 18 other newspapers around the nation

Magazines
Condé Nast magazines group, including *Vogue, Vanity Fair, House &*
   Garden, Glamour, Self, Allure, Condé Nast Traveler, Details, Gourmet
The *New Yorker*
Parade magazine, included weekly with numerous newspapers
   throughout the U.S.
Architectural Digest
Bon Appétit
Gentlemen's Quarterly
Mademoiselle
American City Business Journals, publishing 18 city business peri-
   odicals around the U.S.
Publisher of 3 motor sports magazines
Wired

Cable TV Systems and Other Electronic Media
Time Warner Entertainment–Advance/Newhouse Cable

8. Viacom: From MTV to Mining

Viacom, with its various antecedent corporations and stages of development, is a perfect example of corporate merger mania and conglomerate
empire-building. The corporation is actually several formerly independent companies. Viacom is the company that loosed MTV on the world
via cable TV, and it produces VH-1 (MTV for adults) and Nickelodeon for
children and owns premium movie cable channel Showtime. In 1994, Viacom acquired Paramount Communications, with the major Hollywood
movie and TV production studio Paramount Pictures. Paramount also
included two other big companies: the former Gulf + Western industrial
conglomerate, with business in everything from oil production to mining
to realty investing; and Simon & Schuster publishing group, which
included the major academic publisher Prentice Hall. Also in 1994, Viacom acquired Blockbuster Entertainment, the largest video rental and

recorded music store chain. Through 1996, the corporation also owned ten radio stations; but it sold them to large radio-chain owner Evergreen Communications in 1997. Viacom also owned some cable TV systems but sold them as well, to reduce Viacom's huge debt load. In May 1998, Viacom sold the educational part of its Simon & Schuster publishing group (Allyn & Bacon and the educational part of Prentice Hall) to the big British media company Pearson and sold its professional and reference sections to the rapidly growing media investment group Hicks, Muse, Tate & Furst. The consumer ("trade") book division of Simon & Schuster—and that well-known name—remained with Viacom; Viacom would use consumer publishing in coordination with its Paramount, MTV, and other media properties.

Viacom is led by Chairman Sumner Redstone, who owns 67 percent of the stock. He had a personal wealth of $3.4 billion in 1997, according to *Forbes* magazine. The corporation generated well over $13 billion in revenues in 1997. Some readers might question Viacom's number eight ranking, since the corporation does not have a truly powerhouse news and public affairs outlet. But, besides the UPN TV network, Viacom controls one of the two most-watched media channels on the planet, which is also a major presence for, and influence on, the next generation: MTV. MTV has also inserted an increasing amount of public affairs content in its programming, some of it constructively innovative (such as the "Rock the Vote" series). In 1996, Viacom signed a deal with number two German media giant Kirch to provide programming for Kirch's European networks, including its digital TV endeavors.[20] Viacom's wide range of media and nonmedia holdings are detailed below.[21]

Viacom

MEDIA HOLDINGS

Broadcasting
11 TV stations, 7 in the top 12 media markets (plus 2 other stations under their managmnent)
50% of United Paramount TV Network (UPN), with 159 local affiliates as of early 1997. 10 of Viacom's TV stations are UPN affiliates. Paramount TV production studios also provide the entertainment programming for UPN.

Cable TV Networks/Channels
MTV in the U.S, Europe, and Latin America; plus MTV-2 (or M2)

Showtime

The Movie Channel

Nickelodeon

Flix

Joint venture in Comedy Channel (with Time Warner) and All News Channel

Joint venture in Sundance Channel.

Movies, TV, and Video Program Production

Paramount Pictures major movie studio and TV production studio

Spelling Entertainment Group: Aaron Spelling Productions, Republic Pictures, Big Ticket Television, and Worldvision Enterprises

Desilu Productions

Smaller production companies, including Atlantic Home Video, and "Are We Having Fun Yet?" Productions

Video and Recorded Music Rentals and Sales

Blockbuster Video stores

Blockbuster Music stores

Blockbuster Entertainment Inc.

Blockbuster Family Fun Inc.

Blockbuster Productions Corp.

Many other Blockbuster companies, from Blockbuster Adventures to Blockbuster Global Services to Blockbuster Park Holding Corporation to Blockbuster Promotions

Publishing

Simon & Schuster trade book publishing, along with CD-ROMs, etc.

INDUSTRIAL AND COMMERCIAL HOLDINGS (NONMEDIA)

Theme Parks

Paramount Parks—5 regional theme parks, each with attractions related to content media properties of Viacom

Other

There are too many and varied companies to list separately; the following list illustrates the range of Viacom businesses:

A.S. Payroll Co.

Abaco Farms, Ltd.

Antilles Oil Company Inc.

Avalon Vertriebs GmbH (Germany)

Bombay Hook Ltd.
Brookvale Developments No.1 Pty, Ltd. (Australia)
BS Hotel Inc.
Caloil Inc. (Canada)
Capital Equipment Leasing Ltd. (Britain)
Cayman Overseas Reinsurance Assoc. (Cayman Islands)
Center for Applied Research in Education
Cityvision Videotheken Ges.M.B.H (Austria)
Direct Response Associates
Dynamic Soap Inc.
Energy Development Associates Inc.
G & W Natural Resources Co.
Glendale Property Corp.
Gloucester Titanium Company
Gulf + Western Holdings
Kilo Mining Corporation
New Jersey Zinc Exploration Co.
St. Johns Realty Investors
Timber Purchase Co.

**Notable Financial Connections with Other
Megamedia Corporations**
Other 50% of United Paramount Network held by BHC Communications, a subsidiary of Chris-Craft Industries (leading maker of boats and yachts)
MCA is Viacom's partner in USA Networks (although there is a lawsuit over who owns how much).
HBO–Time Warner is Viacom's partner in the Comedy Channel.
NYNEX (New York regional telephone company) has a $1.2 billion investment in Viacom.

9. Microsoft

Microsoft is, of course, the company founded by Bill Gates and Paul Allen in 1975 and built into the ultimate corporate sultan of software. Microsoft is certainly one of the extraordinary business success stories of the twentieth century. By 1997 it was generating over $11 billion in revenues. But until quite recently, it had not been much involved in mass media that are prime sources of news and public affairs information, or other content. That is why it is ranked "only" ninth in the megamedia pantheon.

More recently, however, Microsoft has been moving out of the realm of pure computer software, and there are indications that Gates and Microsoft may become much more major players in general mass media. The corporation certainly has the financial might to do so; it had the second highest return on revenue of all of the Fortune 500 corporations in 1996, and as of late 1997, it had the awe-inspiring fluid resource of $9 billion in cash.

As *Broadcasting & Cable* magazine noted in mid-1997: "Recognizing that he will need smart content to drive demand for his smart TVs, Gates has been pouring money into content-oriented ventures." Back in 1995, Microsoft bought a piece of DreamWorks SKG, the multimedia company of Steven Spielberg and partners, and they established a 50-50 joint venture. In 1996, in collaboration with NBC, Microsoft and its on-line service, Microsoft Network (MSN), launched MSNBC, a combined cable and on-line Internet news and features channel. MSN includes a magazine—"Webzine"—called *Slate*, edited by the former editor of the *New Republic* magazine. (In March 1997, *Slate* even carried a debate on the subject, "Are media conglomerates bad for us?") By late 1997, MSN also included eleven other "channels" and fourteen Web site "shows," including the first regular live comedy Webcast, *This Is Not a Test,* coming from the interactive arm of the *Saturday Night Live* people.

In April 1997, Microsoft bought WebTV for $425 million. The key reason: WebTV held five patents "that substantially improve the display of Internet content on a TV set." This was intended to keep Microsoft on top of the movement toward making smart TVs through which people can gain access to the Internet; "now, electronics manufacturers that want to incorporate [Internet] surfing capabilities directly into TV sets can turn to Microsoft for the software." Gates and company have also been vigorous voices in the debate about digital broadcast standards, seeking to make sure that the coming standards are compatible with the way PCs handle video. In early 1997, the corporation began setting up entertainment and arts information Web sites for local areas called, for example, "New York Sidewalk" or "Seattle Sidewalk," competing in part against established local area magazines.

In summer 1997 Microsoft took two further steps. First, it agreed to invest $1 billion in Comcast, the fourth largest cable TV systems owner, with 4.3 million subscribers. This should boost sales of Microsoft's on-line and interactive software and services. This investment is also to help Comcast accelerate its development of fiber-optic cable to expand high-speed access to the Internet, which may facilitate a further stage in the convergence of the TV and the computer. Gates said this gives Microsoft a ready market for a version of the WebTV device to hook into the Comcast cable system. The WebTV software, which gives TV watchers access to the Internet and the capacity to perform other on-line functions, is to be put into new set-top boxes from cable companies, thus enabling subscribers to cruise both cable TV and the Internet. A late-1997 agreement between TCI and Microsoft apparently gives Microsoft an even stronger hand in that realm (see chapter 6). Gates is also a major investor in Teledesic Corp., which intends to put up a system of hundreds of low-orbiting satellites that will offer Internet access at a thousand times the speed of today's facilities. And Gates has begun buying up companies that own visual images, like the Bettmann Archive, the important archive of historical photos, and electronic reproduction rights to visual images, such as great works of art.

The second notable step in summer 1997 was Microsoft's investment of $150 million in Apple Computer. As part of the deal, Apple will use Microsoft's version of Java computer language and place Microsoft's Internet Explorer on Apple computers. The latter was a significant boost in Microsoft's battle with Netscape for preeminence in the Internet world. It continued to extend its influence. Analysts suggested that the Apple computer investment was also a little insurance policy against antitrust moves against Microsoft; with Macintosh computer operating systems still viable, Microsoft did not totally control the operating systems on all the world's personal computers. But later in 1997 the Justice Department's Antitrust Division charged Microsoft with violating a consent decree in their design and marketing of the new Internet Explorer 4.0. In May 1998 the Antitrust Division and twenty states' attorneys general announced a formal antitrust suit against Microsoft.

Some close observers might suggest that the number nine spot for Microsoft on this megamedia list is too low—or at least that the ranking will be left far behind in the next few years as the corporation skyrockets upward and expands outward. At the end of 1996 a *Newsweek* assessment of the Gates-Microsoft trajectory suggested, a little frighteningly:

> Critics of its power may not want to hear this, but only now is the 21-year-old company . . . poised to really take off. Some of its executives privately believe Microsoft could double both its size and its market valuation in the next five years . . . But even that would not begin to address the strength and breadth of an entity that sits at the hub of the information revolution.
>
> "It's difficult to think of a company in the history of the world that's positioned to influence so many aspects of life as Microsoft is at the end of the 20th century," says Michael Moritz, a venture capitalist.

In March 1998 Bill Gates's estimated personal wealth was an almost incomprehensible $45 billion, mostly dependent on Microsoft's high-flying stock price. The more important question is, How much of American public expression and information will he control as we move through the first decade of new millennium, and what else around the world will be effectively controlled or influenced by mammoth Microsoft and Mr. Gates?[22]

The following details Microsoft's holdings—although in this case, the formal holdings are far from the whole story. As of early 1998, Microsoft did not have an elaborate conglomerate structure.[23]

Microsoft

Computer Software and Related Products
The principal Microsoft company is divided into 4 main groups:
1. Platforms Product Group: operating system and digital media, Internet software; related technologies
2. Applications and Content Product Group: business software, interactive entertainment and information products, and the Microsoft Network on-line service. Also includes software enabling PCs to receive and transmit various forms of television. Software for broadcast, film producton, and other high-end animation applications, and the integration of visual images, text, sound, and special-effects technology. *Microsoft Encarta* multimedia encyclopedia data base; Bookshelf multimedia reference library; Microsoft Cinemania (an interactive guide to the movies)
3. Sales & Support Group
4. Operations Group

Note: TCI, number 12 of Dominant Dozen, owns 20% of Microsoft Network L.L.C. on-line service.

Other
Sidewalk local entertainment guide in several cities
Microsoft Press book publisher
Owns rights to Bettmann Archives, most important collection of historic photos
Operations in France, Germany, Great Britain, Ireland, Switzerland, and elsewhere
Web TV
In mid-1997, Microsoft committed to establishing a research lab in collaboration with Cambridge University and invested $16 million in a venture fund to back technology start-up companies in that area.

Joint Ventures

Joint venture in MSNBC cable channel and Internet news and features service, in 50-50 collaboration with NBC

Investment in DreamWorks SKG, with 50-50 joint venture in the offshoot DreamWorks Interactive, which develops interactive and multimedia products

$1 billion investment in cable TV systems owner Comcast

$150 million investment, plus other financial arrangements, with Apple Computer

Other investments and joint ventures

10. Matra-Hachette-Filipacchi: From France to the World

Hachette, whose origins go back far into the nineteenth century, is the second largest megamedia group in Europe; but as Matra-Hachette, it is also an industrial conglomerate roughly comparable to what Westinghouse was, with a touch of Chrysler. Hachette began as a modest bookseller. After World War II, it got into magazines in a bigger and bigger way. Then, after it became associated with Matra in 1980, Hachette expanded into other media. Matra by itself in 1988 was the thirty-fifth-largest industrial conglomerate in France. It is involved in military and space hardware, telecommunications and information technology, automobiles, and transportation systems. In 1980–1981, the head of Matra, prominent industrial leader Jean-Luc Lagardère, gained effective control of Hachette, while keeping the two corporations essentially separate. In 1992 the two companies were merged, and by 1994 Lagardère had gained virtually total ownership and control so that Matra-Hachette is formally part of the Lagardère Group conglomerate.

Lagardère had a colleague in the 1980–1981 buyout of Hachette: Daniel Filipacchi, the flashy-dressing, flamboyant head of Filipacchi Publications group. Filipacchi Publications was the eighth largest print media corporation in France, and it included the leading newsmagazine, *Paris-Match.* In the 1980s and early 1990s, Filipacchi Publications operated independently. In spring 1997, it fully merged with the Lagardère Group's Matra-Hachette. The conglomerate now has three basic divisions: (1) the high-technology group, including most of the Matra business in military and space armaments and technology, communications, and information technology; (2) the Matra vehicle-production unit; and (3) the media group, now called Hachette Filipacchi Medias.

After Jean-Luc Lagardère gained control of Hachette, he "made use of Hachette to turn himself from a national figure into an international media mogul." From the 1960s on, Lagardère was adept at political matters and connections, as well as public relations. Two European media scholars report that he has shown how valuable it is to have friends in high places and say that " Lagardère symbolizes . . . the convergence of state and private sector capital, of industry and media, of high technology and commerce."[24]

Corporate revenues in 1997 were well over $10 billion. Hachette has been known in France for some years as "the green octopus" because of its spread throughout a wide range of media and markets; the name is even more appropriate in the late 1990s. With the merger with the Filipacchi corporation and its two additional national radio channels, as of spring 1997, the Lagardère Group controlled four radio networks with a potential total audience of over 150 million. This exceeded the ceiling set in French anticoncentration law and was under review in 1997. The holdings of the Lagardère Group in general, and especially of Hachette Filipacchi Medias, are shown below.[25]

Matra-Hachette-Filipacchi

Magazines
Paris-Match, leading French newsmagazine
Elle women's fashion magazine, with editions in Europe, North
    America, and several other parts of the world
American Photo
Car and Driver, with plans to bring out editions elsewhere in the
    world; and *Road & Track*
Premiere, movies and movie stars magazine, with plans for editions
    around the world
Family Life
Mirabella
Woman's Day
Tele 7 and *TV Hebdo*, leading French TV-listings periodicals
Over 20 other magazines in France and the U.S., and some existing
    or being developed elsewhere in the world. One example (believe
    it or not): a version of *Car and Driver* in China
Major investor in *George*, John F. Kennedy Jr's. public affairs and
    interview magazine
Hachette Distribution Services magazine distribution company

Book and Encyclopedia Publishing
Hachette Livre, major book publisher in France
Librairie Générale Française, book publishing, and pocket paper-
back books
Several other publishing houses in France and the U.S.
Grolier encyclopedias and reference materials
Salvat, Spanish encyclopedia publisher

Newspapers
Owns 7 newspapers in France

**Radio Broadcasting, Television and Movie Production,
and Cable TV**
45% stake in Europe 1 Communications; operates 2 of France's top
national-scope radio stations, Europe 1 and Europe 2. "Europe"
brand radio stations have also been established in Germany, Russia,
the Czech Republic and other Eastern European nations, and Spain.
With merger with Filipacchi Publications came a third national radio
station, RFM; 85% of the national CHR radio network Skyrock
was also part of the Filipacchi interests.
Owns or has stakes in TV production and distribution companies:
Top Tele, Europe Images, and Hachette Premiere
Hachette Premiere also produces major motion pictures, mostly for
European audiences.
As of 1997, 25% stake in M6, new French cable TV channel for
women

Multimedia, including CD-ROMs and On-line Service
Hachette Filipacchi Grolier, including Grolier Interactive: CD-ROMs,
encyclopedia, software, on-line material, etc.
Internet access provider through Club Internet

Other
Brodard & Taupin offset printing company
Administration d'Affichage et Publicité advertising company

Agreements with Other Megamedia Corporations
Operational agreements with Disney-ABC and Hewlett-Packard

Industrial Holdings (Nonmedia)
C.M.C. SA—service provider, communications equipment, and cellular phones

COFEC—retail sales
MP 65—military products
Matec—military products
Matra Automobile—car manufacturer
Matra Cap systems—military and space imaging
Matra Communication and several other companies—telecommuni-
cations
Matra Datavision, SA—robotics
Matra Defense and several other companies—defense systems
Matra Electronique—airplane electronics
Matra Harris Semiconductors and Matra Design Semiconductors—
electronic components and semiconductors.
Matra Transport—automated urban and interurban transport sys-
tems
Matra Transit—transit systems
Matra Space and several other companies: space technology, etc., in,
France, the Netherlands, and Britain

Note: There are various divisions and affiliates of these media and
industrial companies in many nations around the world.

11. Gannett

Frank E. Gannett started the Gannett newspaper chain in 1906 when he
bought the small *Elmira Star-Gazette* in New York state for $20,000. The
Gazette was a profitable paper, while the competing newspaper in Elmira,
the *Evening Star,* was losing money. Even so, Gannett figured he could
make even more money if his paper were the only print game in town, so
he bought the competitor, merged it into the *Gazette,* and created a
monopoly—which generated so much money that he took that sort of
operation to other locations and began building the Gannett newspaper
chain. Nearly all the newspapers in the Gannett chain are monopoly
newspapers—something they have striven to achieve, through various
means.

It was discovered later that the International Paper and Power Co.
had secretly financed the earlier years of Gannett development into a
large chain. It is a remarkable coincidence that the Gannett papers' editorials strongly supported private power corporations, as opposed to public ownership of power facilities.

In 1957, Frank Gannett died. In 1967, Gannett went public with a stock
offering, and it kept growing. In 1978, Allen Neuharth, a brash, driving,

rather arrogant businessman, became chairman of Gannett. Many thought the title of his autobiography was entirely appropriate: *Confessions of an S.O.B.* In the 1970s and early 1980s especially, "Neuharth favored sharkskin suits, . . . [and more than one journalist] wondered 'where the shark ends and Al Neuharth begins.'" Journalist James Squires observed after meeting Neuharth in those days: "Neuharth struck me as a man with an ability to strut even while sitting down."

During Neuharth's reign, Gannett amassed the largest newspaper chain in America and acquired TV stations, radio stations, a huge billboard operation, and a major public opinion polling firm, to become a multimedia conglomerate. The monopoly newspaper situation that Gannett routinely has or develops, along with the intense demands for profitability Gannett makes on its papers and other media properties, affords the company a high economic return. By 1997, Gannett Corp. had revenues of $4.7 billion and profits of over $940 million. Its profits as a percentage of revenues was 20 percent, the highest in the general publishing realm of American industry; as a percentage of stockholders' equity its profits were 32.2 percent, one of the highest of any sort of commercial enterprise.[26] The following details the Gannett multimedia empire.[27]

Gannett

Newspapers
Over 90 daily newspapers in the U.S., including the national-scale *USA Today, Louisville Courier-Journal, Des Moines Register, Palm Springs Desert Sun, Wilmington (Dela.) News Journal, Fort Collins Coloradoan, Pensacola News Journal, Boise (Idaho) Statesman, Lansing (Mich.) State Journal, Rochester (N.Y.) Democrat & Chronicle, Salem (Ore.)Statesman-Journal, Sioux Falls (S.D.) Argus Leader,* and others from sea to sea

Numerous nondaily newspapers and community advertisers (including one named *Ye Olde Fishwrapper*) in 23 states

Television Stations
16 TV stations, including the following in large markets: KARE-TV, NBC affiliate in Minneapolis–St.Paul; WTLV-TV, Jacksonville, Fla.; WTSP-TV, Tampa–St. Petersburg, Fla.

Radio Stations
5 radio stations, including some in large markets: KTKS-AM and

FM, Dallas; KCMO-AM and FM, Kansas City; KHIT-FM, Seattle

Cable TV Systems:
Cable TV systems in Kansas City and elsewhere with 465,000 subscribers

Other Media
Gannett News Service
USA Today Information Network—electronic information service
Gannett Media Technologies International—development and marketing of software, etc., for the publishing industry
Gannett Digital Xpress—personalized audio, fax, and text information service

Other—General
Gannett Offset—printing
Gannett Direct Marketing Services
Telematch—telephone-number appending, data enhancement, and data processing service bureau
Nursing Spectrum—publisher of periodicals specializing in advertising for nursing employment
Gannett Telemarketing

12. Tele-Communications Inc.—and AT&T

Colorado-based Tele-Communications Inc. (TCI) is the largest of the cable TV systems owners. By mid-1997, TCI, with over 14.3 million subscribing households in its many local cable systems, had nearly $7.5 billion in annual revenues. TCI also owns pieces of a series of cable channels, including QVC home shopping channel, the Discovery Channel, E! Entertainment, Court TV, and Black Entertainment Television. TCI had a significant investment in Turner Broadcasting, which turned into a significant investment in Time Warner–Turner when they merged. Since Time Warner aleady controlled the second largest collection of cable systems, after the merger TCI and its new corporate partner controlled cable systems having no less than 46 percent of all cable customers in the United States. The FTC required some modest restrictions on the corporate connection.

If anything, TCI has been even more dominant in the cable TV world than the sheer numbers suggest. The company has long been run, rather imperiously, by John Malone. Malone was a Yale engineering and economics student and went on to get a Ph.D.; he worked for a while at the famous Bell Labs. TCI's dominance is not due just to size and corporate associations; it is also a product of Malone's operating style. Some—including Vice President Al Gore—have called Malone the Darth Vader of cable TV. As a *Newsweek* article noted: "More intimidating . . . is the way Malone uses that power. As tough as he is brilliant, TCI's chief is regularly accused of bullying those who do business with him—and everyone in entertainment and communications has to."[28]

In recent years, TCI has branched out. Its Liberty Media subsidiaries and related operations have engaged in programming and have stakes in over ninety programming services. TCI has many other joint ventures and equity interests in many other companies. In mid-1997, TCI, in a stock and trade deal, got a 33 percent stake in Cablevision, the sixth largest cable systems corporation; TCI gave Cablevision some local cable systems in the New York City area as part of the deal. Also in mid-1997, TCI bought the Kearns-Tribune Co., owner of the *Salt Lake Tribune* and three other newspapers. TCI has also vigorously engaged in international activities, with ventures in Asia, several parts of Europe, and Latin America.

Note: As this book was in production, the dramatic announcement was made of AT&T's acquisition of TCI. This merger will enable the combined megamedia corporation to be a major player in long-distance telephone service, cable TV service, Internet service, and, through TCI's millions of direct subscribers and millions more affiliated customers, to offer local telephone service to challenge the regional Bell companies and others. The AT&T corporate name is one of the most noted in the world; and with AT&T's more than $50 billion in revenues providing enormous financial resources, TCI's dominant position in cable should be made even more dominant. This will also greatly bolster the effort to extend broadband connections to homes and businesses from AT&T-TCI. Officially, TCI's Liberty Network's programming operation will be run "independently." But it will be headed by TCI chairman Malone, the largest single stockholder in the combined corporation, who will also sit on AT&T's board of directors, and who was referred to as "my new partner" by AT&T chairman Michael Armstrong. Clearly Liberty's programming efforts will also benefit from the merger. The merger was reported to be worth over $45 billion, $11 billion of which was assumption of TCI debt. Initial assessment suggests that this merger puts the new AT&T-TCI as high as the number five position of Dominant Dozen megamedia corporations.

TCI's holdings are detailed below.[29]

TCI

U.S. Holdings
Tele-Communications Inc. cable TV systems—largest in the U.S.,
including Cable Management Corp.
Owns 2 satellites
21% stake in Primestar satellite TV system (with other major cable
systems owners and GE)
Liberty Media Corp., with subsidiaries: Liberty Cable, with financial
pieces of many cable networks (see above); Liberty Programming
corporation; Liberty Sports Inc.; 50% interest in Murdoch/News
Corp.'s fX, fXM, and Fox Sports Net cable channels. In general,
interests in over 90 program services as of 1997
TCI Development Corp.—venture capital company
20% interest in Silver King Communications (a division of HSN
(Home Shopping Network's parent corporation), which has 12
UHF TV stations
Owns 39% of @Home Network (Internet access network for receiv-
ing TV, etc.)
10% of Time Warner
Kearns-Tribune Co., with 4 newspapers
Owns a piece of Netscape, leading Internet browser company

Non-U.S. Holdings and Ventures, through TCI International
Joint venture with Dow Jones in Asia Business News
Joint venture with Sega enterprises to develop and market computer
game channels
Majority interests in cable and programming companies Flextech of
Britain and Cablevision of Argentina
10% of Sky Latin America satellite service (News Corp. and the 2
largest Latin American media companies are the lead corpora-
tions)
7.5% interest in News Corp.'s Star TV satellite service of Asia
Joint venture with Canal Plus of France to produce programming (in
French)
Joint venture with Sumitomo in Jupiter Programming, along with Jet
TV, which is to provide channel broadcasting in various Asian lan-
guages
TCI/US West, Britain—joint venture of TCI and US West for cable
TV and telephone operations
United Artists Communications, Britain—cable TV services

The Second Tier: Other Notable Megamedia Moguls and Corporations

Berlusconi: Media and Political Power, Italian Style

Silvio Berlusconi is the greatest megamedia mogul in Italy, but he started his business career—and got quite rich—in a totally different area: the construction business. From the early days on, Italian broadcasting was the exclusive right of the public TV organization RAI. But an Italian high court decision in 1979 allowed private concerns to establish local TV broadcasting stations. By 1982, four commercial TV networks had been established, three by book and newspaper publishers. But those three had financial difficulties; by 1984, the Berlusconi trust, Fininvest, had bought them all. Berlusconi continued to buy up media properties thereafter. By 1989, Berlusconi's TV networks had 40 percent of Italian TV audiences and the public RAI had 46 percent. Berlusconi also controlled magazines amounting to 16 percent of magazine circulation in Italy, and he had newspaper properties as well. He also invested in some media properties outside Italy.

By the early 1990s, Berlusconi and Fininvest (now called Mediaset) had huge media holdings, along with substantial properties in construction, supermarkets, retail, insurance, and a leading Italian pro football (soccer) team. Some of those holdings were sold off in 1996 and 1997 to pay off debt and expand into digital TV and other telecommunications. As of mid-1997, Forbes listed Berlusconi as one of the richest people in the world, with $4.9 billion in personal wealth.

Most strikingly, in 1994, Berlusconi succeeded in getting himself elected premier (Italian version of prime minister). Clearly, having such a dominant media position was a significant factor in his victory. There was much debate about the impact on democracy of a media mogul using his megamedia properties as a springboard into a powerful government position. But Berlusconi and the political coalition he headed lost the 1996 election. [30]

Cox Communications: Multimedia and More

Cox Enterprises, as it is listed formally, began in 1898 when James M. Cox bought the *Dayton Daily News* of Ohio. Over the next ten years he bought other Ohio newspapers and became quite prominent. Cox then got involved in politics, serving as a congressman, then as governor of Ohio; he finally ran as the Democratic Party nominee for president in 1920, with a fellow by the name of Franklin Roosevelt as his vice presidential running mate. After the loss, Cox went back to the media and expanded his newspaper chain, branching out to Miami and then to Atlanta. With the purchase of the *Atlanta Journal* came its radio station, WSB, which started the multimedia dimension of Cox.

Cox and company later got into broadcast TV stations and then cable TV, while continuing to add to its newspaper collection. Cox also established a business and technical publishing division, a national television ad sales representation firm, and a TV programming operation. And the company went further afield, with a growing auto auction business, a paper manufacturing company, a ranch in Texas, farms, and a Hawaiian land corporation. By mid-1997, Cox Communications was the fifth largest cable systems owner in the United States, with nearly 3 million subscribers; it also owned eight VHF and four UHF TV stations, eighteen daily and six weekly newspapers, parts of several cable program channels, and other media properties. Total 1997 revenues were well over $2 billion.[31]

Hersant and Company: Epitome of the Media Mogul from France

Robert Hersant of France has been very much in the classic media mogul style. As two European scholars put it:

> Blunt in speech yet a trimmer in politics, he is a master in . . . controlling the purse strings of a host of family-owned companies; Hersant is also an adventurer and empire-builder who embarks on costly excursions into new territories (Spain, Portugal, Belgium) or new media (the French commercial TV channel, la Cinq). He epitomizes in the eyes of most French journalists all that is worst in mogulry. He is too bad to be true, and refers to himself as the "J.R." of the French press.

Indeed, Hersant himself has said: "I brook no opposition; I'm self-confident beyond reason. Some say I am driven by the thirst for power. I don't deny it."

By the late 1970s Hersant controlled a series of provincial newspapers and magazines and a major regional newspaper; he then acquired three major Paris-based daily newspapers (out of a total of ten existing at the time), including the leading French newspaper *Le Figaro*. Like Rupert Murdoch, Hersant used his main newspapers, especially *Le Figaro*, to engage in "strident right-wing polemics." In the early 1980s, the French parliament introduced a bill to prevent too much concentration in newspaper ownership—a bill seen by most people as occasioned primarily by Hersant's empire-building combined with his arrogance and polemical use of his newspapers. Hersant lobbied intensely to get the bill defeated or weakened. When the watered-down law passed, he proceeded to flout its provisions. By the mid-1980s, Hersant controlled newspapers accounting for 38 percent of total circulation of national newspapers. He continued to expand his empire through the rest of the 1980s and into the 1990s, including ventures into electronic media; by the early 1990s, he controlled some two hundred companies. In media, his operations were third in size in Europe, after the Bertelsmann and Matra-Hachette conglomerates. Hersant also served for a number of years in the French parliament.[32]

New York Times Co.

The foundation of this megamedia company is, of course, the *New York Times*, universally considered one of the two best newspapers in the United States and one of the best in the world. Long controlled by the Sultzberger family, which has had a strong sense of stewardship and the public trust reposed in the *Times*, the newspaper is one of the most influential media voices in the world. Some years ago, the corporation expanded well beyond the original newspaper. As of 1996, the corporation owned a second major paper, the *Boston Globe*, and eighteen small and medium-sized newspapers in New England, the South, and the West. It is also half-owner of the *International Herald Tribune*. The corporation also owned five TV stations; and it owned an AM and an FM radio station in New York and a video productions operation. Further, it owned a series of sports and leisure magazines, such as *Tennis* and *Sailing World*, but some of these were sold in fall 1997. In 1997, it was a Fortune 500 corporation, with about $3 billion in revenues.[33]

Sony: "Software" Following the Hardware

Sony consumer electronics corporation of Japan has had great success (with the exception of the Betamax VCR). It has used its earnings to venture beyond its foundation of manufactured electronic goods. In 1988, Sony bought CBS Records for $2 billion. In 1989, Sony bought into Hollywood in a big way, purchasing major film studio Columbia Pictures and the TriStar production operation for $4.9 billion. Sony wanted to "marry" media content with its hardware. But in the 1990s Sony was having problems with its new properties; Columbia had not done well financially and was considered poorly run. Perhaps the lack of experience in "software" as opposed to "hardware" was part of the problem. For now, Sony is not a truly major player in megamedia content. But given Sony's financial might, with about $45 billion in revenue in 1997, and its clear interest in getting more into content, it may make some more major moves in that direction.[34]

Times-Mirror: L.A. Times to Multimedia Conglomerate

The foundation of this megamedia corporation is the *Los Angeles Times*. For many years, the *Los Angeles Times* was a mediocre, parochial newspaper that was ruled heavy-handedly by the Otis Chandler family and used as an instrument to express its very conservative political views. In the 1960s, however, the reins were taken over by Otis Chandler. He considerably moderated the political orientation of the paper and dramatically improved the quality of its journalists and journalism; he attracted top talent and gave the journalists much leeway and support. Chandler eventually turned the *L.A. Times* into one of the three best newspapers in the United States. Being the dominant newspaper in the rapidly growing and rich area of southern California made the *Times* immensely profitable.

Chandler also expanded the company's holdings. By 1996, the Times Mirror Co. controlled two other major newspapers, Long Island's *Newsday* and the *Baltimore Sun*, plus six other medium- and small-sized daily newspapers and two weeklies, and it had 30 percent of the major Spanish-language paper *La Opinion* in Los Angeles. The company owned several book publishers; a leading specialist periodical on politics, government, and policy issues, the *National Journal*; and a series of magazines, from *Field & Stream* and *Golf Magazine* to *Popular Science*. In 1996, Times Mirror had revenues of $3.4 billion. In recent years, however, under a new CEO, the company has been criticized for managment moves that seem to compromise the *Times*'s journalistic integrity.[35]

Tribune Co.: Chicago Tribune to Multimedia Conglomerate

The *Chicago Tribune* was founded in 1847 and was led during its initial major period by Joseph Medill, whose bequest later helped found one of the nation's premier schools of journalism at Northwestern University. Medill built up the *Tribune*. He was a prime supporter of Abraham Lincoln; the paper closely followed Lincoln's speeches and debates. Medill's grandson "Colonel" Robert McCormick built the *Tribune*'s power and expanded the company's control of media to additional newspapers— including the *New York Daily News*—and into TV and radio stations. He built the great Gothic office tower that is the symbol of the *Tribune*. He also had a rather Gothic notion of politics and power, using his media empire, especially the *Tribune*, to promote his own (right-wing) political agenda.

By the 1990s, the Tribune Co. had amassed significant media hold-ings, including four newspapers; seventeen TV stations—including Chicago's "superstation" WGN—covering 25 percent of TV households in America; four radio stations; Tribune Entertainment; Tribune Media Services; CLTV News; Knight-Ridder/Tribune Information Services; pieces of other cable and broadcast properties; and the Chicago Cubs major league baseball team. The corporation also owns extensive timber-lands and large paper mills in Canada. In 1997, the Tribune Co. generated revenues of about $2.5 billion.[36]

Washington Post Co.: The **Post** *to Multimedia Conglomerate*

The *Washington Post,* the dominant newspaper in the nation's capital, is the core of this megamedia corporation. The *Post* has been led for decades by the Graham family, especially Katherine Graham, arguably the most powerful woman in the megamedia world. Most notably in the publication of the Pentagon Papers and in the Watergate crisis, Katherine Graham strikingly demonstrated her sense of stewardship of the paper and its public trust responsibilities. Like its two distinguished peer news-paper companies, the Washington Post Co. expanded beyond the core operation from the 1960s on. The corporation owns the second-leading newsmagazine in America, *Newsweek,* which publishes editions around the world. As of 1996, the corporation owned six VHF TV stations in large and relatively large markets, and it had cable TV systems around the nation with a total of over 600,000 subscribing households. It also controls several other media and nonmedia properties, including *VirtualCity,* a magazine for Internet buffs, and the significant Legi-Slate data base of leg-islative and regulatory activities in the United States; and its holdings also include 28 percent of Cowles Media Co.. In 1997, the corporation generat-ed about $2 billion in revenues.[37]

Other Second-Tier Megamedia

There are a series of other second-tier megamedia corporations that are noteworthy. I will simply mention in nutshell fashion three that con-trol substantial media of significance.

- Thomson Corp., based in Canada, had 1997 revenues of about $8 billion. As of 1997, it controlled fifty-eight, or more than half, of Canada's daily newspapers and over sixty daily newspapers in the United States, papers in Britain, and book publishers, leading law book and legal data base company West Publishing, and other operations. Kenneth Thomson, who owns 73 percent of the company, had an estimated personal fortune of $11 billion as of 1997.

- The Kirch Group of Germany, with 1996 revenues of $4 billion and a substantial array of broadcasting properties, "has been the major domo of European television for some time." Kirch also owns 35 percent of the large Axel Springer German newspaper chain, is involved in German digital TV operations, and has huge exclusive film and sports rights for Europe, as well as a majority interest in Italy's only digital satellite TV service. Leo Kirch was estimated to be personally worth $2.8 billion as of 1997.

- The booze-and-beverages giant Seagrams owned Universal entertainment group, which includes Universal Studios, MCA recorded music, book publishing, and theme parks; it gained sole control of leading cable TV channel USA Network in fall 1997. In May 1998, Seagrams bought PolyGram, giving it a second giant of recorded music.[38]

Special Cases: The Telephone Connection

The giant American telephone corporations are in a different category from the megamedia corporations. Telephone operations are not mass media, they are individual point-to-point connections and are common carriers, simply carrying messages from individuals. Although the telephone companies were supposedly going to become players in some of the fully mass media, such as cable TV, that has not generally happened, except for an increasing interest in Internet operations and some overseas ventures. But the sheer size and resources of these industrial giants and their potential to get into mass media operations make them deserving of brief treatment here.

US West–Continental Cable

US West is the Regional Bell Operating Company (RBOC) that dominates local telephone service in much of the Midwest and West. In 1996, US West bought Continental Cablevision, America's third largest owner of cable TV systems, with 5.2 million subscribers by 1997. US West also has a 25 percent interest in Time Warner Entertainment, which includes the megamedia company's cable systems.

A rule in the Telecommunications Act required US West to divest itself of its Continental cable TV systems in the areas of the US West telephone operations to avoid overwhelming dominance of wire connections into homes until there is real competition for local phone connections in the RBOC territories. In fall 1997, US West announced that its cable TV and other media business would be split off into a formally separate company, which would be called MediaOne Group. This spinoff-company approach was a new claim regarding that rule, and many doubted that MediaOne was full separation, but the FCC allowed the arrangement. For 1995, US West Communications by itself had revenues of $9.5 billion, and MediaOne had over $5 billion in revenue, but with substantial debt. In winter 1998, US West began to offer a major Internet service to residential and small business customers in several cities, with a "super-fast Internet service" to follow.

US West entered into a joint venture with TCI in cable and telephone fiber-optic wiring in Britain, but by late 1997 the venture was not reaching subscriber projections and was deep in red ink. US West has other cable and wireless ventures in Europe that are doing better financially.[39]

MCI WorldCom

MCI agreed to a buyout by WorldCom for $37 billion in November 1997. MCI had been attempting to break into local phone markets to compete against the Regional Bell Operating Companies. WorldCom was a rather new, fast-growing company that had acquired other companies at a furious pace. It had become the fourth-largest long-distance company and was the largest provider of Internet services to business. It added to its business Internet dominance when it bought CompuServe, kept the business Internet part and the sophisticated hardware network, and sold the consumer part of the business to America Online. The combined conglomerate will be a giant, aggressive force with huge resources in telecommunications, although at present it does not appear to be planning to get involved in more general mass media endeavors.[40]

Bell Atlantic/NYNEX, Ameritech, and SBC/Pacific Telesis

The 1996 merger of giant RBOC Bell Atlantic and its Northeast phone company neighbor NYNEX for $23 billion was one of the largest corporate consolidations in American history. Combined revenues for 1996 were over $27 billion; combined profits that year were well over $3 billion. This gives the new "Bell Atlantic" enormous financial resources to engage in business all along the eastern seaboard, "the most information-intensive area on the planet," as the Bell Atlantic CEO put it. The combined business gave the company access lines to 39 million customers. Despite opposition to this merger, the Justice Department's Anti-Trust Division and the FCC gave it the go-ahead.

Ameritech, the Chicago-based RBOC, through its New Media division, is the only American telephone company building cable TV systems that challenge existing cable companies to a significant extent. By 1997 the small entry into cable system building by GTE, SBC, and Bell South was declining. Like other regional Bell companies, Ameritech has made huge sums of money and thus can afford to engage in this initiative.

In April 1996, SBC Communications (Southwestern Bell telephone) bought out Pacific Telesis telephone of California for $16.5 billion. This enabled the new corporation to provide telephone service in a series of the largest markets in the United States and gave SBC over 31 million access lines into American homes and businesses in the fast-growing Southwest. With 1996 revenue of $23.5 billion and profits of over $3 billion, it has the resources to be a powerful player in more mass media, if it decides to get involved. Then in May 1998 came the biggest bombshell of phone company mergers: SBC announced an agreement to buy Ameritech. This would put nearly a third of all phone lines in the nation in the hands of a single corporation.[41]

AT&T and TCI

AT&T, with its universally recognized name, $52.2 billion in revenue, and nearly $6 billion in profits in 1996, is one of the largest corporations in the world. It has 90 million long-distance customers and is one of the largest independent Internet providers in the United States, as well as conducting other business activities. AT&T is also involved in major operations on the international stage through alliances with other companies. AT&T has explored the possibility of merging with some local telephone corporation to gain fast access to the local telephone business. AT&T has had some ups and downs in recent years, but it remains a giant with enormous financial resources, and thus it is a force to watch in the general telecommunications realm.[42]

The June 1998 AT&T purchase of Tele-Communications Inc., affords a dramatic expansion of AT&T's media activities and capacities and makes it as much as a top-five megamedia corporation. It should also give AT&T the capacity it has sought to get into the local phone market by the beginning of the new century via TCI's millions of cables.

Patterns: Top Twelve Corporations in Each Media Area

Top 12 Titans in RADIO STATIONS in the United States
(as of June 1997, with updates)

	No. of Stations	Total Audience (Arbitron)
1. Chancellor Media/ Capstar Broadcasting[a]	397	3,575,300
2. CBS	178	3,300,000+[b]
3. Clear Channel Communications	195	1,461,600
4. Jacor Communications	145	941,700
5. Disney/ABC	26	720,500
6. Emmis Broadcasting)	12	541,400
7. Cox Broadcasting	49	536,000
8. Spanish Broadcasting System	9	339,500
9. Bonneville International	17	311,800
10. Citadel Broadcasting	88	289,300
11. Greater Media Inc.	15	282,500
12. Susquehanna Radio Corp.	21	278,400

Sources: "Radio's New Order: Top 25 Radio Groups," *Broadcasting & Cable,* 23 June 1997; news stories.

[a]The product of a merger of the Chancellor and Evergreen radio chains in 1997, along with the separately operating Capstar Broadcasting. Both companies are controlled by Hicks Muse Tate & Furst Inc, Thomas Hicks, chairman and CEO. In August 1997, Hicks Muse bought former seventh-ranked radio chain SFX, with its 72 stations, for the Capstar company.

[b]Some accounts say that the CBS group has the largest total audience of any single radio group; those accounts apparently consider the organizationally distinct Chancellor and Capstar companies separately, but they are both controlled by the Hicks Muse firm.

Top 12 Titans in TV STATIONS in the United States
(as of June 1997)

	No. of Stations	% of TV Households[a]	FCC Calc. (%)[b]
1. News Corp.– Fox TV Stations	22	40	35
2. CBS Stations Inc.	14	32	31
3. Paxson Communications	40[c]	51	27
4. Tribune Broadcasting	17	35	26
5. NBC Inc.	11	25	24.6
6. Disney-ABC Inc.	10	24.2	24
7. Gannett Broadcasting	18	18.2	18.0
8. Chris-Craft Industries BHC Communications	8	19.4	17.6
9. Home Shopping Network/ Silver King	17	31	16.4
10. Telemundo Group	8	21.3	10.7
11. A. H. Belo	16	13.5	10.5
12. Paramount Stations Group	10[d]	19.1	9.1

Sources: "Top 25 TV Groups," *Broadcasting & Cable,* 30 June 1997; news stories.

[a]Total households reachable in media market.

[b]Federal Communications Commission's discount total for UHF stations in its official calculations of whether a corporation has less than the (increased) 35% total of American audience reached that is allowed under the 1996 Telecommunications Act.

[c]Paxson also has several TV stations under its management direction by virtue of Local Marketing Agreements. It also has agreed to 49% ownership of two other new TV stations under construction in Phoenix and Little Rock, Ark.

[d]Paramount has three other stations under its management through Local Management Agreements.

Top 12 Titans in NEWSPAPERS in the United States
(as of June 1997, with updates)

	No. of Dailies	Daily Circulation	Sunday Circulation
1. Gannett	92	5,840,635	5,859,487
2. Knight-Ridder	35	4,300,000+	6,000,000+
3. Advance/Newhouse	25	2,811,832	3,656,574
4. Dow Jones (*Wall St. Journal*, etc.)	20	2,361,445	534,316
5. Times Mirror	9	2,314,303	3,020,664
6. New York Times Co.	21	2,278,094	2,898,008
7. Hearst Newspapers	12	1,743,410	2,569,326
8. Media News Group	33	1,500,000+	1,650,000
9. E. W. Scripps Co.	23	1,451,000+	1,578,000
10. McClatchy Newspapers	11	1,353,506	1,836,957
11. Thomson Newspapers	65	1,338,567	1,349,056
12. Tribune Co.	4	1,270,623	1,891,943

Sources: Facts about Newspapers, 1997 (Vienna, Va.: Newspaper Association of America), 22; news stories; *Editor & Publisher* stories about recent acquisitions.

Top 12 Titans in CABLE TV SYSTEMS in the United States
(as of June 1997)

	Total Subscribing Households
1. Tele-Communications Inc. (TCI)	14,370,000
2. Time Warner Cable	12,300,000
3. MediaOne (former Continental/US West Cable)	5,250,000
4. Comcast (with big Microsoft investment)	4,312,000
5. Cox Communications	3,282,000
6. Cablevision Systems (with 33% TCI stake)	2,865,000
7. Adelphia Cable Communications	1,856,000
8. Jones Intercable	1,488,000
9. Century Communications	1,231,000
10. Marcus Cable	1,198,000
11. Suburban Cable	1,153,000
12. Charter Communications	1,073,000

Sources: "Cable's Top 25 MSOs," Broadcasting & Cable, 16 June 1997; news stories.

Patterns in the Aggregate: Megamedia Control

Finally, let us look at the media holdings of the Dominant Dozen megamedia corporations in the aggregate, that is, how much of the media are controlled, wholly or in part, by those twelve and a few second-tier megamedia corporations.

Television Networks and Station

All six of the national TV networks in America are controlled by the Dominant Dozen: ABC by Disney; CBS by Westinghouse; NBC by General Electric; Fox by Murdoch/News Corp.; UPN by Viacom; and WB (Warner Bros.) Network by Time Warner–Turner, which also controls Turner's CNN-TBS-TNT group (news plus entertainment).

Just six of the Dominant Dozen control a total of 88 local TV stations—67 VHF and 21 UHF—in America. If we add second-tier megamedia corporations Cox, New York Times, Tribune, and Washington Post, just ten prime megamedia corporations control 128 American TV stations, including most of the major stations in the larger media markets.

Elsewhere in the world, Bertelsmann has significant pieces of prime commercial TV stations throughout Europe; Murdoch's News Corp. owns TV stations in Australia; and, of course, megamedia mogul Berlusconi is the dominant force in Italian TV, as well as being part owner of TV stations elsewhere in Europe.

Cable TV Systems and Channels

Just two of the Dominant Dozen, Time Warner and TCI, and second-tier companies Cox and Washington Post have cable systems with over 30 million subscribing households, which is nearly half of all cable subscribers in America.

Additionally, all of the most widely disseminated and viewed American cable channels—and the most influential—are controlled by just five of the Dominant Dozen: ESPN (Disney-ABC); Nickelodeon, MTV, Showtime (Viacom); TBS, TNT, HBO, Cinemax, and CNN (Time Warner-Turner); CNBC (GE-NBC); and the Family Channel (Murdoch-News Corp.). USA Network is controlled by second-tier megamedia conglomerate Seagrams. Those five plus TCI also control or have interests in other cable channels. C-SPAN is jointly paid for by the cable industry as a whole. As the entertainment and media periodical *Variety* summed up in early 1997: "Mergers and consolidation have transformed the cable-network marketplace into a walled-off community controlled by a handful of media monoliths."

Satellite TV and Satellites

DirecTV is the leading direct broadcast satellite (DBS) TV distribution system in America. While the owner is not one of the Dominant Dozen or even one of the second-tier group, it is anything but some little start-up company like those apparently envisioned by the legislators behind the Telecommunications Act of 1996. DirecTV is an operation of Hughes Electronics, a subsidiary of General Motors; and a modest-sized piece of it was owned by AT&T until the end of 1997. One of the other two principal DBS operations is PrimeStar, which was spun off by TCI and is owned by TCI, Time Warner Cable, and some of the other major cable TV corporations, plus GE, with Murdoch's News Corp. being the latest part of the deal. PrimeStar was aimed at rural subscribers who did not have access to a full-scale cable system, but recently it began operating as a full satellite TV service. One major satellite TV supplier is an independent: USSB (US Satellite Broadcasting). USSB was the original DBS service, launched by Stanley Hubbard's Hubbard Broadcasting of Minneapolis–St. Paul. The Hubbards, who also own the ABC-TV affiliate in the Twin Cities and operate a news service for local media around the country, have been visionaries in media technology and use. Murdoch dominates satellite TV in several other parts of the world, especially Britain, India, and China, and he has almost half of Vox in Germany, fully half of Foxtel in Australia, and a third of Sky Latin America.

Radio Stations

The concentration in radio station ownership grew rapidly after passage of the Telecommunications Act in early 1996. Just five megamedia corporations control about 650 radio stations around the United States: Dominant Dozen corporations CBS and Disney-ABC, second-tier megamedia companies the Tribune Co. and Cox Communications, and giant, two-part radio group Chancellor/Capstar. Their holdings include most of the largest radio stations in the nation. But even more striking is the concentration in some locales (see chapter 5).

Newspapers, Newsmagazines, Magazines in General

Just four of the Dominant Dozen control a total of 127 daily newspapers. If we add Cox's 22 papers and the 35 papers held by number two newspaper chain Knight-Ridder (a Fortune 500 corporation), 184 daily newspapers are controlled by just six megamedia corporations. They also own approximately 100 weekly newspapers. Further, all of the most influential newspapers in America are now owned by second-tier megamedia corporations: *New York Times* and *Boston Globe* are held by New York Times Corp.; *Los Angeles Times* by Times Mirror Co., *Chicago Tribune* by Tribune Co., *Atlanta Journal and Constitution* by Cox Enterprises, and *Washington Post* by the Washington Post Co.

The two largest (in circulation) and most influential newsmagazines in America are also controlled by these same megamedia corporations: *Time* by the Dominant Dozen's Time Warner–Turner, and *Newsweek* by second-tier Washington Post Co.. The important public affairs and literary magazine, long a veritable institution in America, the *New Yorker,* is controlled by the Dominant Dozen's Newhouse empire. And Disney, Time Warner, News Corp., Bertelsmann, Newhouse-Advance, Matra-Hachette-Filipacchi, and Berlusconi control a sizable majority of the other major and not-so-major magazines in America and Europe, and they—especially Hachette—are advancing on the rest of the world. In fact, by the early 1990s, Ben Bagdikian reported, just three corporations in America had the majority of annual revenues in the magazine industry.

Matra-Hachette-Filipacchi controls leading French newsmagazine *Paris-Match,* and together the Dominant Dozen's Hachette and Bertelsmann, along with Hersant of the second tier, control a major portion of the prime magazines in France and Germany, as well as elsewhere in the world, including the United States. In fact, by the early 1990s, Hachette had become the largest magazine publisher in the world. Murdoch's News Corp. controls about two-thirds of the newspapers in Australia and owns newspapers with nearly 40 percent of the circulation of the popular press in Britain, as well as several newspapers elsewhere in the world. Hersant controls leading French newspaper *Le Figaro,* two other major papers in Paris, and enough other French newspapers to amount to nearly 40 percent of national daily circulation and about 20 percent of provincial daily circulation. Hachette owns seven other papers in France, and Bertelsmann has one of the major newspapers in Germany.

Book Publishers

Just five of the Dominant Dozen control most of the major book publishers in America and many of the minor publishers: Time Warner's holdings include Time-Life Books, Little, Brown Publishers, and Warner Books.; News Corp. has HarperCollins (the largest English-language publisher), Scott Foresman, Basic Books; Bertelsmann has Bantam Books, the world's largest paperback publisher, Doubleday, Dell, Random House, Alfred A. Knopf, Pantheon, Crown Publishing, Times Books, Ballantine Books; and Viacom has the consumer publishing units of Simon

& Schuster along with Pocket Books and Charles Scribner's Sons. By the early 1990s, Bagdikian found that out of "more than 3,000 book publishers in the United States, only 5 companies account for more than half the annual revenue in the book industry." In the English-speaking world, Britain-based second-tier megamedia company Pearson, after acquiring the educational publishing of Prentice Hall and Allyn & Bacon, became the number two force in publishing. By some estimates, more than one in three books sold in America in 1997 was produced by foreign-owned publishers—a ratio that would increase significantly with the Bertelsmann purchase of the Random House group.

In Europe, Bertelsmann and Hachette control a major chunk of book publishing, both have book clubs there, and Bertelsmann has clubs in Latin America.

Film, TV, and Video Production

Just four Dominant Dozen megamedia corporations plus second-tier Sony control nearly all the major film, video, and TV production companies: Disney Films, Miramax, Touchstone, and others are held by Disney-ABC; Warner Bros. film studios and others by Time Warner; Twentieth Century Fox and others by Murdoch's News Corp.; Paramount Pictures, Spelling Entertainment, and others by Viacom; Columbia Pictures and TriStar by Sony; and Universal by Seagrams.

Bertelsmann, Hachette, and the Kirch Group control or have big pieces of most major and minor film and TV production and distribution companies in Europe.

Recorded Music

Just three of the Dominant Dozen plus second-tier Sony and Seagrams control nearly all the major recorded music companies in the world and many of the smaller ones: Walt Disney Records and Hollywood Records are held by Disney-ABC; Warner Bros. Records, Atlantic Recording, Elektra Records, and others by Time Warner; RCA Music, Arista Records, and several other American and European music companies, are controlled wholly or in part by Bertelsmann; CBS Records is held by Sony; and MCA and PolyGram are held by Seagrams. Those conglomerate subsidiaries and Britain's large Thorn-EMI (not part of a conglomerate) distribute 95 percent of all recorded music found in American stores and 80 percent or more globally. Further, "their elaborate global distribution, production, and promotional networks made it difficult for new competitors to succeed"; independent labels generally had to make deals with the giants to succeed—and have usually been swallowed by the majors sooner or later.[43]

Thus, the Dominant Dozen and the second-tier megamedia corporations control most of important media in all forms through which news, public affairs discussion, and social, artistic, and entertainment expression are presented.

4

Opening the Floodgates:
The U.S. Telecommunications Act of 1996

···

The Precursors, Politics, and Power of Policy Change

The basic law under which mass media, telephones, and other telecommunications operated in the United States through 1995 was the Communications Act of 1934. There had been amendments to parts of that law in the years since, but through the first half of the 1990s, there was a growing sense that technological developments in communications, as well as economic and jurisdictional developments, required a fundamental reconsideration and rewriting of U.S. telecommunications law.

Further, media operated under what communications law professor Thomas Krattenmaker calls "legal balkanization." That is, certain media and media companies were limited to certain functions: TV stations could not operate local cable systems, regional telephone companies could not offer long-distance telephone service or cable TV service in their telephone areas, and so on. These restrictions arose over the years in piecemeal fashion, with the intent either to protect the public in terms of price or quality of offering or to protect the media operation from unfair competition from another type of media company that might have a structural advantage. But by the mid-1990s, Krattenmaker and other analysts, some members of Congress, and various communications industry people thought the developments in technologies, economics, and jurisdictional matters had rendered the legal balkanization out of date and obstructive of progress.[1]

Exactly which rules were now unreasonable and how they should be changed were, however, subjects on which there was a wide range of opinion. Economic developments such as increasing multimedia ownership and transnational corporate control of prime mass media added complexity to the issue, as did jurisdictional developments. For example, satellite broadcasting made it possible to transmit TV signals into a nation from well beyond its borders, making regulation of broadcasting very difficult for the particular nation's political authorities. All these developments began to render some basic tenets of the old telecommunications policy in

America, as well as in Europe and elsewhere, problematic as regulatory regimes and as guides to operations in the 1990s and beyond.

But there was another factor that had a tremendous effect on what policies government would adopt to deal with all those changes and what policies it would not adopt—money. The economic developments most prominently included the growing concentration of control over media by giant corporations, which increasingly included conglomerates. When an organization has hundreds of millions or billions of dollars in revenues, controls thousands of jobs, has a high public profile, and produces substantial tax revenue in its locale (and congressional district), the organization's principals typically have a lot of influence in the political system. That is especially so in the United States, where money is such a key element of the political process. Large "contributions" to election campaigns have been a common use of great financial and other resources. Prime access to key policymakers is one result. And when that organization also controls mass media, it is a very powerful force in the political system. There is a good chance that it will be able to get a great deal of what it wants from governmental processes. With the evident potential of financial gold mines and increasing economic might promised by the burgeoning electronic media, powerful media corporations wanted quantum changes in the law. In the Telecommunications Act of 1996, although there were some disputes among the organizations on specific points, they got most of the changes they wanted.

First, let's look at the money side of the politics and policy process. As Nancy Watzman of the Center for Responsive Politics has noted: "The telecom bill was to the 104th Congress what health care reform was to the 103rd Congress, in terms of attracting a lot of big money contributors." Just in the first half of 1995, telecommunications corporations contributed more than $2 million to members of Congress, a sum that was exceeded in the second half of the year. No less than $640,000 was given to the forty-five representatives and senators on the House-Senate conference committee that finalized the bill in fall 1995. Further, as scholars Snider and Page have detailed, during the first half of 1996, when the "giveaway" of the spectrum for high-definition TV was in contention, the National Association of Broadcasters (NAB) spent no less than $2.62 million in lobbying Congress. That included the work of forty-four lobbyists. And the NAB gave over $265,000 in political action committee (PAC) contributions to legislators. Those totals were added to by the PACs of such individual corporations as General Electric–NBC, Westinghouse-CBS and other media conglomerates. And those totals do not include money given by media executives as individuals, which considerably increases the influence money handed out.

Additionally, the enormous financial resources of the megamedia corporations assured significant inside connections, allowing them to hire special talent. Examples: the lobbyist for Murdoch's Fox operations was Peggy Binzel, who formerly served as legislative director for Representative Jack Fields, seven-term member of the House Telecommunications Subcommittee. The networks made use of CBS Senior Vice President Martin Franks, who had served as head of the Democratic Congressional Campaign Committee, which helps Democrats get reelected to Congress, especially helping with fund-raising. And in early 1996 while the spectrum-giveaway issue was still in doubt, the National Association of Broadcasters spent at least $2 million, and about $2 million more was spent by local TV stations on "public service" ads proclaiming the need to "preserve free TV" (i.e., preserve the spectrum giveaway for the broadcasters); and broadcasters did considerable lobbying of legislators in their local districts. It must be noted, however, that consumer groups contributed little in the way of money in the Telecom Act arms race.

One analysis noted that the Telecom Act as a whole

> is filled with provisions that make no sense from a public-interest point of view but make perfect sense for the industries involved. Consider the deregulation of broadcasting. In the name of "competition," limits on TV station ownership were raised so much that networks like ABC and NBC will be able to buy twice as many stations. (CBS, whose new owner, Westinghouse, already had stations of its own, needed the limit raised just to avoid having to sell off stations.)

In fact, the CEO of Westinghouse explained his company's purchase of Infinity Broadcasting's large radio station chain largely by reference to the "recent telecommunications law" and its loosening of broadcasting ownership restrictions. Similarly, in its annual corporate report to the Securities and Exchange Commission, Gannett explained its increasingly aggressive moves into broadcast media by saying, with frankness not intended for general public consumption: "The 1996 Act deregulated radio and television ownership rules so as to permit larger ownership groups, and, in the top 50 television markets, more TV-radio combinations than were permitted under prior FCC rules." Indeed, as *Broadcasting & Cable* magazine noted in late July 1995, before the Telecom Act was passed but while all that furious influence-peddling was going on: "It's begun. Even before Congress changes the rules, the big players are jockeying for position in The New Broadcasting." The megamedia corporations were already in merger mania.

The most striking provision was the one that handed to the networks and other TV station owners free new channels for the transition to, and transmission of, digital, high-definition TV. The heading of a column by

conservative writer William Safire summed it up: "Media Giants Orchestrate Major Ripoff." As Safire pointed out in the January 1996 piece, published shortly before the deed was officially done:

> If the powerful broadcasters' lobby gets its way, media giants would be
> given tens of billions of dollars of the public airwaves free, while the
> individual viewer would be forced to junk his old television set and buy
> a new digivision set. The ripoff is on a scale vaster than dreamed of by
> yesteryear's robber barons. It's as if each American family is to be taxed
> $1,000 to enrich the stockholders of Disney, GE and Westinghouse.

And a later Safire column added: "In the past two years [1995–1996],
according to the Center for Public Integrity, this portion of the lobby's
'spectrum grabbers' donated $7.6 million to federal campaigns and party
committees."

About that time the raw exercise of power by networks and other TV
station owners got even more interesting. Snider and Page provide us
with this story: Senator Robert Dole came out publicly against the broadcast spectrum giveaway in December 1995; he called for auctioning off the
spectrum and thereby generating substantial revenues for public purposes. After he made public that position and as he was campaigning in Iowa
for the presidential nomination, Senator Dole was presented with a star-
tling letter. The letter came from a Mr. Evans, the head of Spectrum Communications, a media company that owned eleven TV stations, several of
which were in Kansas, Dole's home state, and in Iowa, where the presidential caucuses were to be held shortly. Evans was also on the board of
the National Association of Broadcasters. The key part of Evans's letter
said: "If over the next few days your position on spectrum has not
changed and been made public, you will have lost my support. *I will be
forced to use our resources to tell the viewers in all of our markets of your plan to
destroy free over-the-air television*" (emphasis added).

Republican senator John McCain, chairman of the Commerce, Science and Transportation Committee, was clearly dissatisfied with the
process that led to the Act's passage and said: "It was clear to me all along
that it was the . . . special interests that were driving this train." He
"deplored the wheeling and dealing that produced the final version of the
measure."[2]

The U.S. Telecommunications Act of 1996

The U.S. Telecommunications Act of 1996 represents a major change in
telecommunications policy. Significant provisions in the Telecom Act are

the basis for much that is happening in media control in the later 1990s, and they raise serious questions. The longer title of the bill when introduced capsulizes the central ideas behind the law: "The Telecommunications Competition and Deregulation Act." Law professor Michael Meyerson summarizes well the central notions the proponents of the Act had in mind:

> This law represents a vision of a telecommunications marketplace where the flexibility and innovation of competition replaces the heavy hand of regulation. It is based on the premise that technological changes will permit a flourishing of telecommunications carriers, engaged in head-to-head competition, resulting in a multitiude of communications carriers and programmers being made available to the American consumer.

This is a paraphrasing and slight elaboration of the introductory statement of intent in the Act.[3]

The Act has five principal sections, or titles. Title I focuses on telephone service and the potential of the existing telephone corporations to move into new functional areas, Title II is about "broadcast services," Title III deals with "cable services," and Title IV concerns "regulatory reform." The final principal title is on the special issues of "obscenity and violence" in the media.

Development of Competitive Markets

The real centerpiece of the telephone section of the Act is a set of provisions intended to open up the Regional Bell Operating Companies (RBOCs) and other major regional telephone corporations to competition. Indeed, the major part of title I is called "the development of competitive markets." These provisions require US West, GTE, and other companies offering local telephone service to provide comprehensive "interconnection." That is, access to the existing regional telephone lines, switches, and other hardware was required, at a reasonable cost, so that other companies could offer competing telephone services. The idea was to subject the local telephone monopolies to real competition. Additionally, the Act sought to protect the long-established public value of "universal service," essentially meaning that local residential telephone service is a basic service everyone should have at affordable rates, even if that service needs to be subsidized in some fashion. (The new law changed the mechanism of the subsidy.) The Telecom Act also allowed the regional telephone corporations to get into other types of telephone service, such as offering long-distance service in competition with AT&T, MCI, and Sprint, and allowed them to get into cable TV and other non-telephone-business areas. But there were provisions to protect consumers from monopoly predatory practices due to the telephone corporations' unparalleled wire access to all homes and other "natural" advantages.

Elimination of barriers to entry into a given market is a keystone to opening the market to full competition. This section requires the FCC to review regulations that might serve as barriers to entry of new companies into the local telephone and other media markets. But all barriers other than government regulation, including total economic might, dominance of the market, and other factors, are ignored.

The Act was supposed to dramatically open up competition in the local phone markets monopolized by the "Baby Bells," GTE, and others. By the end of 1997, however, as an Associated Press article summarized: "One after another, the nation's largest long-distance phone companies have pulled back from selling local phone service to residential customers. The retreats signal the failure of [the Telecom Act] intended to bring more phone choices and lower prices by removing barriers to competition." AT&T was the latest to pull back from such efforts, after it had "spent up to $4 billion trying to break into the local phone markets." As of mid-1998, there was still talk by AT&T, MCI, and others of entering the local telephonemarkets, but the barriers to such entry remained high. The AT&T-MCI merger in mid-1998 provided the opportunity and the likelihood that there would finally be some meaningful competition in various local phone markets by 2001 or so, as AT&T uses TCI's increasingly upgraded cables to offer telephone service, in addition to cable TV service.

Another development shows that whether competition is viewed as good depends on whose market is being invaded. In June 1997, US West announced it was entering into a joint venture with United International Holdings to offer telephone service in the Netherlands. This service would "break the Royal PTT Netherlands NV's monopoly" on nonbusiness phone service. US West said this would "give Dutch consumers an alternative telephone service for the first time." That is an interesting thought in light of the intense complaints that US West, like other RBOCs, had been obstructing the entry of other companies intending to offer alternative phone service in its American territory. Indeed, in May 1997, a report by consumer groups said US West had been "pursuing a deliberate, multistate strategy to delay competition as long as possible through legislative, court, and regulatory actions."[4]

National Policy

A very significant provision in the Act is given the heading "National Policy." Section 257, subsection (b), says: "the Commission shall seek to promote the policies and purposes of this Act favoring diversity of media voices, vigorous economic competition, technological advancement, and promotion of the public interest, convenience, and necessity." "The public interest, convenience, and necessity" was language carried over from the original Communications Act of 1934. It is rather vague language, but that brief mention and a few similar uses in the Act, are the only things resembling recognition of the genuine public purpose of mass media. The ways that phrase is applied in various parts of the Act also lead to some serious questions.

Title II of the Act placed in the category of promoting the public interest, convenience, and necessity the multibillion-dollar giveaway of the broadcast spectrum to the existing networks and other TV station owners for the transition to high-definition TV—in suitably obtuse legislative language. One hundred twenty-eight of these stations were controlled by six Dominant Dozen and four second-tier megamedia corporations. A later provision (title II, section 336 [2]) of the Act states that the FCC "shall adopt regulations that allow the holders of such licenses to offer such ancillary or supplementary services on designated frequencies as may be consistent with the public interest, convenience, and necessity." Now, a normal person reading that would say, "I guess that sounds sort of reasonable (whatever it actually means)." Columnist William Safire explained what it means:

> Back when we were worried about Japan's high-definition TV making our sets obsolete, the FCC set aside space on the broadcast spectrum for American companies to change from analogue to digital transmission of signals.
>
> But then technology leapfrogged; it was discovered that each channel replacing the broadcaster's old channel could be split six ways, able to handle cellular phones, pagers, computer modems, the works. Each broadcasting oil well was transformed into six gushers.

Thus, an extraordinary amount of the scarce broadcast spectrum—which has long been recognized as public airwaves—was given away to existing TV station owners, most of whom are huge national corporations, allowing them to use multiple channels for electronic business in addition to their TV broadcasts. This is so even though the original technical rationale for ceding the added spectrum had changed. Estimates are that, if this spectrum had been auctioned off, as the part of the spectrum for wireless communications devices had been, the auction would have yielded anywhere from $11 billion to $70 billion for public purposes. But further, in summer 1997 the corporate broadcasting powers got Congress to insert a clause in a tax and budget agreement that added so many conditions for returning their old analog channels, as required by the original agreement, that many analysts thought the companies would be able to keep them longer term. With complaints about the digital spectrum giveaway intense, President Clinton appointed the Presidential Commission on Public Interest Obligations of Digital Television Broadcasters to hold hearings in mid-1998 and turn in recommendations by 1 October.

And while the national policy clause recognizes the basic democratic and social value of having a "diversity of media voices" (one of only two incidental mentions of that value in the Act), the provision giving away the broadcast spectrum and other provisions seem effectively to work against such diversity.

The Telecom Act substantially loosened restrictions on ownership concentration in broadcast media. Ownership limits had already been raised twice in the previous dozen years: In 1984, the limit of seven TV stations and seven AM and seven FM radio stations per owner was raised to twelve of each. The combined audience reach of the TV stations owned by one corporation could not exceed 25 percent of households in America with TVs. In 1992, FCC raised the radio limit to eighteen AM and eighteen FM stations per owner (with the 25 percent reach restriction retained). The Telecommunications Act of 1996 completely eliminated the ceiling on total radio station ownership nationwide. The results of that policy change are dramatically evident in the table "Top Twelve Titans in Radio Stations" (see page 88). In a nod to restricting overwhelming radio dominance in a single area or market, the Act established graduated ceilings for large, medium-sized, and smaller markets. For example, in an area with a total of forty-five or more radio stations, one owner could hold up to eight stations—no more than five in AM or FM. No total audience restrictions were included, however, so one corporation could own the stations with the eight largest audiences.

It is interesting to consider the claimed value of "diversity of media voices" in light of the concentration patterns, particularly in smaller markets. The Act said that in a radio market with fourteen or fewer commercial radio stations, one owner could control no more than five stations and no "more than 50 percent of the stations in such market." So one corporation could own fully half of the radio stations in a small market. In fact, as the post–Telecom Act merger mania proceeded, a high level of concentration of radio ownership developed in some of those markets. Following the buyout of Evergreen radio, giant radio chain Chancellor Media and its organizational cousin under common ownership, Capstar Broadcasting, controlled no fewer than ten radio stations in Huntington, West Virginia, population 54,000, and seven stations in Wheeling, West Virginia, population 34,000 (the radio market area [or, in FCC-speak, "principal community service contour"] would have a somewhat larger total population and potential audience). The FCC has sometimes given waivers—temporary or longer term—to corporations that gain such ownership concentration through mergers but has also required occasional divestitures.[5]

On the TV side, the Act (title II, section 202) completely eliminated total TV station ownership limits per se, and it raised the former limit on national audience reach from 25 percent to 35 percent, with a "discount" for UHF stations. The Act invited the FCC to consider whether to drop the one-TV-station-to-an-owner rule for a single area; indeed, the Act invited the commission to "extend its waiver policy [on the one-to-a-market rule] to any of the top 50 markets, consistent with the public interest, convenience, and necessity." There is that phrase again, used another time in the context of leaving the door open for even more concentration of media ownership, and suggesting this is in the public interest. The Act (section 202 [f]) also allowed a given corporation to "own or control a network of broadcast stations *and* a cable system" (emphasis added).

Another provision in this section (section 202 [h]) directs the FCC to review every two years the rules it adopts to carry out the ownership policies of the Act to "determine if any of such rules are necessary in the public interest as the result of competition." Although its intent is to find reason to institute still more deregulation, this provision could be used by concerned citizens, scholars, analysts, and media watchdog groups to give some feedback to the FCC—and Congress—on the effects of the ownership provisions. (Hopefully, this book itself will serve that purpose!)

Broadcast Stations

In past years, licenses to operate TV and radio stations were the official regulatory instrument the FCC had to assure that broadcast stations operated in the public interest. Radio station license renewals were completely eliminated in the 1980s. Originally, TV station licenses to operate on the public's airwaves were given for a three-year term; in 1984, the license term was increased to five years. At license renewal, the station's performance "in the public interest" was supposedly reviewed. But the FCC has revoked a TV station's license only with extreme rarity, and it has never given a license to a new applicant organization, which might have a superior plan to serve the public interest, in a "comparative" license challenge. By the 1980s, TV station licensees had "an expectation of renewal," almost completely regardless of their actual performance. Only criminal behavior or something approaching it would lead to license revocation. The 1996 Telecom Act effectively formalized that pattern, making an existing owner's license to operate a TV station on a scarce channel of the broadcast spectrum a virtual right and pushing still further into the background even a rudimentary consideration of whether the owner was using the broadcast license to serve the public interest.

Further, the 1996 law actually prohibits the FCC from considering alternative organizations that might have a better plan for programming in the public interest, as presented in a comparative license challenge (section 204[a][4]). This provision is, then, an incumbent-licensee-protection article. There is a revealing action that was a direct precursor to such provisions in the 1996 Telecom Act. In the 1980s the commission canceled the requirement that an owner who buys a broadcast station must hold it for at least three years before reselling. This in turn "opened the door to quick in-and-out deals [resulting in a] burst of buying and selling of stations" after that rule change; in short, it was a prelude to the fully opened floodgates of the Telecom Act. That action was in profound contradiction with the rationale underlying the routine granting of license renewal and the refusal to consider seriously any comparative license challenges. That is, the expectation of renewal was instituted to encourage sustained ownership that would really invest in the station and be involved in the community. Instead, the elimination of the three-year-holding rule encouraged owners to treat as commodities those TV stations that were supposed to be public trusts, which led to a raw horse-trading orientation and a focus on sheer profit advantage-taking in the burgeoning TV market. The 1996 Act then formalized that pattern and orientation. How this serves the "public interest" is not at all clear; it is very clear how it serves megamedia interests.[6]

Cable TV

The Act makes three noteworthy changes with respect to cable TV. First, cable system rates were partially deregulated, in a different fashion for each of cable TV's three tiers of offerings. Rates for the premium channels like HBO for which subscribers pay separately had been deregulated earlier; cable systems may charge whatever they can get away with for those channels. Rates for the "basic tier," including the regular broadcast TV stations, imported superstations like WGN and WTBS, and channels offering public, educational, and governmental access programming are still subject to regulation by local government franchise authorities, which must abide by FCC guidelines. Rates for the middle tier, standard cable channels like ESPN, TNT, and MTV, are regulated by the FCC. Rates for the basic and standard tiers are supposed to stay at "reasonable" levels.

The Act set a "sunset" date when both of those cable TV tiers would be completely deregulated: 31 March 1999. As one analyst revealingly articulated it: "*On the belief* that there will be true competition for delivering 'cable-type' programming to consumers after April 1, 1999, governmental rate regulation of cable programming service will be no more." By fall 1997 there was some serious reconsideration of that sunset deadline due to a pattern of steep cable rate increases and cable operators' continued arrogance. Indeed, from passage of the Act in early 1996 to fall 1997, cable TV systems jacked up their rates by more than three times the rate of inflation. Senator McCain of Arizona said in a 1997 Senate committee hearing: "I want this committee to do what we *didn't* do in the formulation of the 1996 law, . . . put the *consumer* first and everyone else second— so that we don't have a repetition of continued increases in costs to the consumer, which has been the direct result . . . of the 1996 Telecommunications Act." It should be noted, however, that Senator McCain tended to think even more deregulation would accomplish that goal.[7]

Second, a key phrase in the Act says that cable TV systems can be completely relieved of rate regulation right away if they are subject to "effective competition" from a comparable, multichannel TV distribution service, such as another cable TV system operator or direct broadcast satellite service. But "effective competition" is not defined in the Act. FCC rules offer these criteria: Such an "effective" competitor must offer service to at least half of the cable operator's franchise area and actually provide service to at least 15 percent of the area's households. The latter requirement is, of course, a very low threshold for claiming an entrenched cable system has *effective* competition.

The third basic provision repeals the former rules against the telephone corporations entering the cable TV business. It provides several optional regulatory approaches for telephone companies to choose from, depending on how they structure any cable TV distribution activities. There is also an interesting relation to the "effective competition" provision: If a telephone company offers a comparable video programming service, either directly or through an affiliate, the regular cable operator will be considered to face effective competition. The kicker is that "Unlike the 1992 Cable Act's provisions regarding other multi-channel competitors, the telephone company need not serve any particular number of video subscribers. Instead, the telephone company must simply 'offer' service: that is, be physically able to provide video programming service with only minimal additional investment." That is, to put it mildly, an extremely low threshold for "effective competition."[8]

Now, a reality check. A key element of the rationale behind passage of the Telecom Act was the idea that loosening the ownership restrictions and regulations in general would result in a great flowering of competition in media markets. One of the centerpieces of that movement was to be that regional telephone monopolies and monopoly cable TV companies would engage in vigorous head-to-head competition in both arenas. It hasn't worked out that way; in fact, two years after the Telecom Act was passed such competition was actually retreating from pre-passage levels. When US West announced that it was splitting off its cable TV and other media business into a separate company, very revealing comments were made by US West's CEO: "Five years ago it was our belief that not only would the network architecture [of cable television and telephones] converge, but so would the regulatory ones. Neither of those things has taken place."

Thus, US West acknowledged that the telephone business was not going to be a big competitor to cable TV and technology was not, in fact, driving things in that direction. Ameritech has entered the cable market to some degree; telephone giant SBC got in, then retreated somewhat, prompting *Broadcasting & Cable* magazine to remark that "the once-vaunted teleco threat against cable crumbled further." Mark Stahlman, president of New Media Associates consulting firm, had a blunter assessment: "Convergence [of telephone and cable operations] was a hoax from the beginning. Those businesses are as different as automobile and aircraft manufacturing." Further, Ameritech has been the only telephone company to build competing cable systems. Having some, if rather isolated, direct competition for cable TV systems is welcome. Unfortunately, Ameritech's cable systems have committed even less to the public, educational, and governmental channels and facilities than has customarily been required of cable systems. As a result, existing cable systems in their region are lessening their own commitment to those public service responsibilities: "In effect, communities' willingness to grant Ameritech franchises has 'lowered the bar' for cable operators on those responsibilities." Thus, another of the central rationales for the deregulation of cable and other media lay in tatters. (The AT&T-TCI merger offered a different approach: combining a major telephone company with a major cable company.)[9]

Regulatory Reform

Title IV, the final main part of the Telecommunications Act of 1996, is on "regulatory reform." In the spirit of the Act as a whole, it explicitly keeps open the possibility that the FCC can "forbear from applying" some of the remaining regulations if their enforcement "is not necessary to ensure that charges, practices" and so on are "just and reasonable" and if the FCC determines that not enforcing the respective regulations "will promote competitive market conditions" (section 10). The possibility that market conditions themselves might dramatically worsen the "just and reasonable" provision of services and intensify the degradation of public service programming is entirely ignored. The Act also calls for biennial review of "all regulations issued under this Act" (section 11).

A Basis for Public Debate? News Coverage of the Telecom Act

What did the news media tell the public about the prime policy issues involved in the Telecommunications Act? What information were they provided with to enable them to have a meaningful say in the decisions Congress and the president made?

With respect to coverage of the spectrum giveaway, scholars James Snider and Benjamin Page report: "As best we can tell, *no* national TV network covered the issue of the giveaway versus spectrum auctions." They also found that the networks' newsmagazines did not cover the spectrum giveaway issue either. Elite newspapers like the *New York Times*, the *Washington Post,* and the *Wall Street Journal* gave the spectrum auction issue some coverage, but the networks did not. Senator Robert Dole, who had been vocal in his opposition to the spectrum giveaway also spoke on the Senate floor about "the broadcast blackout" of the issue.

The telecom bill in general received very little in the way of news coverage in the three network news shows from the time it was introduced in May 1995 until the bill was passed on 1 February 1996. A search of the Vanderbilt TV News Archive was conducted for this book. On *all* three networks during that *nine-month* period, a grand total of twelve stories were found with a total of *nineteen and a half minutes* of material primarily on the Telecom Act. (Each network also did a story the evening after passage.) A good percentage of that material was on the issue of the V-chip that blocks out TV programs with violence and sex in them; while this was of interest to people, it was really a side issue to the rest of the Act. To illustrate, network coverage on a Senate vote in June 1995, when the public would have had time to participate meaningfully if they had adequate information about the bill's provisions and likely impacts, was pitifully inadequate. A story on NBC News on 15 June 1995 reported on the Senate vote on the bill, some elements affecting the deregulation of television and telephone, and pornography on computer services. That ounds good, but the report was a total of twenty seconds long. This did not convey meaningful information to the public. Further, the network controlled by the largest industrial conglomerate devoted the least time to the telecom bill: over the nine months it was pending in Congress, General Electric's NBC News gave its 12 million to 15 million viewers a total of three minutes, fifty seconds of news material on the bill.

Republican Senator John McCain said: "What troubles me is that the voters never got a clear picture of this giveaway on television. 'The Fleecing of America' [NBC News series], 'It's Your Money' [ABC News series]—where were they?!" Even outgoing FCC Chairman Reed Hundt, who had been largely quiescent in the face of the megamergers and other actions of media corporations, said: "Worse is that there have been no major televised discussions of the issue. The No. 1 missing piece of the puzzle is, why wasn't this story about TV covered on TV?" The self-interest of the megamedia corporations and the selective focus of their products are evident, and the implications are troubling for other policy issues.

It is also revealing to note that the networks, and many local TV news shows, through summer 1997 aired abundant news coverage of the congressional hearings on campaign finance and alleged Clinton-Gore fundraising excesses, coverage whose theme was the large sums of money spent by special interests to influence government officials and policies and whose tone was condemnatory. But those network newshounds were consistently mute about the large sums of money and massive lobbying effort expended by the National Association of Broadcasters and the individual networks to get what they wanted out of the Telecommunications Act of 1996.

Snider and Page, using a NEXIS search of more than one hundred papers, investigated how newspapers that are part of media corporations with significant TV properties editorialized about the Telecom Act provision on the spectrum giveaway. "The results on editorials are very strong; . . . in fact, among newspapers that editorialized on the subject, every one whose owners got little TV revenue editorialized *against* the spectrum giveaway, whereas every one with high TV revenues editorialized in favor of giving broadcasters free use of spectrum." Yale political scientist Martin Gilens similarly compared coverage by newspapers that are part of media corporations with significant TV ownership compared with those without significant TV ownership. He focused especially on the provision in the Act that eased broadcast station ownership ceilings. He did not find substantial differences in the simple amount of news coverage, but he found some interesting differences in what they discussed. Gilens found that newspapers from corporations with substantial TV ownership were decidedly less likely than those without such ownership to mention that the Telecom Act would mean each media corporation could own more TV stations than before, which would probably lead to more concentrated TV station ownership.[10]

While there was not much news coverage, the public did hear something from broadcasters about the Telecom Act. The National Association of Broadcasters, the networks, and many local TV station owners individually sponsored and aired thousands of TV advertisements that promoted preservation of the spectrum giveaway and general support of the telecom bill. These broadcaster ads—more like industry propaganda— were billed as "public service announcements." The ads misleadingly called the proposal to auction the spectrum rights "a TV tax" and claimed the auction would "destroy free TV." When Snider and Page searched the NEXIS data base for newspaper stories about the broadcaster ads, they "found no cases in which broadcasters presented opposing points of view" on the spectrum giveaway. Thus, broadcasters were using the powerful mass medium of TV they controlled—the public airways—to purvey their industry interest in this bill, but they generally refused to let alternative viewpoints have a say, let alone an equal say, in the prime forum of television.[11]

Final Words and a Little Perspective

The language of the Telecom Act and an omission in it say something very significant about the forces and effective orientation behind the Act and about directions in the American political economy in general. Business and the "American consumer" are regularly referred to, but the term *"citizen"makes not a single appearance in the Act*. The rare and primarily consumer-oriented, not citizen-oriented, mentions of the "public interest" in the Act and the single, incidental mention of the basic democratic value of having a "diversity of voices" in the mass media are also troubling.

First, in the telephone part of the Telecom Act, one clause (section 254[k]) institutes what seems like a fairly simple and reasonable requirement (and it's even stated in clear English): "Subsidy of Competitive Services Prohibited. A telecommunications carrier may not use services that are not competitive to subsidize services that are subject to competition." This is primarily directed at the regional telephone corporations, whose telephone business continues to operate under some regulation. Thus, when a regulated monopoly like a regional telephone corporation is guaranteed a "reasonable rate of return"—and in fact, has long made substantial sums of money—then it is not fair competition for that corporation to use that money to subsidize its activities in another business area where its competitors must operate under different circumstances. Thus, the telephone corporation could, through such a cross-subsidization, offer its other business product or service at or below cost and drive the competing company out of business, while sustaining themselves from their regular, semiregulated monopoly profits.

That basic principle is vital to fair economic competition, and it is significant that the Telecom Act explicitly recognizes the illlegitimacy of such cross-subsidization. But the Act fails to address another area in which the logic seem to apply the principle. Under the Act, megamedia conglomerates are able to subsidize their forays into the media markets with profits from everything from military contracting to mining and real estate, in some instances areas in which they are the dominant force in a less than fully competitive market. Various of those conglomerates are also in some media areas, like local cable systems, where they are effective monopolies. This issue is explored in the next chapter.

Second, in an attempt to spell out criteria for how this policy of decreased regulation and hoped-for increased competition "serves public interest goals," law professor Thomas Krattenmaker wrote: "Government has an important role to play in fostering access by speakers to mass media. [Here,] 'access' means the ability to reach any willing recipient by any speaker *willing to pay the economic costs of doing so.*" Addressing the issue of diversity in the media marketplace, Krattenmaker said: "Diversity is achieved when people are allowed to bid for any information or entertainment they desire." In other words, it is only pure financial resources that determine who controls the mass media and who can effectively speak to society and contribute in the democratic process, as well as bid for desired entertainment.

But should what speakers communicate to society about public affairs be decided in the same fashion as determining what entertainment to offeror what shovel or candlestick to buy? Is there no key distinction to be made here? The Krattenmaker–Telecom Act logic leads to that conclusion, but that raises troubling questions about the central principles of democracy. Indeed, political communications scholar Denis McQuail wrote in his major, systematic assessment, "Mass Communication and the Public Interest": "The case for equating press freedom with property rights is far from conclusive, especially since property rights are generally conditional and are often subject to intervention on grounds of 'public interest.' Other arguments for press freedom, in the Western value system, are actually much stronger." And as he points out, "free media will be prepared to offend the powerful, express controversial views, deviate from convention and from the commonplace." That is part of the democratic marketplace of ideas. But does deciding on a pure money basis who is able to control media or obtain speech channels tend to encourage such diverse discussion and challenges to convention, or does it tend to retard such democratic dialogue? For example, one notable goal of the FCC and the Telecom Act has been to spur minority ownership and operation of media. Just two years after the Telecom Act was passed, however, and after the frenzy of radio-station buying by media conglomerates, the percentage of minority-owned stations had actually decreased from 3.1 to 2.8 percent.

Further, Krattenmaker's use of the word "speaker" masks the reality: unlike the 1780s when many individual print shops easily published broadsheets and other news and information sources, it is not individual speakers who control the prime means of mass communication today, it is large economic organizations. This is so precisely because of the "willingness to pay" criterion he articulates. Using individualist terms hides the reality of the patterns of corporate concentration that affect economic competition and competition in ideas.[12]

5

Media Conglomerates and Competition

....

Premises and Promises

It is important here to remember the central premise of the new media policy contained in the Telecommunications Act. As Meyerson related, the Act was "based on the premise that technological changes will permit a flourishing of telecommunications carriers, engaged in head-to-head competition, resulting in a multitude of communications carriers and programmers being made available to the American consumer." And we must remember that a fundamental democratic premise is to have a diversity of truly independent sources of news and ideas on public affairs, as well as diverse sources for creative expression. And for that diverse "marketplace of ideas" to operate effectively, there must be a genuine capacity and opportunity for a wide range of people and organizations to compete for attention (and sales).

Economics and Conceptions of Competition

For many years, economists have studied and theorized about economic competition in the capitalist marketplace. The assumption just noted that underlies the Telecom Act is close to the classic conception of economic competition in the relatively pure marketplace, what economists have called "perfect competition." The conception goes back to the prime founding father of marketplace economics, Adam Smith. "Smith proclaimed the principle of the 'invisible hand.' It says that every individual in selfishly pursuing only his or her personal good, is led, as if by an invisible hand, to achieve the best good for all." American Nobel Prize–winning economist Paul Samuelson spells out the key elements of this epitome of competition: "There are *numerous* buyers and sellers *on each side, well informed about quality and* about each other's *prices, and having no reason to discriminate in favor of one merchant rather than another* and *no reason to expect that variations in their own bids and offers will have appreciable effect upon the prevailing market price"* (emphasis added).

The real world tends to be messy, however, and "imperfect competition" frequently exists. The structure of ownership of businesses in various areas of the economy and other economic factors can signficantly distort ideal marketplace competition. Economies of scale and economies of scope are two prime factors that can result in distortion of pure marketplace competition. *Economies of scale* permit a large corporation, with its abundant resources, to produce large amounts of goods or services at a lower per unit cost than a small company. *Economies of scope* result from producing different products and/or services involving similar processes in a single corporation. Samuelson uses the example of a company that produces cars and trucks. It has a cost advantage if it also produces buses and tanks since the specialized knowledge and machinery used in the production processes can be employed for all those different products. Research and development, marketing and advertising operations, and widely known brand and company names are also shared across product and service lines, giving further economies of scope. The sheer magnitude of financial and other resources gives great advantage to the largest corporations. Thus, "pervasive economies of scale or scope are inconsistent with perfect competition." In such cases, sheer market power seriously distorts marketplace competition.

John Kenneth Galbraith, among others, has discussed how huge resources for advertising and for marketing in general can have a sizable impact on the demand side of the supply-and-demand economy, and even on the price of economic offerings. Samuelson also discusses how product differentiation creates imperfect competition, whether that difference is in the substance of the product or service or more in the perceptions of the consumers. The great resources for marketing that Galbraith speaks of, especially as used in massive, clever advertising campaigns costing millions of dollars, such as the Marlboro Man or "Bud Lite: Tastes Great/Less Filling," obviously affect people's perceptions of products. Further, as Samuelson details, when a few giants dominate given product or service markets, there are tendencies to collude in setting prices or various aspects of production. Such "collusive oligopoly" can be seen by the big corporations as a way to avoid "cut-throat" competition—that is, to "manage" competition and maximize prices and profits. Overt collusion is a violation of antitrust law, but there are ways to engage in subtle or tacit collusion that are much harder to detect. In either case, very imperfect, distorted competition is the result.[1]

Concentration, Competition and Antitrust Law

American antitrust law has recognized the general consequences of a concentrated business structure and particular practices that severely distort competition. The Sherman Act of 1890, the original American antitrust law, basically prohibited monopoly and related contracts and combinations "in restraint of trade." The later Clayton Act (1914, with subsequent amendments) spelled out key aspects of anticompetitive structures and practices. As legal scholars Gillmore, Barron, Simon, and Terry sum up: "The Clayton Act includes among its categories of illegal activities: anticompetitive corporate mergers, interlocking directorates [people sitting on the boards of directors of one another's corporations], discriminatory pricing [including "predatory pricing," where rates are set below cost to drive a competitior out of business], and tying (the connecting of the sale of one product or service to the purchase of a second product or service)." Additionally, Gillmor, Barron, Simon, and Terry point out an important related issue, while specifically focusing on forced combination ad rates—a version of tying. They said such forced combination ad rates "violate section 2 of the Sherman Act *prohibiting the use of monopoly power in one market to gain advantage in a second*" (emphasis added).

Section 7 of the Clayton Act says: "No corporations engaged in commerce shall acquire, directly or indirectly, the whole or any part of the stock or other share of capital . . . of another corporation engaged also in commerce, where . . . the effect of such acquisition may be substantially to lessen the competition or to tend to create a monopoly." Further, an amendment called the Celler-Kefauver Act of 1950 added the directive to try to "arrest a trend toward concentration in its incipience." The Supreme Court, in its interpretation of the Celler-Kefauver Act, said:

> The dominant theme pervading congressional consideration of the 1950 amendments was a fear of what was considered to be a rising tide of economic concentration in the American economy. . . . Other considerations cited the desirability of retaining 'local control over industry' . . . Throughout the recorded discussion may be found examples of Congress' fear not only of accelerated concentration of economic power on economic grounds, but also of the threat to other values a trend toward concentration was thought to pose. . . . Congress made it plain that [the amendment and section 7 as a whole] applied not only to mergers between actual competitors, but also to vertical and conglomerate mergers whose effect may tend to lessen competition in any line of commerce in any section of the country.

It is interesting that at midcentury the Court noted concern about "a rising tide of concentration in the American economy." That concentration is much greater at the end the twentieth century, and it increasingly extends into the realm of the mass media.

Business activities like discriminatory pricing or collusion on pricing and other aspects of oligopolistic business are examples of *competitive practice* issues in antitrust. A second basic category of antitrust issues involves *structural* matters. Mergers and accquisitions that dramatically increase the concentration of ownership in a given mass medium and/or in a given geographic market are the prime sorts of structural antitrust issues in the media realm. Structural antitrust questions can be raised by *vertical* mergers and increased concentration, such as when one corporation owns not only a TV network but also principal programming companies that supply its programs and/or distribution systems to carry the network and its programs to the public (local TV stations, direct broadcast satellite systems, and so on). Structural antitrust questions are also, and more obviously, raised with *horizontal* concentration whereby a corporation takes control of other media companies and operations in the same mass medium and geographic area, for example, a newspaper buying out its competitor in its metro area or one corporation (such as CBS or Chancellor/Capstar) controlling a substantial percentage of the radio stations in a particular market area.

The Bureau of Competition of the Federal Trade Commission (FTC) and the Antitrust Division of the Department of Justice and, indirectly, the Federal Ccommunications Commission in media matters are the executive branch agencies in charge of enforcing antitrust law.

There have been two big problems in antitrust law enforcement and related court rulings, however, especially with respect to media. First and more generally, especially since the early 1980s, there has been a disinclination to pursue antitrust cases aggressively. The Reagan administration was unsympathetic to antitrust law and was quite sympathetic to big business, largely allowing corporate wheeler-dealers to have their way. Indeed, despite a great increase in the number of corporate mergers during Reagan's presidency, as economics writer Robert Kuttner notes: "William Baxter became head of the Justice Department's Antitrust Division. The department virtually ceased blocking mergers or bringing [predatory pricing] cases. The Federal Trade Commission . . . also went into a deep coma." And the Clinton administration, despite some bolder talk, has done little to enforce antitrust law vigorously. President Clinton named Robert Pitofsky chair of the FTC in 1995. Law professor Pitofsky's previous writings indicated that there might be more vigorous pursuit of antitrust, but the initial two years have shown only modest intensification of such antitrust actions in the FTC and very little intensification in the media area. The notable exception to that pattern in Justice's Antitrust Division was the spring 1998 action against Microsoft.

The second big problem in antitrust law, especially as interpreted by the federal courts, is that it has tended to deal only with economic impact quite narrowly conceived of. Impacts on independence and diversity of news and expression under the First Amendment have not generally been regarded as being within the purview of antitrust law. Damage to the heart of the democratic process through great concentration of ownership of media is not a significant enough antitrust problem, but concentration in some garden-variety business area apparently is. For example, in mid-1997, the FTC moved to block the merger of two large office supply companies, Staples and Office Depot, even though the Office Max chain and many independent office stores operate in that market. But neither the FTC nor Justice's Antitrust Division have seen fit to challenge the series of huge megamedia mergers that have occurred. Since the 1996 Telecom Act and FCC documents refer to "the Commission's core concerns with diversity and competition," one might think the FCC would use its powers, perhaps including the license allocation and periodic review process, to deal with issues ignored by antitrust authorities. It has not, however, and the Telecom Act makes things worse by extending license terms and going even further to establish automatic license renewal for existing broadcast station owners.

To be as clear as possible, one final point must be prominently emphasized. The preceding discussion drew on antitrust law and its implementation regarding business in general, as well as noting some particular applications to the media realm (or nonapplications). But keep in mind that, as the First Amendment to the U.S. Constitution emphasizes, the mass media are in a unique and profoundly important special category of business activity. The future of the democratic republic and much of cultural expression depends fundamentally on the control and performance of the media; such is not the case with office supply companies.[2]

Megamedia and the Realities of Imperfect Competition at the End of the Twentieth Century

> "The greatest fascination of the study of law is to watch some great event from the real world intersect with existing legal doctrine."
> —First Amendment law scholar Harry Kalven

As we end the twentieth century and move into the new millennium, Professor Kalven's thought of some years ago is even more strikingly relevant, especially in the realm of the media. The developments in the structure of control of the media detailed in earlier chapters, and the practices of those megamedia corporations that are discussed in this chapter and the next, are great events that raise profound questions about the adequacy of existing laws and their enforcement for dealing with threats to fundamental elements of the democratic process and diverse creative expression. Those developments also raise questions about the impact on fair, "level-playing field" economic competition.

There is a need for substantial, systematic studies of the greatly increased concentration and conglomerate control of media and their impacts on economic competition. The work developing material for this book did not have the resources to conduct a full-scale study of that sort. But this chapter offers much material on the impacts on economic competition, and it draws on various systematic studies already conducted of some aspects of the subject. The material in this and the following chapter also draws on an extensive set of reflections of current and former media company leaders, editors, producers, reporters, and so on from most types of media, describing and assessing the patterns they have participated in or observed in operation. Since News Corp., Time Warner and other megamedia are not inclined to let analysts sit in on their decision processes or pore over their records and files, this testimonial material is some of the best evidence we have on what has been going on. The effort is to develop a full framework for assessment and show particular areas that should be thoroughly explored in any future such studies.

In spring 1997, the U.S. National Telecommunications and Information Administration called on the FCC to study "how the [Telecommunications Act's] media deregulation provisions have affected concentration, minority ownership and TV viewers before taking steps to further deregulate." I hope that this book will help stimulate more interest in, and significant, tangible support for, such studies, as well as major systematic studies of impacts on competition in the realm of information and ideas.[3]

Principal Elements of the Framework for Assessment

This chapter discusses five principal elements of the sheer concentration in control of media and of conglomerate control of media that have significant impacts on genuine economic competition. They are: (1) horizontal integration or concentration of ownership; (2) vertical integration or concentration of ownership; (3) product or service extension by megamedia, meaning extending a company's media products and services into other media realms, while competitors in those realms may not have the capacities to counter the economic thrust of the megamedia corporation; (4) geographic market extension by megamedia, that is, extending a corporation's economic activities into other geographic markets, while competitors in those markets may not have the capacities to counter the thrust of the megamedia corporation; (5) industrial-media conglomerate structure and capacities, bringing various economic resources into a given market that a competitor in that specific market may have no way to counter. Each of these five factors tends to distort the pure supply-and-demand market function in the specific markets, to the great advantage of megamedia corporations.

Concentration, Magnitude of Megamedia Resources, and Competition

> "I'm in a business where the big are getting bigger and the small are disappearing. I want to be one of the survivors."
> —Ted Turner in the late 1980s, a few years before the Time Warner megamedia corporation bought Turner Broadcasting System

> "I guarantee you that if [the lessened or eliminated ownership restrictions in the Telecom Act] stand, a dozen years from now we will have six, maybe eight major companies owning most of the television stations in America. That is not a march toward competition; that is a march backward towards concentration."
> —U.S. Senator Byron Dorgan, February 1996

> "The days of mom-and-pop ownership of a small-town newspaper that was deeply rooted in the community are over."
> —Roy Rode, former editor of the *Dallas Times Herald*[4]

Radio

The magnitude of concentration of media and other properties in a few megamedia corporations is prima facie evidence of lessened competition. The case of radio especially demonstrates that point. After the Telecom Act eliminated all national ownership limits, the United States went from a limit of 18 AM and 18 FM stations per owner as of early 1996 to a situation where one two-section radio chain, Chancellor/Capstar, controlled about 400 radio stations by early 1998. The other largest group owner of radio stations, with well over 170 stations and nearly as great a total audience as Chancellor/Capstar, is network TV, TV station, and radio megamedia corporation CBS. But despite some of the specifications of earlier antitrust law and congressional concerns, FCC largely ignores the high level of national concentration and focuses on local media markets.

There, too, ownership has gotten dramatically more concentrated. As of late 1997, Chancellor/Capstar had eight or more radio stations in San Francisco; Jackson, Mississippi; Lynchburg, Virginia; Huntington, West Virginia; Chicago; Philadelphia; and Washington, D.C. They also had six or seven stations in Detroit, Honolulu, and Minneapolis–St. Paul. In some of those same areas, Dominant Dozen Westinghouse-CBS also had six or more stations—for example, seven in Chicago, eight in San Francisco, and six in Detroit; and after CBS bought American Radio Systems in September 1997, it had eleven stations in San Francisco. Having just two megamedia corporations with fourteen or more stations in one area is not enhanced competition; it is lessened competition, especially when they own some or many of the larger stations in various major metropolitan areas. An illustration of another anticompetitive dimension of this concentration, which is also important in the diversity issue, is found in Disney-ABC's control of several radio stations in the Los Angeles area, two of which used to be competing talk-show-format stations. Now, however, under common megamedia control, those two stations "complement" each other, rather than competing. With megamedia gaining control of more individual stations and even swallowing medium- and large-sized radio chains, the collection of formerly competing stations under one ownership and consequent loss of genuine competition will be seen more and more.

Officially, under the Telecom Act, any one corporation is allowed a maximum of eight radio stations in a single large market. In some recent megamedia mergers, the corporation has had to unload a media property or two to comply with the law. But the FCC sometimes grants waivers on such matters. For example, it has granted nine "temporary waivers" (as of this writing) to Westinghouse-CBS to permit it to own a TV station and multiple radio stations in the same market. As of early 1998, the FCC was considering whether to ease restrictions further on such multiple broadcast media ownership in a market, along with perhaps easing the "duopoly" rule against owning more than one TV station in the same market. For that reason, the Westinghouse-CBS "temporary" waivers were still valid a year and a half after being granted.

Cable Television

In cable TV systems, as *Broadcasting & Cable* magazine pointed out in June 1997: "As this issue's tabulation of the top 25 multiple [local cable] systems owners has it, those companies account for 88% of the industry. Worse than that, the top 10 account for nearly 75%." And it commented: "It may be great for Comcast and Bill Gates, but it doesn't do much for diversity." After passage of the Telecom Act, cable companies raised their rates so sharply that even Representative Billy Tauzin of Louisiana, whom columnist Molly Ivins calls "that wholly owned subsidiary of the telecommunications industry," said that "consumers, in many cases, have a legitimate gripe." The general cable concentration patterns and the area monopolies are surely related to those skyrocketing rates. The attitude of TCI's corporate leaders supports that conclusion. Following the 1992 reregulation of cable (after its first deregulation in 1984), TCI's attitude was: "We can blame [the rate increases] on re-regulation and the government. . . . We cannot be dissuaded from the charges simply because customers object. It will take a while, but they'll get used to it."

Broadcast Television

Similar concentration patterns are seen in TV stations. Murdoch's Fox system controls 22 TV stations reaching 40 percent of the American public, and six of the top seven TV station owners are among the Dominant Dozen or second-tier megamedia corporations. Just six of the Dominant Dozen plus four of the second-tier corporations controlled no fewer than 128 TV stations in America, including the majority of the prime stations in the largest and fairly large markets in the nation. The top nine TV station owners (some not among the true megamedia) own over 150 TV stations. Senator Dorgan's observations were right on track.

Multimedia Dominance in Local Markets

But it is particularly troubling when two or three giant media corporations overwhelmingly dominate all main media in a single metropolitan. The Chicago area is is a striking example. Just three of the megamedia, Westinghouse-CBS, the Tribune Co., and Chancellor/Capstar Radio, control two prime VHF TV stations; sixteen radio stations, including the leading radio station in the area and one of the largest in the nation, WGN; and the dominant newspaper in the metro area, the powerful *Chicago Tribune*. (The other metro newspaper, the weaker *Sun-Times*, is owned by huge Canada-based newspaper chain Hollinger International.) It is safe to say these three megamedia corporations dominate mass media communications in the Chicago metro area of more than six million people. This concentration surely represents a serious constriction of competition in the marketplace of ideas and seems to lessen pure economic competition in the media realm.[5]

When I was researching this book at FCC headquarters, an FCC employee (who was being pleasantly helpful) in a senior position in the radio division was not aware of that Chicago area situation. This is an illustration of how the FCC regularly loses sight of the forest for the trees. Because the FCC is so compartmentalized, and because its personnel do not do an adequate job of putting these several patterns of concentration in perspective, the agency misses such constrictions of competition and threats to diversity, even in the local markets on which it tends to focus narrowly.

A traditional way to measure concentration in an industry is to look at the percentage of the industry's total revenues in a market area garnered by the top four and the top eight companies (called "concentration ratio 4" and "concentration ratio 8," or CR4 and CR8). If the four-company ratio is 50 percent or more, or if the eight-company ratio is 75 percent or more, then the market is considered highly concentrated. Media economics scholars Alan Albarran and John Dimmick looked at the data in each media market/industry and found that:

> [I]n 1994 all but four industries (newspapers, book publishers, consumer magazines, and miscellaneous communications) were found to be highly concentrated based on the CR4 ratio. Using the CR8 ratio, . . . only five industries were below levels of high concentraion (cable systems, newspapers, book publishers, magazines, and miscellaneous communications). In five industry segments (cable networks, recorded music, professional publishers, advertising agencies, and interactive digital media) the top eight firms controlled over 90% of all revenues in the segment.

Since 1994, concentration in each of those industries has increased significantly; in fact by mid-1997, in cable systems, the top three owners controlled over 50 percent of cable subscribers, in addition to their typical local monopolies in cable. And cross-media and conglomerate ownership have risen at an even faster rate.[6]

Resources

It takes huge sums of money to play in the media big leagues. Time Inc., paid $14.1 billion for Warner Communications and later $7.2 billion for Turner Broadcasting Systems; Viacom paid $9.6 billion for Paramount Communications; and Murdoch's News Corp. paid $2.5 billion for New World Communications' ten TV stations. Individual broadcast and print media properties are also costly. For example, in 1993 KDFW-TV in Dallas plus KTBC-TV in Austin, Texas, sold for $335 million, and Boston's WHDH-TV station alone sold for $204 million; and in the years since then, prices have risen sharply. Even in small markets, the costs can be huge. For example, two TV stations in Portland and Bangor, Maine, sold for $112 million in 1997; and illustrating another trend, they were bought by Gannett from the local Maine Radio and Television Co. And mere radio stations are selling for huge sums. KASE FM and KVET AM and FM in Austin, Texas, the 51st largest radio market in America, sold for $90 million at the end of 1997—bought by giant Capstar from a smallish regional company. Besides distorting or overwhelming competition, such megamedia entry into local markets obviously affects local control of the area's media. Newspapers have also entered the big leagues in cost: In April 1997, number two newspaper chain Knight-Ridder paid $1.65 billion for the *Kansas City Star*, the *Fort Worth Star-Telegram*, and two smaller papers.

A look at the general pattern in broadcast media buying after passage of the Telecommunications Act is particularly telling. As *Broadcasting & Cable* reported in 1997: "Consolidation swept broadcasting last year, with 1996 radio and TV station deals topping $25 billion. . . . Brokers and group owners described the year as the busiest and most lucrative ever— with a more-than-200% increase over 1995 in the amount spent on TV and a 315% increase in radio spending." The jump in radio occurred, of course, after all national ownership limits on radio stations were eliminated by the Telecom Act. In newspaper buying, *Business Week* noted: "Halfway into 1997, 71 daily papers have changed hands in 30 transactions totaling $3.4 billion—exceeding the highest full-year sales figure of $3.2 billion set in 1995. Those numbers don't even count the flood of weeklies being traded."

A key question is, traded to whom—lots of different, modest-sized companies that own individual media outlets and compete vigorously? Not by any means; as just illustrated, these media properties are increasingly bought up by huge media chains and megamedia conglomerates. In the newspaper realm, for example, *Editor & Publisher* summed up in mid-1997: "Instead of chains buying up independent newspapers—a decades-long and continuing movement—big chains are taking over smaller chains. Now that the number of independent dailies is down to 300 or so, and they're mostly tiny, it's logical that these companies would gobble up smaller chains."

Given the staggering sums of money involved, only bigger and fewer corporate conglomerates have the resources to get into this game. After Renaissance Communications, a sizable but not megamedia-level corporation, had tried unsuccessfully to expand by buying media companies, its chairman told the *Wall Street Journal*: "I'm a buyer who can't buy. Every time I try to buy, a bigger gorilla gets in the way." In July 1997 (roughly a half year after the Telecom Act opened the floodgates) Renaissance itself was bought out by second-tier megamedia corporation the Tribune Co.[7]

The dramatic increase in ownership concentration in radio also has implications for advertising. With Infinity's large chain of radio stations added to the big Westinghouse-CBS chain, the conglomerate's strategists decided that, by controlling 30 to 40 percent of the major-market radio audience, they can offer advertisers one-stop shopping and a full selection of listener demographics and prime radio formats. Indeed, by late 1997, Westinghouse-CBS had 30 to 40 percent of the radio revenues in New York, Chicago, Philadelphia, Boston, and Los Angeles, as well as sizable pieces of other markets. Confronted with complaints about high ad rates and pressures for package deals on most or all of the CBS stations in Chicago, where CBS controls ten radio stations with 32 percent of radio revenues, the Antitrust Division of the Justice Department finally awoke and began investigating in later 1997. Similar concerns were expressed about ads on CBS stations in New York and Los Angeles; and the CBS acquisition of American Radio Systems gave it control of 60 percent of total radio advertising revenue in the San Jose, California, market area. (As of March 1998, the FCC had not yet officially approved CBS's acquisition of American Radio Systems.) In early 1997 the head of the Westinghouse-CBS radio group told *Barron's* business magazine: "It used to be that [stations] competed, that media buyers would play off against each other. Now we have the [CBS stations'] ad sales managers talk to each other every morning. That adds up to higher prices and better [profit] margins." That also adds up to evidence that megamedia constrict competition.

That evidence brings up a point Professor Krattenmaker made in his generally laissez-faire observations on the Telecommunications Act of

1996. He said that we need to look beyond the simple number of media properties: "Also important . . . are the percentage shares of the market that each controls. Not all firms are created equal and the impact on market behavior of commercial practices or mergers is partly dependent on whether the firms engaged in the questioned behavior are among those who were created more equal than others." That is, if one corporation controls even seven or eight of the largest stations, it is probably in a dominating competitive position. Thus, Krattenmaker says, the Telecommunications Act "largely perpetuates a method by which regulators measure acceptable levels of concentration by how many stations a firm acquires, not by the size of those stations." That is one reason Krattenmaker criticizes the Act for its "failure to engage in serious competition analysis at several points." Indeed, the FCC, in a March 1996 Order (FCC no. 96-90) "eliminated the definition of a radio station's 'audience share' for multiple radio ownership under the current rules."

With the increasing dominance of big national radio chains, national programming has grown considerably, crowding out genuinely local, community-based programming. For example, Mel Karmazian, head of CBS broadcast stations, wants to push national programming like Don Imus and Gordon Liddy through his 25 percent stake in distributor Westwood One. In fall 1997, Chancellor Media announced it was forming a national radio network, and more of such local impacts seem on the horizon.[8]

A special case of the structure of concentration and the sheer magnitude of resources factor is that of the huge regional telephone corporations in America. Since the breakup of AT&T in the early 1980s and the creation of the "Baby Bell" Regional Bell Operating Companies, the profits of the regional phone companies like Southwestern Bell and US West have been decidedly higher than those of other regulated utilities and of industrial companies in general. From 1988 through 1992, the RBOCs averaged 14.0 percent return on equity, well above the average of 11.5 percent for all kinds of industry for that period. When the enormous size of these corporations is taken into account, it becomes clear that they have made an immense amount of money in absolute terms. How are they spending these profits? Economics writer Robert Kuttner relates:

> In the mid-1990s, US West invested $2.5 billion to acquire a share of Time Warner, $1.8 billion to buy a cable company, . . . and billions more on overseas ventures. During the same period, hundreds of installers and customer service representatives serving US West phone customers were laid off, and tens of thousands of customers for basic telephone service were made to wait weeks or even months for installation. . . .
>
> During this era of partial deregulation, the net outflow of capital

from regulated Bell operations to nonregulated activities has significantly increased. In the 1987-1989 period, the first two years when Baby Bells were freed to pursue outside ventures, $1.733 billion flowed out from rate-base operations to nonregulated activities. In 1990-1992, that doubled to $3.579 billion—money that was diverted from maintaining, expanding, and upgrading the phone grid.

In many cases, then: (a) these giant phone corporations have used their special regulated monopoly status to amass huge profits; (b) they have used those big bank accounts to finance economic adventures in other market areas, including mass media; and (c) they have not used those funds to maintain and enhance the phone system that was supposed to be their primary responsibility. Again, in their purchase of cable TV companies, etc., this was not level-playing field economic competition. US West later set up an officially separate operation for their mass media endeavors, but the foundation of those operations came from the monopoly profits. How does this square with section 2 of the Sherman Antitrust Act prohibiting the use of monopoly power in one market to gain advantage in a second?[9]

It remains to be seen how the rather vaguely worded provision in the Telecom Act restricting use of regulated monopoly resources to compete in nonregulated market areas will be monitored and enforced. This provision would seem to apply to the owners of cable TV systems, with their own version of a sometime and semiregulated monopoly. Kuttner noted that they "were using their [exceptional profits] less to build the information highway than to finance an acquisition binge." This included grabbing full or partial ownership of many of the cable channels they distribute on their systems, resulting in more vertical concentration of ownership. As the trade periodical *Variety* notes: "Mergers and consolidations have transformed the cable-network marketplace into a walled-off community controlled by a handful of media monoliths."

Krattenmaker also asked: "Why would we not simply leave formal and informal consolidation to the antitrust authorities [rather than having the FCC involved], as we do for most other U.S. industries and markets?" I would answer, first, that we largely have done just that. Second, we should not do so, however, since those authorities focus narrowly on pure economic behavior and tend to ignore impacts on competition in the marketplace of ideas, diversity, and independence of information sources. The mass media are not the same as "most other U.S. industries and markets"; they are in a profoundly and constitutionally recognized special category. This is fundamental; the failure to adequately comprehend that fact and its implications is dangerous to democracy, as well as diverse cultural expression.[10]

Two Pieces of Good News about Competition in TV (Sort of)

From the 1980s into the 1990s the traditional three broadcast TV networks and their prominent news shows that had the field to themselves were challenged by three new entrants. Beginning in 1980, Ted Turner's CNN went up against the network news programs; then the Fox TV Network was set up and challenged ABC, CBS, and NBC in entertainment shows; then the United Paramount Network (UPN) was established. CNN has added considerably to the news and public affairs material available to the American public, although it does not have a very large audience on a daily basis. There is bad news regarding the other two, however. First, the two newer TV networks don't qualify well as genuine, diverse, alternative voices, since they are subsidiaries of Dominant Dozen megamedia corporations News Corp. and Viacom. Second, many think the Fox TV Network has degraded American TV as much as it has contributed some additional shows to the total available to viewers. Leading TV critic Tom Shales said, "Fox TV established new lows in taste on TV." Further, UPN still had rather limited programs and reach as of late 1997. And, until Murdoch belatedly started Fox News, neither of those new networks made much of a contribution to news and public affairs. By 1998, Murdoch was putting some emphasis on Fox News and asking his local affiliates to do the same. But there are also doubts about the neutrality and quality of Fox News, given Murdoch's record of interference with his news properties, his vow of having Fox News serve as a conservative counter to what Murdoch perceives as liberal leanings of the other networks, and the overwhelmingly ideoogical cast (conservative variety) of the principal personnel.

A second apparent bit of good news in economic competition has been the establishment of satellite TV systems as some competition for cable TV systems. The cable systems, epitomized by TCI, have been widely criticized as arrogant monopolies that charge excessive prices and provide poor service. Although as of late 1997 and early 1998 satellite TV had only a tiny fraction of cable's subscription numbers, it was growing steadily. It appears to have had some effect on cable operations, most notably by beginning to make the cable systems feel that they had to provide better service. But cable systems still raised their rates sharply in 1996. Also, two of the three principal American satellite operations are controlled by giant corporations. Primestar is owned by megamedia member TCI, other major cable system owners, News Corp., and General Electric; DirecTV is controlled by the Hughes Electronics division of General Motors. The other satellite operation, USSB, is, however, run by genuine and innovative independent Hubbard Broadcasting of St. Paul,

Minnesota. However, by early 1998, USSB and DirecTV, which share a satellite and the DSS dish system, did not really compete between themselves but complemented each other's offerings; consumers using the DSS system commonly had to buy both DirecTV and USSB to receive the most-requested channels. In Britain, Europe, Asia, and Latin America, Murdoch's News Corp. is a or the dominant force in satellite TV, and in most of those areas, cable TV was only a marginal player as of early 1998.[11]

Concentrated Control of Newspapers, Impacts on Competition, and Gannett and Newhouse Methods

For many years the newspaper realm, like the rest of the media markets, has been growing increasingly concentrated, although in absolute terms it is not quite as concentrated as in some other media. As in other areas, in the later 1980s and 1990s the pace of concentration in newspapers quickened. In 1977 the eight largest newspaper chains in America, ranked by total circulation, controlled 189 dailies and somewhat over 19 million in circulation. But by 1997, the top eight chains controlled 247 dailies and over 23 million in circulation, and the top twelve controlled over 450 dailies, which is about a third of all daily newspapers in the United States. Further, several of those big chains also control numerous weekly papers. Two of the top twelve, Thomson and Hollinger (temporarily number thirteen in America in early 1998), control well over 50 percent of dailies and weeklies in Canada, as well. In fact, by 1998, Hollinger, controlled by Canadian mogul Conrad Black, had 58 of Canada's 106 dailies with 37 percent of total circulation, and his chain was the third largest worldwide, behind News Corp. and Gannett.[12]

Local newspapers in America have increasingly become newspaper monopolies. One notable result has been higher ad rates in those monopolies, as some studies by journalism professors have shown. For example, in 1990, journalism professor John Busterna studied matched samples of Gannett's chain newspapers and independent newspapers (that is, papers in the same size categories and in communities with similar relevant demographics). He found that the Gannett papers "charged a national advertising markup of about 10% more than did the independent newspapers." He pointed out that an independent daily that tried to charge an exorbitant price to a national advertiser would likely be skipped over by the advertiser, since it could still achieve good national coverage. But if a chain the size of Gannett, Knight-Ridder, or Newhouse/Advance Publications charged higher prices, the national advertiser might not be able to avoid paying the high prices if it wanted national exposure. Thus, huge chains like Gannett "have the market power to control price" to a meaningful extent. And Gannett, like others in the Dominant Dozen, also controls significant outlets in other media: sixteen TV stations, five radio stations, and cable TV systems, further increasing its market power (although there is only partial carryover to different media in some types of national ads).

A recent assessment of these patterns by journalist Richard McCord also focused on Gannett. McCord compared the ad rates of the Gannett paper in Green Bay, Wisconsin, which did have a competitive paper, with Gannett papers of comparable size in comparable cities around the nation. He found a significant difference between the Green Bay paper's rates for local and national advertising and the average rates at similar-sized monopoly papers in the chain. As more media are controlled by fewer corporations, there is a constant reduction in the number of sellers of ad space and time in prime media. This spells lessened economic competition. And the economic impact extends beyond the media. Using the ad rate averages, McCord calculated the savings to the Green Bay community merchants resulting from having a competitive newspaper in the city: "By my estimate of the *Press-Gazette*'s annual revenue, the dramatically lower rates meant that the Green Bay business community was paying at least $7 million a year less than it would if Gannett were free to operate at its monopolistic norm." Much of that money was staying and circulating in the community instead of being sent back to the Virginia headquarters of Gannett.

How is a newspaper monopoly created in the first place? The Newhouse/Advance Publications empire and the Gannett chain are two prime exemplars of the resources of megamedia corporations and ruthless economic actions that have led to a monopoly newspaper situation in a number of cities. They show the ways megamedia corporations can and do distort economic competition, along with the competition in ideas and information.

Gannett's behavior in Salem, Oregon; Little Rock, Arkansas; Green Bay, Wisconsin; Santa Fe, New Mexico; and elsewhere is documented in Ben Bagdikian's *The Media Monopoly* and in greater detail in Richard McCord's *Chain Gang: One Newspaper against the Gannett Empire*. In Salem, Gannett controlled the morning and afternoon daily newspapers. They had sharply increased ad rates, provided sloppy copy, cut costs and local news with them, etc., as they did in other areas. With their local newspaper monopoly, "Gannett's attitude toward its [ad] clients in Salem was simple: Take it or leave it. With no other place to turn, the clients were taking it." All this led local merchants and others to encourage the initiation of a competitive local newspaper in Salem. Thus was born the weekly, the

Community Press. Before long the *Press* had nearly a fifth of the ad market in the city. This was unacceptable for a megamedia corporation that, as one Wall Streeter commented, has management that "lives, breathes and sleeps profits, and would trade profits over Pulitzers any day." As observers of the Gannett operations have said: "All over the country the big chain has been buying up newspapers in small-to-medium-sized towns. The objective . . . is to monopolize the smaller markets, cut costs at the expense of news coverage, and drive out any competition."

In response to the new weekly's challenge to their monopoly in Salem, Gannett initiated Operation Demolition to destroy the new partial competition. This effort, court records showed, included giving instructions to the Gannett paper's ad sales force to use whatever means possible to "eliminate advertisers from the *Community Press*"; giving various advertising inducements to some businesses to keep them from advertising in the weekly; and other, more unsavory methods. As the *Press*'s situation deteriorated under this onslaught, intimidation was resorted to. The last major advertiser in the *Community Press* testified that the Gannett people told him: "Basically, all the major advertisers are now back with the [Gannett paper]. Because of this fact, the *Community Press* cannot stay in business much longer, . . . and if we didn't return our advertising to the [Gannett paper], there would be nothing for us to advertise in should the *Community Press* go out of business." The national media chain also used its megamedia status and other resources to get national companies, like K-Mart, whose local stores advertised in the local papers to pressure the Salem store manager to cease advertising in the weekly.

The Salem case was some years ago, but Gannett used similar, if a bit more subtle, tactics in other cases, such as Green Bay (end of the 1980s and on into the 1990s). A court case in the Salem developments provided an inside look at Gannett actions and attitudes and provided a perverse keynote to the story. Gannett's high-priced lawyers succeeded in getting the case file sealed. Now as McCord said when he was told of the sealed court record: "I thought that was what a lawsuit [on a case like this] was supposed to do—get stuff like this on the public record." But Gannett got the file sealed by claiming it "contained trade secrets." Revealing them might "damage Gannett's 'competitive position' in the marketplace." The irony of Gannett complaining about "protecting their competitive position," in light of what they had done to the *Community Press*, was apparently lost on the corporation.[13]

The privately owned Newhouse media empire has shown a similar intense drive to buy or make local newspaper monopolies and an equally great disdain for ethical behavior and a vibrant, independent press in America in doing so. These patterns are documented by Thomas Maier in his well-researched book *Newhouse*. Maier says that it is important to consider

> Si Newhouse's attempt to secure a virtual monopoly on daily newspapering in Cleveland—a prize undoubtedly worth millions of dollars in added revenues for the Newhouse empire. The series of ethical compromises and other legally questionable actions . . . would prompt a federal antitrust investigation. . . . Overall, this air of manipulation and editorial compromise surrounding the Plain Dealer compelled some of its most talented journalists to leave. . . .
>
> The actions in Cleveland would forever mark Si Newhouse and his company as unworthy stewards of a public trust, a flawed vessel for so important task as the free flow of information in a democratic society.

The tale of the Newhouse empire's role in Cleveland's newspaper scene is a complicated one best understood by reading Maier's book, but I will summarize it here. Through the 1970s, Cleveland had two competing metro-wide newspapers, the *Cleveland Plain Dealer*, owned by the Newhouse empire, and the *Cleveland Press*. But as in other places, the rise of television and other pressures had made maintaining a strong second paper more difficult, even in a large city like Cleveland (metro area population: over a million). In the early 1980s, manufacturer Joseph Cole bought the *Cleveland Press*. He made prominent statements about his commitment to a second paper that could serve as an alternative voice for Cleveland. In a publicized speech, he said:

> A publisher's potential for mischief is no less than that of anyone else if the conditions are right. Give a publisher . . . a monopoly and you run the very real risk of seeing a square deal converted into a rigged deal . . . a plain deal into a raw deal. Simply said, I don't like monopolies.

Unfortunately, in the background Cole was taking things in a quite different direction. Cole initially approached Newhouse and asked about a collaborative operations agreement. This might have been intended as a joint operating agreement, an arrangement authorized by Congress to permit two newspapers to consolidate some operations while leaving the editorial activities separate in a city where there was a threat of the loss of one of them. Newhouse at first indicated that he had no interest, thinking the Newhouse empire's superior resources would sustain it until the Press withered on the vine. But a little later, Newhouse saw advantages and paid over $22 million for "an all-but-worthless subscription list and a newly formed bulk-mail advertising circular from Cole—in return for

Cole's promise to shut down the *Cleveland Press*."

After the *Press* was closed in 1982 and many smelled a rat, a federal investigation was launched. The two on-site investigators, assistant U.S. attorneys, saw ample reason to conclude there was antitrust activity that should be vigorously pursued in court. Federal district judge Ann Aldrich, in considering a related lawsuit, found: "The record is replete with facts from which the jury could conclude that [Newhouse's] *Plain Dealer*, Press Publishing, and Cole conspired together in restraint of trade." But the Justice Department did not seriously pursue the case, and the assistant U.S. attorneys both said "their attempts to bring the full case before a grand jury were stymied by higher ups." The new Cleveland newspaper monopoly was profitable for the Newhouse media empire: Newhouse's *Plain Dealer* raised its advertising rates by 28 percent in less than two years and increased its circulation by more than 80,000. It also increased total advertising in the paper, since supermarkets, department stores, and others had no other place to go for the daily print media ads they rely on.[14]

Book Publishers and Bookstores

Just five of the Dominant Dozen, along with three other megamedia companies, control nearly all of the major and many not-so-major general book publishers in America and many of the publishing companies in Europe and elsewhere. The Dominant Dozen members are Time Warner, News Corp., Bertelsmann, Viacom, and Hachette. The other three dominant forces in general book publishing are:

- British second-tier megamedia corporation Pearson P.L.C., owner of Penguin Books, Viking Books, Putnam Berkley Group, and so on, with 1996 revenues of $2.9 billion

- one of the original media chains, Hearst Corp., owner of William Morrow, Avon Books, six TV stations, and other media properties, with 1996 revenues of over $2 billion

- the other German giant in book publishing, Von Holtzbrinck, owner of Macmillan Co., St. Martin's Press, and Farrar, Straus & Giroux in America, plus a series of publishers and other businesses in Germany and elsewhere in Europe, with 1995 revenues of over $17 billion

In scientific, academic, and reference books, there are four dominant corporate forces, especially in America and Europe: Pearson, Viacom,

McGraw-Hill, Harcourt General, and newly merged Reed Elsevier–Wolters Kluwer. Worldwide, despite language differences in publishing in various nations, the ten largest book publishers had 25 percent of book sales. In America and Europe, the concentration is greater. With the acquisition of the Random House group, Bertelsmann alone will control 10 percent of the $21 billion total book market in America, and it will account for 15 percent of the book units and total dollar sales of Barnes & Noble's book business. Half of the leading American publishers, with over a quarter of the total U.S. market, are now controlled by foreign corporations.

In America, the only remaining fairly large independents are the two distinguished publishing houses W. W. Norton and Houghton Mifflin. Fortunately, a number of other modest-sized independents survive, and some work hard to produce books that actually matter and enhance our culture. Despite the long odds in battling the giant conglomerates, the independents may be on to something, as more and more people, especially those better educated and more attentive to the book world, see the increasing focus on fewer "star" authors and celebrity books, with less support for quality books that may not have high sales. As *Newsweek* has noted, various smaller presses continue to operate and are boosted "as authors flee the conglomerates." It is a genuine David-versus-Goliath battle for the independents to hold their own against the giants that have such massive resources and that can draw on other parts of the conglomerate both for content and for marketing and general distribution.

Then there are the bookstore chains. Like the rest of megamedia, the bookstore business is intensely consolidating. Besides the higher level of concentration in general, the giant chains are increasingly driving independent, community-based bookstores out of business. As recently as 1991, over 30 percent of all general-audience books ("trade books") for adults were sold in independent bookstores; but by 1997, the total had sunk to barely over half that. The four biggest bookstore chains, Barnes & Noble, Borders Group, Crown Books, and Books-A-Million, increased their sales by 180 percent from 1986 to 1996. The biggest bookstore gorilla, Barnes & Noble, increased its revenues by 24 percent just between 1995 and 1996. Barnes & Noble also owns the B. Dalton chain of smaller mall bookstores. But the independent stores were going under—two hundred in the United States in 1995 and 1996 alone. As the manager of one smallish bookstore commented: "When I read the industry newswire sometimes, it's like reading obituaries. All across the country, small bookstores are constantly going out of business." Indeed, in my hometown, Minneapolis–St.Paul, the invasion of the giant Barnes & Noble and Borders Books stores have driven out of business such respected independent local stores as Odegaard's Books, a major store that was a fixture for decades in the Twin Cities.

In five basic ways the giants can overwhelm the independents and distort fair, level-playing-field competition. First, they can offer volume discounts. Second, they can get volume discounts from the publishers. Third, they receive payments from the publishing giants for displays, along with cooperative advertising, and even for having the publishers' books shown face out on the store shelves; these payments amount to an average of about fifty cents a book, but the independents don't get any such help. Fourth, they can guarantee long-term leases at more reasonable rates with national commercial firms for real estate space. Fifth, they can spend large sums on advertising and other forms of marketing that the independents cannot begin to match. These are classic economies of scale, with a couple of special twists.

But beyond that, in their invasions of local areas the chains often appear to be targeting the independent bookstores, pointing their big guns at those independents rooted in the local community. And the efforts seem especially to target the best of the independent stores to eliminate at least some of the most serious competition in the area. For example, Barnes & Noble intentionally put a "superstore" within a couple of blocks of an Odegaard Books store in the Twin Cities. And then, as Dan Odegaard noted: "They put billboards all around where we were located," among other direct targeting. Other independents have testified that similar patterns of targeting occurred in other locales. Whether they involve distinctly predatory pricing or other formal monopoly practices, all those methods amount to predatory targeting. Indeed, in March 1998, California independent bookstores joined with the American Booksellers Association in a lawsuit filed in California against Barnes & Noble and Borders. The suit claims preferential pricing and other treatment secured from publishers by the two huge chains are "keeping the playing field far from level" and are driving independents out of business.

The Barnes & Noble chain plans to continue the onslaught around America by opening three hundred to four hundred new superstores through 1999. Further, in October 1997, they signed an agreement with Microsoft that makes Barnes & Noble the exclusive on-line bookseller in Microsoft's increasingly encompassing Internet world. They also signed a deal with the *New York Times* for a "transactional book site" on the Web where users can purchase books they read about in the *Times;* the Barnes & Noble operations are directly linked to the *Times* site. Further, Barnes & Noble has started an affiliate network to do the same with a number of other newspapers such as the *Chicago Tribune, USA Today,* and the *Los*

Angeles Times. All of that stacks the deck even further in the world of bookselling competition.

Some independent stores have held on, though, an excellent example being The Hungry Mind bookstore in St. Paul, Minnesota. Perhaps such stores are now partly sustained by some degree of backlash against giant bookstore chains and megamedia of various sorts. In fact, in February 1998, The Hungry Mind announced it was expanding to an adjacent store area for its bargain-book section.

But the giants can not only overwhelm the independents with their massive resources but can even, in some cases, literally shut them out. Newspaper columnist Doug Grow of the Twin Cities *Star Tribune* reported that in 1997, the area magazine for the Twin Cities, *Mpls–St. Paul,* decided to do a sixteen-page special section in conjunction with Children's Theatre. The Red Balloon Bookshop of St. Paul, managed by Roxy Markle, specializes in childrens' books. *Mpls-St. Paul* magazine approached the local bookstore about advertising in that special section. But after Markle had signed her contract to run the ad, giant bookstore chain Barnes & Noble came in and said they wanted to sponsor the entire section—exclusively. The magazine then bounced the Red Balloon's ad—refusing to run the ad at all in the special section, which was an excellent venue for getting the word out about the specialty bookstore. As columnist Grow summed up: "The Red Balloon's efforts to buy an advertisement in the July issue of *Mpls–St. Paul* magazine shows how lopsided the fight against the giants can be." As Red Balloon's manager colloquially remarked: "This is just like the playground and world politics. The big guy gets what he wants."

On the other hand, while there are good grounds for being concerned about the dominance of the giant chains, in some cases at least, there can be some positive effects. An example will illustrate. I spent some years in the Fargo, North Dakota–Moorhead, Minnesota, area. It is a metro area of about 140,000, and it is the location of two state universities and a private college, as well as being a general regional center. In the 1980s and into the early 1990s, there was not a single comprehensive bookstore in the area; there were a few small independent new or used bookstores and a standard modest-sized B. Dalton store in a mall. Then Barnes & Noble put in a superstore. It did, apparently, help drive one independent store out of business, but in truth, that store had a very limited stock. The Barnes & Noble store provides the community with a very large selection and thus has to be characterized as a significant improvement in book availability and a net enhancement of competition in the area.

It is also possible that the huge Barnes & Noble and Borders Books chains, with their great resources, prominent presence, and additions of bookstores in many large and not-so-large metro areas, have helped generate more attention to books in general and perhaps have increased book buying in this age of television. In 1996, total U.S. book sales exceeded $20 billion, the highest ever. However, the giants and their resources, their special arrangements and other circumstances denied to independents, and so on do seem to distort the level playing field of economic competition. Further, those circumstances and patterns do not deal with *what types* of books the giants are pushing or allowing in their stores, a subject we take up later in the next chapter; and the giants surely do not have the fundamental roots in and commitment to the local community that The Hungry Mind does—or Odegaard's had—to the Twin Cities or like local stores have in other communities.

The realm of book distributors is even more concentrated. For general trade books (nonacademic), two huge companies dominate wholesale distribution: Ingram and Baker & Taylor. Mark Crispin Miller relates the experience of the owner of small Barricade Books, which had trouble collecting money Ingram owed him: "Ingram is so huge, they feel you can't do business without them. But we can't stay in business if we keep dealing with them."[15]

The Internet World

The "new medium" of the Internet has been touted as a significant new outlet that provides a dramatic diversity and open possibilities in answer to the high concentration of control in the main media realms. In some ways this is true; in others it is not. While there are an increasing number of Web sites and anyone can send out messages, the means of access to, and use of, the Internet in general and the possibility of very strong or dominant presences on the World Wide Web suggest caution in reaching those optimistic conclusions.

In general, there are many Internet access providers, including some independent local ones in each sizable area. However, as of the end of 1997 and after acquiring CompuServe's consumer service, one company, America Online, has over 10 million subscribers, giving it half the on-line consumers in the United States and 20 percent of the world's on-line population. And in the realm of Internet services for business, in March 1998, the Justice Department's Antitrust Division "intensified" its investigations into MCI WorldCom's dominance of business Internet access. In June 1998, European antitrust regulators required MCI to sell its Internet holdings; WorldCom's UUNET was retained. More specifically, competition for Internet access business is heating up even among the major players. US West and some other major regional phone corporations have stepped into the competition and are building high-speed Internet wiring and connections, as is US West's former division Media One. Some cable TV providers also were planning to enter the fray as of spring 1998.

Additionally, there is the now-notorious new edition of Internet Explorer 4.0 that Microsoft unveiled in fall 1997. Nine out of ten computers run Microsoft's Windows; that 90 percent market share will soon have Microsoft's Explorer built in, and Microsoft's 1997 deal with Apple Computer means Macintoshes will also have Explorer built in starting in 1998. Thus, the Internet guide from Gates's World was heading toward presence on 100 percent of personal computers. Microsoft was demanding that computer makers place the Explorer on the computer systems in the Microsoft way, with the icon for Explorer prominently displayed on the PC's desktop so it is automatically encountered first. The setup is also designed to lead Jane Computer User directly to Web sites belonging to Microsoft or to companies Microsoft has partnerships with. Thus, the design allows Microsoft to program the software so that it favors certain content—with Microsoft connections and benefits—over other content. A computer executive described Microsoft's goal in its demands for full integration and prominent desktop display of the Explorer icon in and on PC operating systems: "I believe that the reason for Microsoft wanting that was because the icon represents the ease of use for the customer. . . . With the icon of the Internet Explorer visible and [readily] available to the consumer, they naturally would migrate to that particular product versus any other product."

Attorney Gary Reback, who specializes in the field and does legal work for Netscape, said: "It's not a good thing for consumers or for America to have one company dominate the entire Internet." In fall 1997, the Justice Department bestirred itself and charged Microsoft with monopolistic practices and violation of the antitrust consent decree the company had signed in 1995. Included in the charges was evidence that computer manufacturers had been threatened with loss of their Windows 95 operating licenses if they did not comply with Microsoft demands regarding use and display of Internet Explorer. In May 1998 the Justice Department filed a major antitrust suit against Microsoft; it was joined by twenty states' attorneys general.

In a March 1998 hearing of the Senate Judiciary Committee, a further aspect of Microsoft's strategy of Internet domination—and some dissembling tendencies of Mr. Gates—were brought out. At least ten times, committee chairman Orrin Hatch asked Gates whether Microsoft was using its software monopoly/oligopoly to pressure big media companies like Disney-ABC and America Online to choose Microsoft's Internet software and services over Netscape. All he got was evasions. "Gates's evasions

prompted an angry response from Hatch and chuckles from the audience, but [Senator] Leahy . . . finally got Gates to acknowledge that Microsoft's contracts bar media companies from paying Netscape for similar services." In another forum, Microsoft's chief operating officer, Bob Herbold was asked in an interview with Bloomberg News Service how small software companies could compete on products that Microsoft wants to fold into Windows. Herbold said the companies "could either fight a losing battle, sell out to Microsoft or [some other] larger company or not go into business to begin with."

There are additional dimensions of the concentration issue and constricted control and competition on the Internet. One of the most interesting of the new magazines on the World Wide Web ("Webzines") is *Salon* (www.salon1999.com), founded and edited by David Talbot and "designed to revolve around ideas, and especially books." Speaking of the days in the early 1990s, Talbot said: "The Internet comes along, and I launch Salon for a fraction of what it would have cost us to launch it with print. . . . And foreign investors aren't asking me every week, 'When are you going to turn a profit? What do the focus groups say?'" Talbot continues, however: "These are the golden days, and the bar that is going to be raised is the cost of marketing, because there's such a glut of things on the Web. *For start-up publications to make it online, they'll have to forge alliances with media giants like Microsoft and Time Warner*" (emphasis added). Or as a *Wall Street Journal* article put it, "online upstarts tap big media companies for funds." In 1996 a prominent research firm estimated that an average business Web site costs $2 million a year to maintain, and most are losing money. And as Edward Herman and Robert McChesney note, big media corporations "can afford to be more patient than stand-alone commercial websites that have uncertain prospects." Time Warner, for example, operates more than 190 Web sites, including one of the largest and most ballyhooed, Pathfinder. With Time Warner–Turner's massive resources and its vast stable of other media outlets to give publicity to its Web sites and direct attention to them in the maze of thousands of other Web sites, it is gaining a preeminent presence even in this paragon of "new media."

The new cable on-line industry is also dominated by a very small number of companies. In December 1997, Time Warner Cable's Road Runner cable TV venture was combined with MediaOne Express cable on-line service (US West's sister company) "to create the largest cable on-line business with 3.6 million potential customers now and 27 million eventually." The other dominant group is At Home Corp., which is a venture of other big cable TV systems owners, with TCI as the dominant backer. (Then in February 1998, word leaked out that Time Warner Cable and At Home Corp. were in talks about an alliance!) How will people actually receive on-line cable TV? The dominant forces in the equipment and software for reception of cable on-line TV are none other than Microsoft and TCI. TCI brought in various organizations and sought to structure the development of cable on-line so that Microsoft would only be part of a "layer cake" of competitive companies in this new area, which would include Sun Microsystems and Netscape. But a leading independent analyst from Giga Information Group concluded that "Sun's share of this deal is trivial," and *Newsweek* wondered, will "New Age TV be yet another Windows world?"[16]

The "Barriers to Entry" Issue, the Competition Question, and a Little Economic Theory

The Telecommunications Act specifies a concern about keeping "barriers to entry" as low as possible for new companies/competitors that want to get into a given media area; the concept is a key part of the promise of full economic competition in all media areas that underlies the Telecom Act. The concentration levels detailed earlier, the enormous sums of money being paid for media properties, the very large costs of facilities, and the other corporate capacities, along with the advantages of conglomerates, constitute high barriers to entry of new, independent competitors in most realms of the media world. In a study reported in 1993, media economics scholars Ozanich and Wirth found that was indeed the case—and that it was a key factor in media mergers. And since 1993, the inhibiting factors have grown rapidly. Obviously, under such circumstances, in most areas only other very large media chains or industrial-media conglomerates have the resources to enter the market, whether through purchase or new operations. Again, competition is steadily lessened.

Over the past fifteen years or so, some economists have realized that significant parts of the economy just do not follow the neoclassical economic orthodoxy. That is, in reality, they don't operate in the relatively pure supply-and-demand mode, where the collective process of individual market choices "naturally" yields the best products and maximizes benefits to consumers. In various market areas, markets don't self-correct. Economists have found this is especially the case in the high-tech and communications industries.

Economists Brian Arthur, Paul David, and others were keyed in to this major flaw in the market competition function by the QWERTY phenomenon. QWERTY, followed by UIOP, is the arrangement of letters on the top row of a typewriter keyboard. It is not, in fact, the most efficient layout for frequency of letter use and finger movement. But due to the historical happenstance of the original nineteenth-century typewriter layout, that arrangement got locked in—people learned on those old typewriters and it became disruptive to change the layout, despite its inefficiency. This was a good symbolic representation of the general problem: in some areas of the economy, historical happenstance, something in the nature of the design of a technology, or something in the structure of organizational operations in an industry distorts the "perfect competition" of standard market economics. Economist Paul Krugman also saw this phenomenon in aspects of international trade.

The computer market in general and Microsoft in specific is the most emphatic case in point. Microsoft has been able to dominate so overwhelmingly because of "network externalities," as the economists phrase it. The core idea is that a product or service becomes more and more valuable as the number of other people who are using it increases. Often high-tech products have to be compatible with other products, and they are often linked to a network. Because it provides the operating systems for 90 percent of the world's computers, and because software has to be compatible with the operating system, Microsoft had a tremendous advantage; and increasingly, Microsoft was central to the network of such applications in the DOS and Windows operating systems and more generally. What economists call "path dependency" develops—a dependence on a particular path of technology (or other operative system in the economy and society). These phenomena lead to a "positive feedback" process. That is, more and more software is written to fit in with the Microsoft systems, given dependence on the operating system, and more and more people and organizations focus on the Microsoft mode of software in general in an increasing positive feedback process that constitutes a "reinforcement mechanism" for

Microsoft's dominance in this economic area. In turn, this leads to "increasing returns to scale" from that set of business activities, which further reinforces the dominance with accumulating sheer economic power.

Other economists developed game-theory models that showed "how powerful firms could exploit the peculiar nature of high-tech markets to the disadvantage of their opponents."

Generalizing beyond the Microsoft mode and the computer industry, Brian Arthur has discussed how corporations that get to the market first with a product or service, and/or establish major market prominence in given areas, and/or can use great resources to employ massive ad campaigns, and/or use predatory tactics can establish a dominance or even a near-monopoly "which can stifle the very competition that free market advocates swear by." Arthur also refers to "mutually reinforcing elements" and to "learning effects" whereby people's regular, substantial exposure to a given technology (or source of information and cultural expression), along with limited time and inclination to explore other options, causes a "learning" that impels use of that particular technology or source. These concepts seem to apply well to the capacities of Time Warner-type conglomerates to use their large array of media properties to cross-promote and cross-subsidize and to have a dominant presence in mass communications, thus stimulating a learning effect regarding people's use of their media outlets, including the Internet. Some other research by economists indicates that dominant companies can use advertising and marketing in general "as a weapon of predation in order either to drive out [new] entrants [into that market], and/or create a reputation that will reduce the prospective profitability of future potential entrants." Arthur suggests that the communications industries are another area where these patterns occur. He also finds that "perhaps the most important way a dominant firm can exploit its position is by using its monopoly [or dominance] in one market to bludgeon its way into another." Key elements of this pattern of market dysfunction apply more and more to the realms of megamedia.[17]

The Conglomerate Factor and Corporate Practices in Competition

> In the new millennium, there are going to be a handful of global telecommunications companies that have the scope and resources to provide a full range of services virtually anywhere on the face of the globe. *You need to be either part of one, or run the risk of being stepped on.* [emphasis added]
>
> —Amos Hostetter, chairman of
> Continental Cable Television, which was bought
> by US West regional telephone giant in 1996

Beyond sheer high concentration in media ownership, the conglomerate ownership factor adds crucial dimensions to the issues of economic competition and competition in the marketplace of information and ideas.[18]

Conglomerates and the "Synergy" System

Corporate conglomerates provide significant advantages in the economic wars. First, they can provide some extra economic efficiences by spreading technical know-how, marketing, and existing industrial or commercial processes to other products and services, and so on. Conglomerates can shift resources from nonmedia businesses into media realms and affect the media market in artificial ways, in ways that contravene the central justifications for market economics as a good economic choice system. Thus, the economic activity is not a product of pure compection over product or service and price, but rather, the conglomerate interjects sheer economic power and distorts the direct competition over service and product based on price and quality in that particular market segment. Second, when the conglomerate has considerable vertical integration in media areas, this also can distort standard, level-playing-field market mechanisms in several ways.

As megamedia corporations have gobbled up media companies all along the production and distribution line, they have touted the benefits of these developments in vertical concentration to stockbrokers, stockholders, and other economic operators. The buzzword for the value of using all those parts of the conglomerate is "synergy." In biology "synergism" is defined as "the action of two or more substances or organisms to achieve an effect of which each is individually incapable." This suggests why synergy violates the pure economic competition standard and why the vertical integration of conglomerates affords unequal and unfair competition and thus is at odds with the basic premise of the Telecom Act.

The simplest of benefits from conglomerate ownership of media—and a more modest factor skewing economic competition—is the abundant opportunities for cross-promotion of megamedia products and services. Some examples will illustrate the pattern and the benefits:

- Explaining the benefits of synergy, an ABC radio executive said: "What synergy has done for us, particularly here in Los Angeles, with the fact that there's [Disney-ABC-owned] KABC-TV, Disneyland, *Los Angeles* magazine, the Disney movies, and three radio stations, is, it's a great opportunity to cross-promote each vehicle and really help each other." After Disney bought out the ABC network, the *Good Morning America* show traveled to Disney World quite a few times. This cross-promotion even extends to the network affiliates, with a little clever marketing work, as I discovered in Minneapolis–St. Paul. *The Lion King* was a theater production from the Disney entertainment colossus, following the successful animated movie. The week the show opened in the Twin Cities, the local ABC affiliate, channel 5 (not owned by Disney-ABC), gave lavish, daily prime news attention to the show; the station stated it was "exclusive material—the only local TV station allowed inside to videotape the final rehearsals." It is evident why it just happened to be channel 5 that got that exclusive and why the ABC affiliate gave the show such attention. What other, independent theatrical productions got similar elaborate exposure to the public, and hence, a substantial chance to have wide public awareness of their alternative creative expression? None; and it is a distortion of the marketplace dynamic resulting from the vertical integration (including affiliation), geographical and product extension into various markets, and conglomerate capacities.

- The CEO of the new Westinghouse-CBS mega-chain of radio stations indicated that he "will try to cross-pollinate his [radio] stations with CBS television." And "Since his TV network is a little creaky at reaching younger viewers, he can promote David Letterman on his rock stations."

- Seagrams, owner of Universal movie studios, USA Network, and Sci Fi Channel on cable TV, now heavily promotes its movie and TV productions on its beverage products.

The conglomerate capacities and synergy system become more profoundly distortive of level-playing-field competition when a vertically integrated megamedia corporation, which has an array of media outlets, uses those connections for preferential treatment, favoring the corporate cousins in making available products or even offering them at special rates or with in-kind benefits, or when it simply shuts out the competition. Consider the following examples:

Time Warner "kept things all in the family" by selling rights for the U.S. network TV premiere of *Space Jam* and other recent Warner Bros. theatrical titles to Turner Broadcasting. This is something Ted Turner, Time Warner vice president, demanded. The conglomerate also has two of the greatest movie collections in the world, the former MGM and United Artists film libraries plus the Warner Bros. movie library. This gives an enormous economic advantage to Time Warner, which it can exploit throughout its media properties.[19]

In its edifying Darts & Laurels section, *Columbia Journalism Review* (*CJR*) referred to NBC's "embarrassing on-air displays of affection for Microsoft since they got engaged" with the MSNBC cable and on-line computer networks. Did Microsoft really need extracurricular help in getting its products and services attention in the marketplace? *CJR* did note, however, that the *Today* show had a more balanced presentation of Internet providers on a Money segment. How long that will last is the question. When the Justice Department took on Microsoft over Internet Explorer 4.0, NBC News did cover it prominently, but the issue was so big, they could hardly ignore it; the real test is on other matters that are not blazing brightly everywhere.

Reflecting on the array of media properties of Time Warner–Turner, *Newsweek* (*Time*'s rival) noted: "All that production and distribution power could make it more difficult for rivals to get their programs on Time Warner and TCI systems," since TCI owned a chunk of Turner Broadcasting, and now of Time Warner-Turner. The Federal Trade Commission specified a few formal "arm's-length" conditions on the TCI–Time Warner connection after the acquisition of Turner Broadcasting, but these were very modest restrictions. For example, Time Warner's huge cable system in New York City recently eliminated The Box, an alternative rock and rap music channel, and one of the two channels newly put in was the fledgling financial news channel CNNfn, now owned by Time Warner. After Murdoch's Fox system developed his all-news cable channel, Fox News, the New York Time Warner cable system refused to carry the channel. Eventually, after FTC and FCC pressure and some public exposure of the situation (thanks to what is left of competing media, along with the entertaining spectacle of a "Ted Turner versus Rupert Murdoch" story), the cable system added MSNBC to have another non–Time Warner–owned, competing news network on the cable system.

Bruce Erickson, professor of business and government at the Carlson School of Management at the University of Minnesota, has pointed out the potential impact: "If you're a program producer with creative ideas, you may be forced to produce within four or five large conglomerates, rather than take a chance and do your own thing outside the corporate bureaucracies." Indeed, there are now some lawsuits regarding these favorable connections, which are rightly characterized as conflicts of interest. "The vertical integration of all these media companies is leaving creators without negotiating power," said Los Angeles attorney Rita M. Haeusler, who is involved in the suits.

Ultimately, an antitrust-law term captures the consequences of these special connections: "predatory cross-subsidization." Indeed, the increasing tendency to use such special conglomerate connections for special deals, particularly in the cable realm, had, by fall 1997, engendered considerable concern in Congress and elsewhere. Thus, "the [cable] industry is under fire for certain exclusive programming deals that some powerful cable operators are striking." The conservative chair of the House Judiciary Committee, Henry Hyde, said that "serious antitrust questions are raised by these cable programming arrangements, . . . the issue reeks of restraint of trade."

The same sorts of mergers are occurring elsewhere in the world, especially in Europe. For example, in 1997 Bertelsmann added to its broadcasting operations with a merger creating a huge, Europe-leading broadcasting combination, CLT-Ufa. Bertelsmann proclaimed that it could now compete on equal terms with the megamedia corporations of North America. As the co-CEO of the merged broadcasting company commented: "U.S. companies have shown that the key to success is size and the ability to take part in all stages of the media business. Only companies that have stakes in production, programming and distribution will remain key players in the global media scene."

Nicholas Johnson, a former FCC commissioner and rare activist at the FCC in the cause of improving the quality and democratic responsibility of television, provided a perfect summary of these conglomerate patterns that use the benign-sounding name of "synergy." He said that

> synergy is actually the annihilation of competition. . . . When you contract with an author to write a book and sell it in the stores you own, produce the movie in the studio you own and run it in the theaters you own, make it into a video and distribute it through the stores you own, then put it on the cable system you own and the broadcast stations you own, promote it on the TV network you own, and write it up in the entertainment magazine you own, that's pretty tough to compete with.

A case in point is the Batman property. With Time Warner's vast resources and outlets for production and marketing, from its comic book origins Batman was turned into a hit movie, a big-selling and -renting video, a record soundtrack album, a T-shirt, an animated television series, character products in the hundreds of Warner stores, and so on. Media analysts say the number of such cases is growing. Borrowing again from economists Arthur and David, these certainly seem to be examples of conglomerate mass media versions of "network externalities," "increasing returns to scale," "positive feedback process," and maybe even some "path dependency."[20]

Speaking about megamedia trends and their impact on our society, Senator Byron Dorgan said, "You're not going to have local control or much local input" as megamedia gobbles up every media company in sight. At the end of the twentieth century people in America and elsewhere feel buffeted by the forces of huge national- and international-scale organizations and developments. Opinion polls show that people feel big government is not responsive to them and they have no control over it; but polls also show people have similar feelings about other huge organizations, especially big corporations, whose headquarters are located in some faraway place—in every sense. People feel a strong need to have more control over their lives, including over their local realm.

At least partly in response to this need and to counter the march of megamedia and the increasing corporatization of local press, there has been a rise in alternative newspapers. Between 1990 and mid-1997 the number of alternative newspapers around America, typically weeklies, increased from 68 to 111, and their total circulation rose from 3 million to 6.4 million. From the legendary *Village Voice* of New York City to *City Pages* of Minneapolis–St. Paul, these alternative newspapers provide at least partial competition and a different voice in media areas that, in general, have become increasingly monopolized in the local market and increasingly dominated nationwide by giant newspaper chains.

Typically, a prime attraction of these papers is an extensive listing and discussion of the local arts and entertainment scene. Unfortunately, these alternative media sources may be threatened by Microsoft, which has begun "Sidewalk" on-line service, "billed as the definitive online source for local arts and entertainment listings." This service also runs ads from many restaurants and other enterprises in leisure and entertainment. "Sidewalk" has already been launched in New York City, Seattle, Boston, and the Twin Cities; the launch in Montreal has had problems. Other sites in America and elsewhere were in development as of this writing. As the leader of one alternative press company pointed out: "Gates has more than enough money to buy people's staffs out from under them." Indeed, Microsoft has been hiring staff in each site, with attractive money offers. With Microsoft's immense cash reserves, Gates's giant is "putting enormous resources into the development of its various 'Sidewalk' projects, which they are reportedly willing to operate in the red for three years or more." Ironically, Microsoft took out a full-page ad in the Twin Cities for "Sidewalk" a little after its launch—in the alternative weekly *City Pages*! What alternative weekly can match Microsoft in economic competition?

Thus, the software sultan is bringing profits from its monopoly in operating systems and dominance in software to gain advantage in other market areas. Remember what the law professors said about the Sherman Antitrust Act "prohibiting the use of monopoly power in one market to gain advantage in another"; and remember economist Brian Arthur found that "perhaps the most important way a dominant firm can exploit its position is by using its monopoly in one market to bludgeon its way into another." Indeed.

Further, "Sidewalk" and the new edition of Microsoft's Internet Explorer appear to be twin fronts for vastly increasing Microsoft's control of operations and commerce on the Internet.

> According to an internal Microsoft memo obtained by [journalist David] Bank, "Sidewalk" is an integral part of Microsoft's drive to control the broader world of online commerce. Specifically, "Sidewalk" is to be used as an interface to goods-and-services providers such as travel agents and online music stores; Microsoft in turn will exact a fee for every bit of commerce transacted. And that's where the Gates gang is banking on making big money from the Internet—not from online advertising, as so many others are trying to do.

As noted earlier, Microsoft's Internet Explorer 4.0 was designed to take people directly to its own and affiliated sites for "e-commerce"— and the next iteration of Explorer was to intensify that function. As *Editor & Publisher*'s on-line magazine observed: "Microsoft's hydra-like sprawl of Web publishing ventures" is increasingly orienting itself in that direction.[21]

Summations and Significations

This chapter discussed the impact of the march of megamedia on level-playing field economic competition and on competition in the marketplace of ideas. Some summations and some thoughts on what all this signifies are in order before we move on in the next chapter to a special focus on the impact on the news process and creative outputs.

How does competition in media measure up to economist Paul Samuelson's description of the prime elements of fully functional marketplace competition cited at the beginning of this chapter? (1) In many prime media areas, there are *not* "numerous buyers and sellers on each side" able to compete fairly and evenly; rather, there are a few conglomerate giants with vast and multifarious resources and structural advantages on one side that dominate economic relations. (2) Those vertically and horizontally concentrated media conglomerates, with their array of connections, joint ventures, and extension into many other geographic and product/service markets, have every reason to and do indeed "discriminate in favor of one merchant rather than another." (3) Given that they also control the dominant means of mass communication to pervasively purvey messages and images about their products, services and companies, they *do* "expect that variations in their own bids and offers will have appreciable effect upon the prevailing market price." As an Associated Press reporter commented after the Time Warner merger with Turner Communications: "Time Warner's move to remain No. 1 in the face of Disney's expansion also means *it will be hard for American households to avoid one of the industry's giants when they seek news or entertainment.*"

Looking at media merger mania from a humorous angle, Susan Douglas and T. R. Durham have provided a tongue-in-cheek glossary of words from the media wonderland of the 1990s. Their right-on-the-money (so to speak) definition of "synergy": "Current: the transcendental, binding arc of energy that radiates throughout the land and all the peoples in it when two behemoths in the media industry seek to unite in order to clobber all known competition. Obsolete: oligopoly."

The full name of the Telecom Act, at least as it worked its way through Congress, was the Telecommunications Competition and Deregulation Act. Deregulation was a centerpiece of the Act and was supposed to lead to an outburst of competition. Perhaps we can learn some things from some other regulatory areas and efforts at deregulation in the 1980s and 1990s. The contemporary deregulation wave really began at the end of the 1970s, during the later stages of the Carter administration, most notably in the airline industry. Alfred Kahn, President Jimmy Carter's economic policy adviser, led the way on this effort; a Kahn associate was Mark Kehan, who served at the Civil Aeronautics Board, the federeal agency that dealt with airline policy.

As Robert Kuttner relates, in recent years, Kehan ruefully acknowledged that "Of the six intellectual assumptions behind airline deregulation, four have proven completely false." Two of those appear to have special lessons for the media realm: "Deregulators believed that barriers to entry are low in the airline business. Experience has demonstrated that they are very high. Deregulators believed that increased competition would produce low unrestricted fares. In fact, it has produced a bewildering array of discriminatory prices." Alfred Kahn himself has acknowledged that "The persistence—indeed—intensification of price discrimination has been a surprise." He said: "Most of us probably did not foresee the deterioration in the average quality of the flying experience. . . . I should have recognized that the naturally monopolistic or oligopolistic character of most airline markets would continue—indeed expand—under deregulation." All of those factors—discriminatory pricing, high barriers to entry, and the deterioration in the quality of offerings under deregulation—appear to be exactly the trajectory of corporate market activity in mass media in the 1990s, especially following passage of the Telecom Act.

Kuttner also reminds us, "The banking and savings & loan scandals [in the United States] suggest what happens when a necessarily mixed sector of the economy tries to substitute excessive marketization"—dysfunction in the intended service of the sector and a costly disaster. This suggests a lesson for the media industry.

In light of the fact that those sorts of policy schemes are typically the product of some standard economists in the first instance, it is impossible to resist relating the following. Kuttner reports:

> One of the best-documented findings from a long series of game-theory experiments is that most people . . . will contribute a share of windfall winnings to the public good, even though economic theory would predict that each rational individual would "free-ride" and hope that somebody else will worry about the general welfare. The major exception occurs when the experiment is conducted among economics students, who have evidently been conditioned by their training to prize egoist behavior. In one famous experiment, only 20% of economics students chose to contribute to the general well-being, compared with a majority of other students.

Major corporations tend to be economists-in-practice, especially in their basic orientations. Thinking in not-so-standard mode, economist Arthur Okun, who served as chair of the Council of Economic Advisors under President Lyndon Johnson, cautioned that under the raw market approach, "some of our most cherished rights are auctioned off to the highest bidder."[22]

6

Megamedia, News, and
the Democratic Dialogue

●●

> It is my conviction that the Founding Fathers . . . had a reason for
> giving journalists special privileges in the Constitution. The rea-
> son was that we were supposed to find out what was going on,
> here and abroad, and report it, so that the public could under-
> stand and make an informed judgment [on public issues]. It was
> not put in the Constitution so that publishers could make billions
> of dollars or so that journalists could make millions of dollars. It
> was put in the Constitution so we could do serious journalistic
> work.
>
> —R. W. "Johnny" Apple Jr. of the *New York Times*

In the United States and the rest of the world, the concentrated, conglomerate ownership of the media form the basic context in which news
and public affairs material and cultural and entertainment material are
produced and communicated. The marketplace of ideas is forced to operate under the circumstances of the economic market and under the organizational conditions of corporate owners.

Lee Bollinger, dean of the University of Michigan Law School, relates
the principle of diverse, independent sources of news and ideas to that
corporate context:

> We must also consider how press freedom might . . . actually prove to
> be a threat to democracy, a threat to the very values the First Amend-
> ment . . . is supposed to further. . . .
>
> The press can exclude important points of view, operating as a
> bottleneck in the marketplace of ideas. It can distort knowledge of pub-
> lic issues not just by omission but also through active misrepresenta-
> tions . . . It can also exert an adverse influence over the tone and char-
> acter of public debate in subtle ways, by playing to personal biases. . . .
> or by making people fearful. . . . It can fuel ignorance and pettiness by
> avoiding serious issues altogether, favoring simple-minded fare or
> cheap entertainment over serious discussion. . . . Of course, *all these con-
> cerns become more serious as the number of those who control the press become
> fewer.* [Emphasis added.]

The first sections of this chapter take up the issue of the impacts of concentrated and conglomerate control of the media on the production and presentation of news. A later section looks at the impact of that structure of control on cultural and entertainment media processes and productions.[1]

The Evolution and Nature of Corporate Control of Media

In America, and in many other nations, news operations have long been parts of for-profit businesses, except for public broadcasting. But in recent decades, sizable media companies have increasingly gone public and offered stock in their corporations. This tends, sooner or later (usually sooner), to exert a strong pull on those media corporations to be most attentive to Wall Street's concerns; and Wall Street worries, not about quality of news, but about profitability and what looks like an ever more attractive investment. This strongly tends to lead to an intense corporate bottom-line mentality regarding how news organizations are operated. James Squires, journalist and former top editor of the *Chicago Tribune,* observed these developments firsthand. His compelling book *Read All About It!* documents the patterns in striking detail. Squires says of the Wall Street context and its impact:

> In its struggle for relevance and financial security in the modern information age, the press as an institution appears ready to trade its tradition and its public responsibility for whatever will make a buck. In the starkest terms, the news media of the 1990s are a celebrity-oriented, Wall Street-dominated, profit-driven entertainment enterprise dedicated foremost to delivering advertising images to targeted groups of consumers.

In earlier years, newspapers and broadcast companies tended to be individually owned and directed by people who felt a strong identity with the company, and news operations were centerpieces and prized elements of their organizational identities. People like William Paley of CBS and David Sarnoff of NBC took pride in operating the networks and their news divisions with a sense of stewardship of an important institution carrying a public trust, even if they were sometimes less than perfect at following their better instincts. Katherine Graham of the *Washington Post,* the Sultzberger family of the *New York Times,* Otis Chandler of the *Los Angeles Times,* Peter Fleischmann and his father of the *New Yorker* magazine, and others had a similar sense of stewardship. The parent companies also had long experience with running organizations that included news operations.

Over the course of the 1980s and 1990s especially, with megamedia empire-building in full fury, that orientation has, however, given way to a mentality that manifests little concern for such stewardship, or even demonstrates simple disdain for it. Rupert Murdoch is the paramount example. Harry Evans, who served as editor of the *Times* of London under Murdoch, says of Murdoch: "He's a good businessman and a lousy journalist—a lousy journalist in the sense that he doesn't believe in public service journalism. . . . And also, he's a very treacherous person, it must be said." This is in reference to Murdoch's promises to newspapers he has bought that he would not interfere in their editorial process, promises he has repeatedly broken. Si Newhouse, Gannett's Neuharth, and other media moguls have demonstrated similar orientation and behavior, and General Electric's Jack Welch illustrates tendencies at least as severe among the industrial companies that have gained control of media.

Another factor stemming from the megamedia empire-building and the raw corporate finance orientation is debt. This factor also raises questions about the value of various of those big media mergers even for their simple, direct purpose of enhancing the general economic condition of the corporation. In the process of acquiring more media companies, the Dominant Dozen have added staggering levels of debt through borrowing to finance their acquisitions and through taking on the existing debt of the companies they have purchased. Time Warner was left with a mind-boggling $17.5 billion debt after the Turner acquisition, an amount that was reduced somewhat by early 1998; Murdoch's News Corp. had $9 billion in debt in 1997; Viacom had $10.7 billion in debt in 1997, and so on. Financial columnist Christopher Byron has described this merger mania and the attendant financial feeding frenzy:

> You have an entire industry on Wall Street—the investment banking industry—that keeps bidding the prices of these deals into outer space, then raking off absolutely mind-blowing fees for providing the debt financings needed to pay the bill. . . .
> This debt burden is of huge importance, and everyone in the media knows it. In fact, the debt burden on the American media, which began with the junk-bond financing of Drexel Burnham & Co. . . . in the early 1980s, is why the whole industry is in the mess it is today.

That debt burden intensifies the patterns of corporate cost-cutting, major layoffs, and increased problems for news investigation and presentation. Some corporations have also been selling off pieces of their acquisitions or their original assets to buy down debt.

In addition, there are a number of "corporate interlocks" between media and nonmedia corporations through their boards of directors, which are legally responsible for the corporations. That is, many members of the boards of directors of the major multimedia corporations and industrial-media conglomerates also sit on the boards of other corporations. Time Inc., just before its merger with Warner "had so many interlocks it almost represented a Plenary Board of directors of American business and finance, including Mobil oil, AT&T, American Express, Firestone Tire & Rubber, Mellon National [bank] corporation, Atlantic Richfield, Xerox, General Dynamics." Some late 1990s examples, among many, are: (1) Directors of Murdoch's News Corp. include Thomas Perkins, who is also head of Tandem Computers and a director of the huge Philips Electronics Corporation; and Bert Roberts, who is also chief executive of MCI; (2) Directors of Gannett include Andrew Brimmer, who is also a director of BankAmerica Corporation, E. I. DuPont, and other corporations; Drew Lewis, who is also a Director for Ford Motors, American Express, Lucent Technologies, and so on.

Several studies of economic and organizational reasons why megamedia corporations (like other companies) have directors from other economic areas shed light on the implications of these corporate connections. One study found that these interlocking directorates are a significant part of a more general effort to manage the socioeconomic environment in which the corporation operates "by appointing significant external representatives to positions in the organization." By this means the media corporation can "access resources, exchange information, [and] develop interfirm commitments. " A study from the late 1980s of the top one hundred American media companies found numerous such intercorporate directorships and connections. In light of the high debt levels of current megamedia corporations, most interesting was the finding that "among the many firms represented on a typical board of directors, there is usually a representative from a major bank, and these financial proxies exercise corporate power." To finance the tremendous acquisition activity requires vast amounts of capital, and banks and other financial institutions are where the money is. In conceptual terms, this is about "resource dependency"; that is, organizations are dependent on various resources for their operations and acquisitions, and capital is the ultimate resource. This study found a strong correlation between the long-term debt, the debt-to-equity ratio, and like measures in a big media company and the number of officers from large banks and other financial institutions sitting on media boards. A significant presence on the boards of directors of the top one hundred media companies was also found for the biggest advertisers in America; and the number of top one hundred advertisers represented on these boards was strongly correlated with the amount of advertising sales the media corporation had.

Another study, published in 1994, found institutional investors have large investment stakes in a number of major media corporations that own newspapers. Those institutional investors include banks and other financial institutions like Mellon Bank Corp., Wells Fargo Investment Trust, and Fidelity Management. In general, this communications scholar concluded: "If the percentage of the company owned by institutions is very high or significantly higher than inside ownership [i.e., original owners and officers of the corporation itself], institutional owners will have a great deal of influence on the selection of directors and managers and the decisions made by the firm." Cap Cities–ABC (just before Disney took control), Gannett, and Knight-Ridder were among those over 60 percent owned by such institutional investors.

Interlocking directorates abound among media corporations in Canada, as well. The conservative Conference Board of Canada, after reviewing the situation, articulated the general worry that "interlocking directorates [have] a potential for restricting competition or other conflicts of interest." Providing a moral of the story on all this was a wonderfully appropriate observation (from years ago) of American legal giant Louis Brandeis: "This practice of interlocking directorates is the root of many evils. . . . It tends to disloyalty and violation of the fundamental law that no man can serve two masters."[2]

Megamedia Impacts on the News Process and News Content

Richard Clurman was for years a leading figure in *Time* magazine, helping make it a respected and leading newsmagazine; he also had experience with a major newspaper. In an important book on the news media, he said:

> As the news media became bigger and bigger business, the innovative traditions led by creative editorial dominance began to erode. . . . The media had grown from a nicely profitable, creative business into a gigantic investment opportunity. It was becoming harder to think of them as different from any other business in free enterprise America.

Doug Underwood is a former newspaper reporter who became a journalism professor. In his aptly titled book *When MBAs Rule the Newsroom,* he wrote:

> It's probably no surprise that in an era of mass media conglomerates, big chain expansion, and multimillion dollar newspaper buy-outs, the editors of daily newspapers have begun to behave more and more like the managers of any other corporate entity.

Leonard Goldensohn was the lead owner and head of the ABC network from the 1950s into the 1980s and had a strong sense of the public responsibilities of ABC. After Capital Cities took control of the network in the mid-1980s, along with the similar transfers at the other two American TV networks, Goldensohn remarked:

> I fear that one of the most insidious byproducts of the current merger mania may be the loss of a sense of stewardship, a value to which those of us in broadcasting have always been acutely sensitive. Because our business is more than a business. It is a public trust.[3]

Incident in Chicago

An incident in Chicago in mid-1997 illustrates the impact of corporatization and megamedia on the news process. Far more people attend to their local TV newscasts than to the network news shows—about 80 million in the aggregate, compared with about 40 million to 45 million for the network newscasts. Local TV news is a prime news source for large numbers of Americans.

WMAQ-TV of Chicago is one of the local TV stations owned by NBC. Besides the local news, two other shows are filmed in WMAQ's studios: the sleazy Jerry Springer and Jenny Jones talk shows, well characterized as those "festivals of dysfunction." In the era of General Electric's profit-obsessed control of the NBC network, Joel Cheatwood was hired as WMAQ's vice president for news. Cheatwood had been on the rise in the news business by pouring on the crime, sex, and glitz in TV news broadcasts in Miami and Boston. In the May 1997 period of ratings sweeps, Cheatwood decided to do something catchy to generate ratings for the station's "budget-battered newscasts": He reached out to those WMAQ studios used by the netherland of TV and hired Jerry Springer to do commentaries on local issues for the late news show.

The reaction to this major additional step in cheapening broadcast news shows was swift and strong: "When the noise stopped, the station's respected anchor pair of Carol Marin and Ron Magers had quit on principle, the ratings for WMAQ's newscast had slipped significantly," and the top managers at the station were tainted. Marin was particularly public in her criticism, even commenting on the problem in her final night on air. Tom Rosenstiel, former journalist and now journalistic reformer, put the incident in perspective: "It shows that audiences do care, and they do get it. Marin clearly helped undo Springer by raising people's awareness of the whole thing and what the stakes were. She made it emblematic and people voted with their feet. It's an important election." Carol Marin's courageous action, ending a highly paid anchor job, was actually an extension of "a record of fighting against her medium's steady debasement," and the action "received an outpouring of public support."

This story shows that journalists are the first victims of the degradation of the news process. But it also shows that noted journalists, with a little courage, can play powerful roles in bringing the debasement of their news processes into the spotlight and public arena for intense discussion. After such a demonstration of journalistic caring, the public is likely to respond and support preservation of quality news efforts.

Even before the Springer incident, WMAQ's news operation showed the impact of megamedia control on the news process. First, before bringing in Cheatwood, NBC and the station had hired as vice president of WMAQ news someone from Frank Magid Associates, the leading TV news consulting firm—a firm that tells TV news shows how to be attractive, catchy, splashy, but has shown little concern about the quality of the news purveyed. Second, despite the fact that WMAQ was enjoying profit margins that would make most nonmedia corporations turn green with envy, the station head brought in by NBC in 1995, Lyle Banks, proclaimed the station was underperforming (in revenue and profit terms, that is). Two key changes he made as a consequence were: (1) "Stories were being killed on the basis of a photographer's overtime. There was no reinvestment in the [news] product." (2) He increased the story count, from thirteen items to twenty or twenty-five in the half-hour broadcast. Susan Kennedy, a newswriter whose job was lost in a cutback, said the increase meant "the standard voice-over story dropped from thirty seconds to fifteen, roughly three written sentences." What kind of meaningful "news" is imparted in three sentences?[4]

Patterns of Corporate Media Development and the Impact on the News Process

Testimony from numerous sources around America shows that those developments in Chicago represent general patterns in the constant squeeze of newsroom resources and the effort to give newscasts more attention-grabbing stories that appeal to the viewers' supposedly short attention spans and don't tax the brain too much. The basic profit picture at WMAQ-TV is standard for TV stations of substantial size around America. By all accounts, local TV stations have typically earned from 20 percent up to 50 percent profit margins. "Even with the recession that accompanied the beginning of the 1990s, stations in large metropolitan areas were earning average pre-tax profits in the mid-30% range," one report notes. Meanwhile, the average for all types of industries is more like 8 to 11 percent. In short, for much of the past quarter-century American TV stations have been virtual licenses to print money for their owners. But under increasing megamedia control, these stations are being squeezed for considerably higher profits, and in most cases, that means damage to already inadequate personnel and other resources for meaningful (as opposed to gimmick) news gathering and reporting. For example, inside sources testified in late 1997, after CBS Inc. had bought WCCO-TV in Minneapolis–St. Paul and fully taken control, that the pressure was on for a big leap in profits. The station's 1996 profit of 27 percent was declared not sufficiently high; CBS now demanded 40 percent profit levels.

Further, the huge profits at local stations have not been plowed back into the news operation to enhance genuine news gathering and reporting capacities. Most of the money has been taken out of the news operation and out of the community and sent back to corporate headquarters in some distant city; and most of the modest balance of the money has been spent on gimmicks such as "chopper 7" helicopters and the like, rather than on enhancing the quality of journalistic talent and regular and investigative reporting efforts.

The nature of the ownership of most chain-owned local TV stations and the basic mentality of many owners has been described by Ken Auletta. By the late 1980s, only two of the fifty largest CBS local station affiliates were owned by individuals; the other forty-eight were owned by corporate media chains like Group W, Gannett, and Cox. Auletta also noted:

> Run by bottom-line managers, and often burdened by the debt incurred to meet the steep purchase price, stations were constantly trying to better last year's numbers. "It's commodity trading to us," admitted Martin Pompadur, chairman of Television Station Partners, who managed his eight stations from his New York headquarters. "We don't know the community. We're short-term players."

As Auletta also pointed out, those newer corporate owners "lack shared history and old loyalties" in connection with the network, so they more frequently preempt network public affairs shows for profitable entertainment fare and in general have lower or little commitment to the public responsibilities that are part of the heritage of the three networks.

The same basic patterns are seen on the newspaper side. The profit margins in larger markets and many more modest-sized ones range from 12 percent to 35 percent—again, well above most nonmedia industries. Gene Roberts is former executive editor of the *Philadelphia Inquirer* and former managing editor of the *New York Times*. His deep concern about these patterns is evident:

> Chains . . . will tell you they don't interfere with local coverage, they simply insist that each newspaper return an "acceptable" level of profits to the central corporation. . . . This alone is enough to cause newspapers . . . to weaken their coverage by slashing newsholes [the amount of space devoted to news as opposed to ads] and newsroom staff. But there are problems even beyond these.
>
> News coverage is being shaped by corporate executives at headquarters far from the local scene. It is seldom done by corporate directives or fiat. It rarely involves killing or slanting stories. Usually it is by the corporate graphics conference that results in a more uniform look, or by the corporate research director's interpretation of reader surveys that seek simple common-denominator solutions to complex coverage problems. [And] often the corporate view is hostile to governmental coverage.

The impact of such ownership is why, when their paper has been sold to one of the big newspaper chains, journalists have talked about "being sold into chains." That term is a too-revealing metaphor, which is why the Gannett corporate people go to great lengths to avoid use of the term "newspaper chain"; they prefer "newspaper groups."

Richard McCord relates another example of the impact of the corporate financial orientation, a case he saw firsthand. Gannett took over the daily newspaper the *New Mexican* in Santa Fe, where McCord ran a respected weekly newspaper; this worried McCord and his little weekly. The Gannett paper's newshole got smaller instead of being expanded, however, and it contained more wire service copy from afar than local coverage. As a consequence:

> Santa Feans ridiculed it. . . . As [the weekly] got stronger, the Gannett daily weakened. Its circulation dropped. . . . All our gains against *The New Mexican* were the result of journalistic fervor. All along, the obvious way for the daily to curb us was to upgrade its own effort. But five years after Gannett and its limitless riches hit town, the paper was worse than ever.

Why? A former accountant gave the answer. Even though annual revenues at the daily *New Mexican* had soared past $5 million and profits had doubled to 24 percent of income, the accountant was told by Gannett's corporate headquarters back east that they expected a return of 36 to 38 percent, so they would have to squeeze the news-gathering resources even more to bleed the paper of such profit levels.

Media critic Howard Kurtz of the *Washington Post* reflected on those patterns and asked the key question of whether these media companies are willing to invest seriously in quality news operations—"spend real, serious resources on news." He also made an illuminating observation about news and information sources in the "new media," focusing his comment on news media sites on the World Wide Web: "I surf the Web . . . and go onto these sites that have all these great bells and whistles and interactivity. But what you don't see on most of these sites is much or any original reporting." That raises questions about how meaningful a source of news coverage the "new media" really are. Clearly, Web sites and Internet access to data bases and other material provide a significant new connection to information for those citizens/consumers who have the skills and equipment to go on-line. The point Kurtz makes, however, suggests a bit more sober-minded appraisal of the Internet's value as a journalistic outlet than some people have suggested.[5]

Increasing Influence of the Marketing Mode. Further dimensions of the impact of the megamedia mentality and practice on the news process are evident in the marketing connection. The most notable recent example involved what has been one of the most highly respected newspapers in America, the *Los Angeles Times*. In 1995, the *Times*'s parent corporation, Times Mirror, brought in a new CEO, Mark Willes. The new chief executive had been an executive of General Mills, the food products company; he had no experience in the news business. He proceeded to cut 2,200 jobs and quickly shut down the Times Mirror–owned New York City edition of *Newsday*. Then in 1997, Willes set up a reorganization. A top marketing executive was named general manager for news; each section of the *Times* was to have a business executive assigned to be involved in planning for the section, and editors of those sections were to participate in meetings to discuss how to attract new readers. This appeared to breach what had long been considered the news version of the constitutional wall between church and state, that is, the fundamental separation between the news operation and the business operation. To make matters worse, CEO Willes "compared the newspaper to cake mixes and Hamburger Helper, a product to be relentlessly packaged and marketed" (which led some to call him the "cereal killer" of news integrity). Belatedly, Willes began to mention the need for independent news judgment, but profound questions remained. "Whether they like it or not, they've got a conflict of interest," was the assessment of the former national editor. The top editor, the respected Shelby Coffey, resigned early in 1997 after he had "found himself presiding over a series of cutbacks, buyouts and finally, layoffs."

The *Los Angeles Times* is far from an isolated case. This increasing encroachment of marketing on the news process is more and more a factor in American, and other, media. In the *Columbia Journalism Review* in early 1998, Doug Underwood provided a series of examples of that pattern from Knight-Ridder's *Bradenton Herald* and other newspapers controlled by other companies. Remarks by the chief executive of the Thomson newspaper chain and multimedia corporation further illustrate the corporate mind-set: "The editorial department is the biggest problem in a newspaper's marketing dynamic. . . . An effective marketing strategy depends on editorial cooperation; . . . marketing should be the king for all editors."

A related dimension of this increasing marketing menace is the influence of advertisers. Because advertising is the chief source of news media revenue in the twentieth century (unlike American newspapers during most of the nineteenth century), the temptation for advertising influence has long been there. But in the megamedia era, the tendency for advertisers to influence content has taken a quantum leap upward. At the aggregate level, a Marquette University poll of newspaper editors found 93 percent of them indicating that advertisers had tried to influence their news;

a majority said that their management condoned the pressure; and "37% of the editors polled admitted that they had succumbed" to that pressure. Additionally, a Nielsen survey found that 80 percent of TV news directors acknowledged broadcasting corporate public relations video material as news pieces "several times a month."

Chrysler's heavyhanded effort at influence is particularly illustrative. As America's fourth largest advertiser, spending $270 million on magazine advertising alone in 1996, Chrysler is a force to be reckoned with. In early 1997, Chrysler's ad agency, PentaCom, sent a letter to many magazines that included the following demand:

> In an effort to avoid potential conflicts, it is required that Chrysler Corporation be alerted in advance of any and all editorial content that encompasses sexual, *political, social issues* or any editorial content that might be *construed as provocative or offensive.* Each and every [magazine] issue that carries Chrysler advertising requires a written summary outlining major theme/articles appearing in upcoming issues. [Emphasis added.]

The magazines were to sign a form agreeing to do this.

The American Society of Magazine Editors responded to this ominous case and the more general pattern by saying they had "deep concern" about the trend of demands to give advertisers advance notice about upcoming stories. In the context of the march of megamedia, such demands raise grave questions about preservation of free expression and unrestricted investigation and presentation of information. There were real impacts: *Esquire* magazine pulled a short story as a result of this Chrysler demand, "many reputable magazines acceded to Chrysler's wishes," and in a number of cases, "a parent company signed for all its publications"—an ominous development in itself.

Another response to the Chrysler initiative illustrates a second type of danger. A new start-up magazine, *Maxim,* aimed at affluent young men, said: "We're complying. We definitely have to." This is one of several indications that start-up companies or media services are increasingly forced to operate under the rules set by the megamedia corporations and their big corporate cousins in other commercial realms. This is further evidence that megamedia dominance either sharply raises the barriers to entry or, as in this case, constrains and conditions the nature of any new entries.

The basic function of the media for business executives and the source of the essential problem were well captured by a quote provided by ad analyst Leo Bogart in his book *Commercial Culture.* An ABC network executive frankly acknowledged: "The network is paying affiliates to carry network commercials, not programs. What we are is a distribution system for Procter and Gamble," which spends hundreds of millions of dollars on advertising each year. The ominous impact of this orientation was confirmed in a speech by Westinghouse-CBS chief executive Michael Jordan in a speech to business executives in November 1997: "Every CBS program is sent to major advertisers for previewing. "

The executive editor of the Newhouse-owned *Cleveland Plain Dealer* in the mid-1980s eventually resigned from the newspaper largely because of "the repeated attempts by Newhouse business executives to allow advertisers, such as large department stores in Cleveland, to influence the news and how it appeared in the *Plain Dealer.*"

Consumer reporting has presented particular problems in the context of big corporate control of local TV stations. With increasingly complicated products and services involving mechanical and electronic gadgets and chemicals that nonspecialists do not have the expertise to assess, consumer product reporting is needed more than ever. More generally, simply serving as a monitor of questionable business operations that affect consumers is part of the news media's traditional watchdog function. But with the profit obsession, corporate connections with other commercial enterprises, and dependence on advertisers for revenue, consumer reporting, especially on local TV news shows, has taken a big hit. Various examples have come to light in recent years. By 1991 only about 20 percent of TV stations had consumer reporters, down from 40 percent ten years earlier. As one review found: "Those stations that still feature consumer reporters . . . now seem more likely to delete names of advertisers from critical pieces, allow their own sales department to grill reporters, or kill stories outright." And so, in still another way, citizens and consumers are being disserved.

An interesting new wrinkle on the marketing thrust into the democratic sanctuary of news via the conglomerate connection has arisen courtesy of Time Warner–Turner and Murdoch's Fox–News Corp. Some recent movie scripts called for a network news show to announce some dramatic development in the story. In the Warner Bros.' movies *Lost World: Jurassic Park* and *Contact,* several real CNN reporters and anchor Bernard Shaw made appearances. The idea for the cross-promotion came directly from Warner Bros. chairman Robert Daly to CNN president Tom Johnson, "who thought it a dandy opportunity." Fox News was similarly used in *Independence Day* from Murdoch-controlled Twentieth Century Fox. The presence of supposedly serious journalists in a movie from another part of the conglomerate engendered considerable criticism from other journalists and analysts. Marvin Kalb, formerly of CBS News, now director of the Shorenstein Center at Harvard, said:

The line between news and entertainment, between reporters and actors—which has become increasingly blurred in recent years—has been crossed in "Contact." . . . If a reporter is to retain his credibility as a truth-teller, he has to stick to his craft and not confuse the viewer by playing an actor who plays a reporter telling fictional truths about space flight.

[And,] "Contact," produced in Hollywood by Warner Bros., highlights many of the . . . troublesome questions about megamergers suddenly producing too much corporate power.

In late summer 1997, after the prominent criticism, CNN announced that it would put restrictions on such movie appearances. But where will the next break in the line between supposedly serious news and entertainment occur, where will the next conglomerate action come to cross-promote and enhance the general corporation's bottom line, resulting in a breach in the integrity of the news process? Given Murdoch's record of interfering with his news operations and the low-grade entertainment material he has regularly made a part of his newspapers, there is little reason to think more such breaches will not be forthcoming, especially from the News Corp.–Fox connection.

Increasing megamedia arrangements with other corporate endeavors and joint marketing agreements further threaten the preservation of consumer reporting and the unfettered independence of news operations. For example, in fall 1997, the *Chicago Tribune* made an exclusive marketing agreement with Starbucks: the *Tribune* would be the only Chicago daily paper sold in the 80 Starbucks coffee shops around the Chicago metro area—thus shutting out the *Trib*'s rival the *Sun-Times.* Then, on 7 October, the paper's Tempo section carried "an oversized, overheated, and oversweetened profile of Howard Schultz, Starbucks CEO," as *Columbia Journalism Review* put it in its Darts & Laurels media-watchdog section. When Disney-ABC establishes a big-bucks, ten-year deal with McDonald's to provide for elaborate promotion of Disney products in McDonald's thousands of fast food emporiums throughout the world, will there sooner or later be pressure, subtle or not-so-subtle, for ABC News to ease up on bad news stories about McDonald's, especially any investigative reporting beyond some big public development that can't be ignored?

In general regarding the megamedia impact on news operations, the Gannett chain, again, is illustrative. Consider the case of the *Des Moines Register* in Iowa. For years the *Register* was owned by the Cowles family. For years the *Register* was a highly respected newspaper, especially given its middling size. As former editor Michael Gartner said, "the news side was the watchdog of the state, and the editorial page was the conscience of the state," as a state's major newspaper should be. But then it was sold to Gannett. Gartner's conclusion: "I don't believe either arm is fulfilling that mission today." And he noted that changes came slowly at first because the paper was still staffed by people who "understood the traditions of the newspaper and the heritage of the state." But gradually, some of those people left; at that point "the paper started changing sharply, both its news and editorial page. . . . A lot of the newsroom became disenchanted."[6]

Are Claims about Megamedia Impact Overblown? There is continuing debate among journalists and others about the extent and nature of the impact of megamedia control over news organizations. Some journalists take umbrage at the thought that they could be influenced by corporate central. *Time* managing editor Walter Isaacson, who, to his credit, has participated in several forums on these issues, said:

> I'd like to challenge a widespread but shallow notion that media conglomeration inevitably leads to compromises in editorial integrity. . . . Those of us who work for publications that are owned by big parent companies . . . can sometimes be cozily insulated from editorial meddling (and even financial fluctuations) either because the companies have a heritage of valuing creativity or because they have a pragmatic realization that screwing around with what we write is likely to backfire noisily and be more hassle than it's worth.

As an example of that independence, Isaacson cited a *Time* magazine business writer's article that called Time Warner stock "among the biggest dogs in media since Lassie." He has also noted that the magazine did "a good, tough cover story on the impact of violence and obscenity in movies and music, and on the crusade against Time Warner being led by Bill Bennett."[7]

There is surely more capacity for resistance to corporate encroachment if the journalistic organization is long established as a premier news institution and if the journalists involved are respected and well known. It will also depend on how blatant and major the infraction. Perhaps even more helpful in such resistance is raising the red flag over coverage of an issue that is already prominently in the public arena—like Bill Bennett's values attack on Time Warner entertainment products, a "crusade" that was boosted by Bennett's best-selling book. This was an issue that was already so much in the public eye that it would have looked bad if *Time* magazine hadn't dealt with it rather prominently. Unfortunately, that does not cover the vast majority of issues in this realm; to the extent the factors just noted are lessened or absent, the likelihood of interference probably increases.

There is strong reason to have major worries about a growing corporate influence on the news process. The substantial staff layoffs that have accompanied many of the megamedia takeovers clearly make journalists more concerned about keeping their jobs, more aware of their ultimate corporate bosses, and hence more likely to be subtly or no to so subtly influenced. The Time Warner merger brought in its wake huge debt, and budget crunches throughout many parts of the conglomerate resulted in the loss of 605 jobs in journalism. *Time* magazine alone lost 44 people. (So much for that "cozy insulation" for Time Warner journalists "even from financial fluctuations.") After the conglomerate takeovers of the networks, the corporate-parent-induced layoffs at ABC, CBS, and NBC were quite substantial. Beyond the general network job cuts noted in chapter 3, reductions specifically in the news budgets and personnel were very significant. Capital Cities cut 20 percent from the ABC News budget and eliminated 300 jobs; Tisch cut 215 positions in the CBS News Division; and at NBC after the General Electric takeover, the number of NBC correspondents alone (not total news personnel) shrank from 110 to 70.

These developments create a climate of concern in the newsroom, especially about journalists' jobs, and are likely to result in more anticipated reactions by journalists to the ultimate bosses and more self-censorship. James Fallows, former editor of *U.S. News & World Report*, spoke to this phenomenon in his book on the media, *Breaking the News*. He noted that journalists had heard about corporate officials in various industrial and commercial areas, in this era of "downsizing," telling employees of the need to be "flexible" and to "repackage" themselves for a changing economy. But in the 1990s, journalists "have begun to realize that [these conditions] apply not just to people working at IBM or Chrysler but to employees of CBS and the *Los Angeles Times* as well." Thus: "They have responded to a changed environment as rational people inevitably will: by developing the survival skills necessary if they hope to earn a living in a troubled business. . . . Increasingly they must be economic survivors; . . . the result . . . is a subtle skewing of the news."

CBS correspondent Betsy Aaron spoke from experience on that: "After the corporate takeovers, when there were all those mass firings, it really frightened people. . . . Now we don't take as many chances. . . . If you're worried about the mortgage, the kids, you won't be as good a reporter." Former CBS News producer Richard Cohen testified to the issue more pungently: "News used to be a bunch of strong-minded people with authority problems. Now it's changed. People are more submissive, more willing to play corporate games." Ken Auletta's reporting in *Three Blind Mice* on actions by corporate executives in demanding personnel cuts and other obeisance in the cases of GE-NBC, Capital

Cities–ABC, and Tisch/Loews-controlled CBS detailed the organizational conditions. Lawrence Grossman's service as NBC News president made the point painfully clear to him:

> The corporate culture came to dominate the news business, treating news as a commodity or service no different from "toasters, light bulbs, or jet engines," to quote John F. Welch, chairman of General Electric. . . . For Welch and a good many of his GE colleagues, news—even though part of hugely profitable NBC—was expected to make the same profit margins as every other GE division. As soon became evident, they had no qualms about doing whatever was necessary to achieve that goal, with little regard for journalistic standards, integrity, or taste.

The message from the top is sometimes delivered in very unsubtle fashion. The message is hard to miss when, as noted earlier, the chief executive of General Electric installs as NBC president a GE man who then jabs his finger into the chest of the leader of NBC News and says "You work for GE!" The message is also brutally clear when the General Electric CEO says in a speech to NBC executives, "We're going to demand from you earnings growth every year. . . . You take charge of your destiny. If you don't, we will." And, of course, top news people are hired—and fired—by executives at megamedia or industrial-media headquarters. James Squires, from his *Chicago Tribune* experience, provided an additional illustration of the basic problem:

> John W. Madigan [is] a former Salomon Brothers investment broker who also served as Tribune Company's chief financial officer, and who today is the *Tribune*'s publisher and head of all the company's newspapers. Again and again we butted heads over what I considered conflicts between the interests of the *Tribune* and those of the corporate executive suite.

This also sends a message to the news staff. And when James Squires ended his term as top editor at the paper, what kind of person was corporate central likely to hire? A decidedly more compliant individual is the likely hiree in such cases.

One other point is important to note in response to Isaacson's contention that media conglomeration does not tend to compromise editorial integrity (although he fudged the issue by saying "inevitably"). As was alluded to in the case of the Gannett assumption of control over the *Des Moines Register,* we should not necessarily expect a takeover by a corporate chain to have immediate seismic impacts. It may take a while to wear down the traditional process. Further, since the intensity of scrutiny regarding impacts of a buyout tends to be high right after the change of control, if the megamedia corporation waits a while following the takeover to really get the people and processes under its thumb, there is less likelihood that their actions will be noticed. Frank Rich of the *New York Times* has recognized these transition factors and bids us consider what happens after a period of time of megamedia cost-cutting and control. As he points out, "we are still at the beginning of this phenomenon" of conglomerate conditions of operation for news organizations. While some people from genuine journalistic traditions are still reporters and editors, producers and anchor persons (like Dan Rather), "the question is, will [the new] people who come in be people who have no institutional memory of what journalism is or journalistic values? Will there be a whole new kind of nonjournalistic employee who comes out of a corporate culture?" One can certainly hope for considerable resistance, but the structure of the situation and related tendencies, in the passage of time, do not seem encouraging.

Indeed, a *Columbia Journalism Review* assessment of the effects of Gannett's takeover of both the *Des Moines Register* and the *Louisville Courier-Journal* found that at both papers, especially after the initial years of the chain's ownership, the newer leadership "snaps the last major links to family ownership and signals greater obedience to the mother corporation." After a grace period of those initial years, a just-retired news editor of the *Register* reported: "Now the management mandates have exploded." A further part of the problem is what observers call Gannett's "revolving-door system of executive advancement," whereby editors, chief editors, and publishers are frequently transferred to other papers in the chain (for varied experience, presumably). From mid-1996 through late 1997, the *Courier-Journal* had three different top editors. Michael Gartner, who had edited both papers in the past, pointed out that these news executives do not "stay anywhere long enough to understand his or her town, let alone develop an affection for it." And as he notes, an editor or publisher who doesn't really understand the area and isn't genuinely involved with it and committed to it can hardly provide the kind of news leadership for coverage the community deserves.

The conglomerate budget axes have also meant real losses of journalistic capacity at ABC, CBS, and NBC. As usual, the NBC case is especially striking. Former NBC correspondent Ken Bode said: "When I joined on, the Chicago bureau was forty people. . . . They covered anything that happened in the Midwest. Now it's three people." All three networks also eliminated a series of foreign bureaus, thus reducing their capacity to have their own major journalistic talent (rather than mere stringers), with a well-developed understanding of key nations and regions, give viewers significant foreign news. In reality, ABC News, like CBS and NBC, became less and less "uniquely qualified to bring you the world," as their motto went in the 1980s. At NBC, even the Paris bureau is now just an answering machine. Network news spending may have been a little excessive at times, but such cuts reduce basic news-gathering ability.

On the newspaper side, the *Courier-Journal* of Louisville, which had a history of quality before being gobbled up by Gannett, had five fewer general-assignment reporters in late 1997 than it had in 1990, and vacant positions can go unfilled for months, which looks to insiders like "subtle cost-cutting." *New York Times* editor Gene Roberts reports information that indicates that that conclusion can be generalized to the industry as a whole. In early 1998 he talked with a consultant to newspapers; the consultant had worked with at least one hundred papers in the previous two years. The consultant found that the middle tier of editors (section editors) "seemed traumatized" because of inadequate resources; they "didn't think it was possible to perform at an acceptable standard given the resources at their disposal." Roberts had found the same response was widespread in editors' professional meetings over the previous three or four years.[8]

In the conglomerate context, the possibility of news punches being pulled is a particularly weighty concern. This is illustrated in a case discussed by journalist Elizabeth Lesley. Her introduction to several cases was a good summation of the basic issue, starting with the article's title, "Self-Censorship is Still Censorship." She reported that the problem had happened again and again recently: "A division of a media giant adjusts its agenda to appease its corporate parent. . . . As media giants digest their huge acquisitions of recent years, it will become more and more common for the juicy content of one division to fall victim to the best interests of another." She discovered that in early 1996 CNN's news operation had developed a story for *Moneyline with Lou Dobbs* about an IRS and Labor Department investigation of "possibly illegal use of contract workers at its Time Inc. division." (Subsequently, the government subpoenaed witnesses in the case.) The story apparently would have "cast Time in an unflattering light," and "one issue raised in the reporting of the story was that the probe could affect Time Warner's then-pending merger with Turner Broadcasting, parent of CNN." But CNN did not air the story. CNN news personnel who were involved in preparing the story said that "they were never told why but suspect corporate interference." Unfortunately, this kind of behind-the-scenes look at what was not covered or was killed after material was developed is extremely rare.

Lou Dobbs, who subsequently became a vice president of CNN under the Time Warner regime, later contended that there was no interference and that he had just decided it wasn't enough of a story. In any case, at least the clear and present danger of a conflict of interest is apparent. In fact, communications scholar Joseph Turow's investigation of Time Warner in the early 1990s led him to conclude that anticipated reactions and self-censorship were significant factors in that megamedia company "when it comes to reporting about internal organizational matters." He found that "such efforts to report about the parent organization and internal operations went largely unrewarded" and could "generate the opposite reaction from superiors who are not appreciative of self-disclosure reporting."

Another Time Warner case illustrates the conglomerate connection and dangers for the news and investigation process and also illustrates the government antitrust action, or rather inaction. Steve Brill is head of American Lawyer Media, which includes *American Lawyer* magazine, Court TV, and *Corporate Control Alert* newsletter. In 1996 American Lawyer Media was co-owned by Time Warner. A story on the director of the Federal Trade Commission's Bureau of Competition, William Baer, was scheduled to run in *Corporate Control Alert*. At this time, June 1996, the huge Time Warner merger with Turner Communications was being reviewed by the FTC. In late June, Brill got a call (about which he immediately wrote a memo for the record) from the chief financial officer of Time Warner "at the behest of" Time Warner CEO Gerald Levin. The chief financial officer told Brill that the piece on FTC's Baer "could endanger the merger," and he said: "We are working hard on Baer and anything that gets him nervous or makes him think we don't appreciate him could hurt us. . . . I'm not telling you what to do, but I think you know what to do." Later a Time Warner spokesman denied "the accuracy" of Brill's account; but the memo and Brill's track record for integrity are strong evidence for concluding the incident happened as related. In the end, the story ran—a tribute to Brill's integrity and guts. But Time Warner subsequently bought complete ownership of American Lawyer Media.

Such conglomerate conflicts of interest are, of course, more numerous with the industrial-media corporations like General Electric–NBC, Viacom, and the rest. A simple perusal of the number and variety of GE's industrial and commercial interests, for example, makes that clear. In one instance, the *Today* show cut out a reporter's reference to the fact that some faulty bolts used in airplanes and missile silos were made by GE.

Then there is what we might call the knife-edge of conglomerate ownership for media personnel. When formerly independent media organizations are gobbled up by a conglomerate, there is a real danger that critical voices in those organizations will be silenced. Ben Bagdikian reports that after the Disney takeover of ABC, Disney fired Robert Anson, editor of ABC-owned *Los Angeles* magazine, "presumably, like other Eisner sensitivities, because Anson had once written criticisms of [Disney

CEO] Michael Eisner." The company also fired Texas-based, progressive commentator for the ABC radio network Jim Hightower, who had also been critical of Disney. After Disney took over ABC, Hightower said his boss was now Mickey Mouse: "I work for a rodent." Well, not for long, as it turned out.

It can also be difficult to get a strong critique of a powerful media conglomerate produced, distributed, and taken note of in the main media. This is the story of Thomas Maier's excellent book *Newhouse*, on the Newhouse/Advance Publications media empire. The book won the 1995 "best media book" prize from the National Honor Society in Journalism and Mass Communication. But Maier had a hard time just getting a publisher for the book. "No one would touch it" at the start, he said. In a rather typical response, the Bloomsbury Press in London responded: "We love it, but we're sorry, we do business with S. I. Newhouse." The Newhouse-owned *Vanity Fair* magazine refused even to run an ad for the book, and none of the twenty-five Newhouse newspapers ever reviewed it; "in effect, the Newhouse company banned any mention of this book in their publications." Further, when Liz Smith mentioned the book as the lead item in her nationally syndicated column, none of the subscribing Newhouse newspapers used it. In New York City in general (Newhouse headquarters), the Newhouse book had trouble gaining recognition; the book was not reviewed or mentioned in *New York* magazine, for example. Further, Maier's next book project was a first biography of Dr. Benjamin Spock, who had granted full access, but he had publishing problems with that project on a mere guilt-by-association basis. For example, when editors at Crown Publishing, one of the Newhouse stable of publishers, discovered that Maier was author of *Newhouse*, they canceled his appointment to discuss the Spock bio. This pattern of what one might call "restraint of trade in the marketplace of ideas" seems to be a serious constraint on diversity of voices, and on the democratic society's need to have access to critiques of powerful forces and means of public accountability for such forces—all of which are central purposes of the First Amendment.[9]

Patterns of News Material in the Megamedia Era

Much evidence is now in, and it shows disturbing patterns in what the corporate media are giving the public in the form of news, patterns that appear to have gotten steadily worse from the mid-1980s on—the prime megamedia era. Consider first the American network news shows, the most prominent of the news operations. From the later 1980s on, many observers have increasingly criticized the network news shows for focusing less and less on news material of vital importance for our democratic process and society more generally and instead giving the public more and more crime, sensationalism, and feature-story fluff. Those critics include such former prominent network news figures as Marvin Kalb, Bill Moyers, and Walter Cronkite. Kalb said:

> In the 1980s, . . . the network news shows came to be seen by people outside of the news business as gigantic profit centers. Up until that point, [the news divisions] were never seen as profit centers, we were loss leaders. . . .
>
> See, in earlier years, it was the story that determined whether a story got on the air—it had something important to say. In the 1980s, the judgment changed. If you had something that looked important, that looked appealing—striking images and quick, flashy motion— that's what they went for and the substance often fell into second place. Whereas earlier, substance was first and the picture amplified the substance, by the 1980s, the picture was first and substance amplified the picture. . . .
>
> The idea of making money in the news business is not new. The difference now is that news has never been so powerful, . . . so *there*— with the result that people have the opportunity to make, not just handsome profits, but huge profits, even obscene profits. But if the pursuit of profit be the guiding light of contemporary journalism, it will lose its way.[10]

By 1997, under the conglomerate control of General Electric, *NBC Nightly News* was coming in for especially strong criticism. CBS anchor Dan Rather has publicly lamented the softening of NBC News, calling it "news lite." One might take criticism from a direct competitor with a grain of salt; but Rather has some credibility here as he has also spoken and written publicly warning his own network not to cheapen the network news shows, including an admonishment to CBS executives not to cut resources and decrease foreign news coverage. Speaking of the environment in the news operation under conglomerate control, Rather said: "Part of what's changed here is an acute awareness that every good and decent thing [in news operations and responsibilities] is constantly on the razor's edge of danger, and must be fought for minute by minute."

A *Columbia Journalism Review* article documented quite well the degeneration of NBC News, an explicit product of its "inside-out makeover" giving it a "softer, more user-friendly" approach. "More and more of [NBC's stories] focus on trends, life style and consumer issues, pop culture, and heartland America, " *CJR* noted. An ad NBC placed in the *New York Times* for one major feature story illustrates the pattern: "Marriage 'Boot Camp': Could It Save Your Relationship?" One analyst who tracks the network news shows found that over the first two and a half months of 1997, NBC used a total of 351 minutes of its weeknight news shows for named feature segments; CBS and ABC used only 197 and 185 minutes respectively for such material. The story that got the most airtime in 1996 on NBC News was the Olympics. Take a wild guess which network had broadcast rights to the Olympics that year—another example of synergy.

In defense of this "reorientation," NBC anchor Tom Brokaw says he travels around the country and hears "what people are talking about and what interests them," and "a whole lot of that has very little to do with what we would routinely put on the air ten, fifteen years ago." But getting stories on saving the marriage, pop culture, health tips, and the like is not why the network news broadcasts have been given a special place in public affairs and the democratic process. Such fluff stuff masquerading as material for a major national news institution does not distinguish the network newscast from the dozens of other shows, magazines, and supermarket tabloids that give that kind of "you news" and features. Further, especially with the severely limited time—twenty-two minutes of actual news time, minus ads—this direction seems likely to encourage the softening and muddling of the serious news pieces that newscasts still cover. Such an approach does not seem likely, in the long run, to maintain a loyal following, since people can get the same stuff elsewhere, presented less pretentiously. As *Nightline*'s Ted Koppel pointed out, in a speech away from the ABC newsrooms: "Our managers. . . don't seem to realize that their network will only flourish by being visibly stronger, deeper, and of better quality."[11]

Some systematic measures of network news material demonstrate the pattern of news content in the era of conglomerate control. Robert Lichter's Center for Media and Public Affairs does a continuing content analysis of the network news shows. The center found that crime was by far the leading story throughout the first six years of the 1990s; no fewer than 9,391 stories on crime were carried on the network news shows during that time, nearly 50 percent more than on the economy and business. In past decades, crime was primarily a local news story, but not in the megamedia era, when attracting ratings with splashy stories is the norm. Even more telling, there was a sharp increase in those crime stories in 1993 and thereafter, but during that same time, the actual crime rate was going down, according to FBI statistics. Not incidentally, the center found a major decline in foreign news coverage, with NBC's News Lite having by far the thinnest foreign news total (15.6 percent of stories compared with over 20 percent for ABC and CBS). This failure of foreign coverage comes at a time when international relations, international economics, and events in foreign nations affecting trade, jobs, and the like are far more abundant and critical than ever.

Beyond the regular news shows, these trends are evident in the increased use of "TV newsmagazines" on the networks. The major hour-long documentary in which the networks did much of their most distinguished work in the 1960s and early 1970s has almost totally disappeared. On the surface, it looks like ABC, CBS, and NBC have attempted to make up for that loss by airing a substantial number of newsmagazines; no fewer than ten aired each week, as of fall 1997. But most of the material shown on those newsmagazines falls far short of consistent, meaningful journalism, to put it mildly.

John Dancy, a principal correspondent for NBC News from 1965 into 1996, recently assessed those developments and concluded: "America's over-the-air television networks . . . have abandoned any serious attempt to deal with major issues facing the country in a search for audience, ratings, and profits." He noted that these newsmagazines are about half as expensive to produce as a regular entertainment show, and that is the principal reason we are seeing more of them. *Dateline NBC*, for example, made a $50 million profit for NBC and General Electric in 1995; considering costs, that amounted to a stunning profit margin of 66 percent. Dancy monitored *Dateline NBC* for three months in late 1996 to find out what subjects the show was covering. He found that it aired a total of 109 stories during that time. The show had three staples: crime (14 stories), celebrity and celebrity trials (27 stories), and medical stories (13 stories); there were also 8 pieces he aptly called "gee-whiz" stories. There were 10 stories categorized as "consumer" pieces, although there was no information on their quality. *Dateline* is clearly not a substitute for the traditional documentaries; it is tabloid TV masquerading as a newsmagazine. Another analyst who regularly tracks the newsmagazine shows (not just *Dateline*) offered this assessment: "The trend in network newsmagazines is toward more tabloid-style stories and fewer big picture pieces. . . . It's getting harder to tell the difference between 'Inside Edition' and the network newsmagazines." Former NBC News president Reuven Frank said of *Dateline NBC:* "I can't watch it. I just plain can't . . . because it's thin, because it's cheap. . . . Cheap in attitude."

The current president of NBC News, Andrew Lack, in a 1995 speech to the Radio and Television News Directors Association, made something of a confession of guilt regarding these patterns and practices. He noted that, in theory, "fiery pictures and prurient stories" were needed as a "hook" to get people into the news or newsmagazine programs; then they could follow with the serious stuff. But, he said:

Unfortunately, it seems to me, we got too good at producing hooks. More and more of the audience has taken the bait and television news seems to have convinced itself that that's what it does best—tap emotions. Someone else can tap their brains. And as a result, much of our news was never more shallow. . . . I think television news, wittingly or unwittingly, is contributing to the dumbing down of America.

These processes at the networks have been well described by Bill Moyers:

> Instead of the role of gathering, weighing, sorting and explaining the flux of events and issues, we began to be influenced by the desire first to please the audience. . . .
>
> Pretty soon, tax policy had to compete with stories about three-legged sheep, and the three-legged sheep won. . . . And now we're trapped. Once you decide to titillate instead of illuminate, you're on a slippery slope, you create a climate of expectation that requires a higher and higher level of intensity all the time until you become a video version of the drug culture and your viewers become junkies.

And then there is local TV news. The *Washington Post*'s media watcher, Howard Kurtz, reviewed five big-city newscasts, all of them megamedia-owned. To assess the degeneration of local TV news, he evaluated them for tabloid stories, which he defined as those involving crime, sex, disasters, or public fears. He found that "On the late-night newscasts, the proportion of tabloid stories ranged from 74% in Miami to 46% in Washington, excluding sports and weather." "Voyeur Murder," "Tollway Murder," and "Serial Rapist" were typical fare for lead stories. A *New York Times* review of six New York City news shows found similar results. A study from the Rocky Mountain Media Watch group analyzed one hundred local TV stations from around America on the same evening in September 1995 (for comparability) and discovered the same pattern. They found an average story length of only forty-seven seconds; and on fifteen of those stations they found more airtime is actually given to commercials than the news segments (not counting weather and sports). Combining crime, disasters, and like stories into an appropriately titled "mayhem index," they found that for thirty-three of the stations, news shows were over half mayhem, and the average for medium- and large-city TV news shows was 46 percent. They called this, along with the additional fluff stuff that adds to the total, "a constellation of excess" and "tabloid fever" news. In summary, as the saying now goes, "if it bleeds, it leads"; or, as I say, "what we mostly get these days is flash, trash, and crash news."

A *New York Times Magazine* article from early 1998 on trends in TV news provided a revealing comparison over time. Writer Michael Winerip went to the Museum of Television and Radio in New York City and reviewed local TV news from twenty years ago, before megamedia control. He "was shocked [at] how much things had changed." He found that "In that era, there were fewer pieces and they were much longer; there was far less crime news and local news was local," and there were more and bolder watchdog pieces for consumers about businesses, including a substantial piece on one station about misleading commercials.[12]

Further (as I have discussed elsewhere, as well), the megamedia mentality and the tabloid tumult on TV have resulted in a drastic failure of reporting on governmental and political matters, especially on the state level. Thus, for prime example, by the end of the 1980s, all out-of-town news stations in California, even the big network-owned ones, had abandoned their long-standing news bureaus in the state capital. Far less coverage of state government was the consequence. Further, there was minimal coverage of the 1994 U.S. Senate race in California in which one candidate spent $28 million, mostly on ads; the public was inundated with campaign ad propaganda but heard little election news from the TV stations because they were so busy chasing O. J. Simpson stories.

Most unfortunately, the failure of local TV news to cover state government and politics comes at precisely the period when America has been more and more engaged in "devolution," that is, passing responsibility for policy programs and social problems from the national government down to the state and local governments. At a time when good coverage of state and local government has become more important than ever, megamedia-controlled local TV news has drastically reduced such coverage; these stations have abdicated their responsibility for informing the public on these matters.

Doug Underwood, who has experience in both journalism and the academic world, has documented similar patterns of news material in the newspaper realm, as have other analysts. There is reason to believe those patterns are not confined to American newspapers. The poster boy for mayhem and sleaze in newspapers is, of course, Rupert Murdoch. But, in addition to tabloids, Murdoch owns the *Times* of London, a genuine institution of democracy in Britain. After a visit to Great Britain, Anthony Lewis of the *New York Times* concluded that the *Times* "has degenerated under Murdoch's ownership from one of the world's great newspapers into a shrill, hatchet-wielding scandal sheet." Other observers suggest other newspapers in the "quality press" in Britain have also degenerated in quality of coverage and focus on scandal, crime, and fluff. There is some debate over how substantial this trend is, but the basic direction seems clear. Extreme commercialization and its consequences also seem to be spreading around the world, as Herman and McChesney, among others, report.

Washington Post Watergate reporter Carl Bernstein summed up these basic news patterns in an article in a public affairs magazine:

> We have been moving away from real journalism toward the creation of a sleazoid info-tainment culture in which the lines between Oprah Winfrey and Phil Donohue and Geraldo Rivera and Diane Sawyer and Ted Koppel . . . are too often indistinguishable. In this new culture of journalistic titillation, we teach our readers and our viewers that the trivial is significant and that the lurid and loopy are more important than real news.[13]

The Corporate Connection and Impacts on the News: What the Formal Studies Say

Some university scholars, especially those in journalism and mass communications, have recognized the significance of the issues raised here. A number of their studies have sought to apply more systematic social science methods to investigating these issues. There have been two principal difficulties with these research efforts, however: (1) They have fairly often had a difficult time conceptualizing, defining, and operationally specifying key elements of journalistic process and content so that the study captures adequately what is expected of a quality news production; and (2) it is difficult to obtain enough research funding to cover the subject well—retrieving and content analyzing a large and representative sample of newspapers, newsmagazines, and/or TV news shows, along with other research requirements, is very expensive. Additionally, the great majority of the research has focused on newspapers. TV and the rest of the media have received relatively little attention, and full implications of conglomerate ownership have received minuscule academic research efforts. This is partly because academics tend to focus narrowly on a subject for which data are more available and on which the issues are more manageable.

John McManus's book *Market-Driven Journalism* provides some of the most compelling evidence and has a rare focus on television news. The study did not specifically look at the influence of megamedia on news operations but examined the general question of whether American news media, especially local TV news shows, are chiefly focused on ratings and commercial considerations while serious, substantive journalism is given low priority. McManus intensively researched four TV stations in very large to medium-sized media markets. For a full month he closely observed the stations' operations and reporters' efforts in the field. He also conducted surveys of key participants at the stations and content analyses of the news shows produced.

McManus noted that a significant part of serious journalism in covering the local territory is an active "discovery function" in which reporters and editors actively seek out significant developments in the area. At the station in the medium-sized market, he found the effort level was low with respect to investigating issues of significance, monitoring government agencies, developing important sources, and other hallmarks of serious journalism; 74 percent of the stories aired involved low discovery effort, and only 4 percent involved high discovery effort. Similar patterns were seen in the news operations of the other stations. "Taken as a whole, the case studies describe a minimal commitment to actively examining the doings of local government and business." Despite healthy profits, resources were not being allocated for genuine journalistic digging: "The market model overwhelmed the journalistic model." The station in the largest market did a little better on those measures of journalistic initiative. But when the station's news director was asked about the general consequence or significance of various stories, his reply clearly revealed the dominance of the commercial mentality: "I don't know what consequence means. Take the [Roxanne] Pulitzer trial [a lurid Palm Beach divorce case]. . . . What was the consequence of that? It was the greatest story in the world! I'm not here to improve society. I'm here to tell good stories. It's television. It's pictures. That's the business." McManus also reported that the news directors' descriptions of news production changed radically between his first visit and the final interviews. At the beginning, all but one of the news directors explained their news process in overwhelmingly public service terms. But, "in each of the stations . . . economics steadily replaced journalism over the course of the visit as the primary explanation for news production." And after McManus presented the preliminary results of his research: "'You've got it,' said the news director at the station serving as the pretest for the study. 'The purpose is to make as much money as possible.'" That was a more candid comment than most. The more common reaction to his evidence was, "I know you're right. But I hate to think of myself that way."[14]

As noted, most studies have focused on newspaper chains. While the conclusions of the studies have been somewhat mixed, the weight of the evidence leans decidedly in the direction of suggesting that newspaper ownership by big media chains tends to have deleterious impacts on newspaper quality, diversity, and editorial independence. The validity of that general conclusion was documented in a review of principal studies by Professor C. Edwin Baker, then of the Shorenstein Center at Harvard.

He also showed that, when their data were closely analyzed, even some of the studies that concluded there was no significant chain influence actually provided some evidence of the impact of such chains.

For example, a study of front-page leads and op-ed pages in the Canadian *Windsor Star* before and after it was taken over by the Southam Press chain found a slight increase in material from Canada and in "editorial vigor." But "The single biggest change in source of content in the *Windsor Star*'s front page leads was the increased reliance on Southam News Service." Indeed, the chain's news service moved from the least used to the largest source of front-page leads. This suggests a significant increase in chain influence and uniformity in news in the chain's newspapers.

More generally, Baker found the weight of the evidence was toward significant impact of chain control on homogeneity, profit orientation, and news quality. Regarding homogeneity, Baker summarized: "Of the six main studies reviewed, the three best [in methodology] . . . all provide clear evidence that chain ownership has homogenizing effects," and the other three, on balance, "provide some evidence pointing toward troublesome homogenizing effects of chain ownership." For example, a study by a journalism professor and two doctoral students compared the editorial positions taken on three public issues in 1989 by 56 newspapers in the Gannett chain with a matched set of 155 other newspapers. They found the Gannett papers more likely to take editorial positions and much more homogeneous in the positions taken compared with the nonchain newspapers. This is at odds with the diversity of editorial voices.

Second, on the whole, the studies supported the hypothesis that chain ownership intensifies a paper's profit orientation. "The research does suggest that independents are less likely to sacrifice quality or public trust responsibilities to profit maximization," Baker reported. David Pearce Demers's research found somewhat greater profit orientation, but also, drawing on John Kenneth Galbraith's and Max Weber's theories of big corporate and other organizations, he warns that we should consider the different goals of executives and editors in large organizations and the separation of ownership (usually in the form of stock) from direct managers. He concludes that these organizational factors moderate the pure megamedia impacts on individual news outlets. Still, the bulk of the research points in the direction Baker indicated.

The third issue, the quality of the news produced, is the most difficult on which to devise satisfactory research methods. It is also the case that the results of the studies are a little more mixed. A couple of studies found no significant difference in six specific measures of quality, such as size of newshole, size of editorial page newshole, and even proportion of local news to total news. Another study by three journalism professors that measured "content inputs" like number of full-time news staff, library staff, subscriptions to wire services, and access to data bases found a small correlation with chains minimizing investment in news gathering, but they decided the differences were too small to justify a clear conclusion of negative chain impact. That is interesting, because some have suggested that a benefit of big chain control is access to superior resources, but at best the evidence is very mixed on whether that provides any real benefits, especially benefits that outweigh what strongly appears to be a greater bottom-line obsession.

In fact, other studies have found significant such impacts. For example, one substantial study of 101 mostly large metropolitan newspapers "found that chain size had a statistically significant negative impact on the total size of newshole . . . and on staff size," showing reduced investment in news gathering under chain ownership. Another study looked at Great Britain's London-based "quality" newspapers. It yielded telling results: "Examination of front-page articles from composite weeks in [1987, 1989, and 1991] showed that independently owned dailies covered stories that required more reportorial effort than did dailies owned by conglomerates." The independent papers also had more articles by their own staff, rather than relatively generic news-service stories, and they used more enterprise news sources, doing more journalistic digging rather than just relying on standard, especially official, news releases.[15]

In the effort to discern megamedia impact it is also important to consider what subjects, issues, and developments were *not* covered. This is, of course, a difficult enterprise, and it sometimes involves judgment calls. Project Censored: The News That Didn't Make the News—whose founder, Carl Jenson, coined the term "junk-food news"—monitors the issues and developments that should have received prominent news treatment but that were largely ignored by the main media. It has been conducted for years out of California's Sonoma State University, and it employs a panel of notable and expert national judges to determine the top twenty-five stories that did not receive the attention they deserved. Each year the project produces the *Project Censored Yearbook*, which discusses those issues and related matters, giving us a fine sourcebook.[16]

Megamedia and Impacts on Books and Other Creative Production

Publishing houses, including some old and distinguished ones, have also been very much subjected to the relentless, big-corporation bottom-line approach. The most eloquent testimony on that pattern comes from Andre Schiffrin, who was for years managing director of Pantheon Books, a division of Random House, which was acquired by the Newhouse empire in the 1980s. It was during the 1980s and on into the 1990s that U.S. publishing companies, under new megamedia ownership, "came to resemble the mass media." Reflecting on general developments, Schiffrin concluded: "The changes that have taken place in our media culture during my professional lifetime are so vast that it is hard to comprehend fully how extensive they have been." He said:

> The editorial process has been skewed by the fact that at large companies, decisions about what to publish are made not by editors but by so-called publishing committees, in which the financial and marketing people play a pivotal role. If a book does not look as if it will sell a certain number—and that increases every year—these people argue that the company cannot "afford" to take it on, especially when it is a new novel or work of serious nonfiction. What the Spanish newspaper *El Pais* perceptively called "market censorship" is increasingly in force. . . . The obvious success and the well-known author are the books now sought; new authors and new, critical viewpoints are increasingly finding it difficult to be published in the major houses.

And, for specific example from Schiffrin's direct experience, he observed:

> Newhouse bought the Random House [publishing group] for some $60 million. Ten years later, his holdings had increased in value to over $1 billion. But this did not suffice. Greater annual profits were expected of each of the publishing units, so each of the houses changed its [book] list accordingly, until the group as a whole had altered its character completely.

Two other examples come courtesy of Murdoch's HarperCollins publishing corporation. In summer 1997, HarperCollins canceled more than one hundred book contracts to make a better profit picture for the company (and to recoup some oversized advances to well-known authors). The second is a more ominous example of the overall corporate interest compromising editorial integrity. In March 1998, HarperCollins dumped a book by the last English governor of Hong Kong, Chris Patton, which was scheduled for publication. Patton's memoir was assessed by HarperCollins's top editor, Stuart Profitt, as "the most lucid and intelligent" he had ever read by a politician and a sure best-seller. But the book criticized the Chinese government, which Murdoch had been cultivating so that his spreading satellite TV empire could gain a foothold in

China. When Murdoch ordered editor Profitt to tell Patton his book was not acceptable, Profitt refused; he was then suspended from his job. The book was pushed out of HarperCollins publication and was subsequently picked up by another publishing company. Novelist Doris Lessing, whose work had been published by HarperCollins, said the Murdoch corporate intervention was "so shocking I can't find words for it." A noted British historian called for authors to avoid the publishing house and said: "HarperCollins has quite simply ceased to be a member of our open society."

Ben Bagdikian reports the other general theme song of megamedia-owned book publishers as we end the twentieth century:

> When Viacom bought Simon & Schuster [as part of the Paramount deal], its new president, Jonathan Newcomb, announced the new philosophy: "The lines between people who are in publishing and those who are in entertainment companies are beginning to blur. . . . That's how we are positioning ourselves."

The corporate book publisher is being matched by the giant bookstore chain. These huge, nationwide chains are having an impact on what books are published, and the interaction between megamedia-owned publishers and big chain bookstores is increasingly reinforcing patterns of superficiality in the production and presentation of books. When the issue was raised for a spring 1997 newspaper article, a Borders Books store manager in Texas pointed the finger at the publishers but also revealed the disturbing pattern at his own Borders stores:

> The way publishers market their books has radically changed. The publishers are backing fewer and fewer books with more and more money, and those are the so-called star authors. The more literary writers who are published get left by the promotional wayside. When a Grisham or Clancy has a new novel, we get 150 to 300 copies to display in our store. We only get seven to ten copies of books by what we call "midlist," or good but unknown authors. So it's hard for the great unknowns to get noticed because of how much display space the Clancy's take up.

Close observers of the big chain bookstores report that if a new title doesn't sell enough copies within the first three months, the book is written off as a loss or sent back to the publisher for a refund—an action that is especially hard on independent publishing houses. This low level of commitment makes it difficult for not-so-well-known authors, especially of serious nonfiction books, to gain at least modest readership.

The head of Barnes & Noble says that their stores give plenty of space to minor authors and publishers, "even university presses." But few university press books, even prominent recent releases, are actually on the shelves. Indeed, an October 1997 search for a book as part of the research for this book illustrated that point and the failure of chain bookstores to keep a title on the shelves, regardless of intrinsic merit, if it doesn't sell quite strongly. Borders Books and Barnes & Noble stores in the Twin Cities were called to obtain *Commercial Culture: The Media System and the Public Interest,* by media analyst Leo Bogart, which was published in 1995 by Oxford University Press, the most widely distributed university press. None had it; Barnes & Noble claimed they officially carried it "because it's in the computer," but none of their Twin Cities stores had it in stock. Barnes & Noble has thirty-five central buyers in the New York headquarters who order the books, in numbers they decide, for all Barnes & Noble stores. Local managers have a limited capacity to add books to that central determination, if the books come out of their own budget.

For fair perspective, we should mention that Barnes & Noble, unlike the other chains, has a distinguished history as a large independent bookstore for decades in New York City and as a publisher in its own right. It is clearly in megamedia mode in the 1990s, however. [17]

Magazines, TV, Movies, and Other Cultural and Entertainment Media. The magazine *TV Guide,* which bridges the realms of journalism and entertainment, is the second-largest general circulation periodical in America, reaching over 14 million households. In its 28 December 1996–3 January 1997 issue, *TV Guide* included a ringing editorial endorsement of a proposed age-based program-ratings system for TV shows, characterizing the TV-industry-backed plan as "familiar," "comprehensible," and "useful." The editorial claimed that the plan was "better equipped to gauge the important subtleties of tone and intent." But it ignored the alternative system that was being seriously considered in Congress that would label programs with regard to sexual and violent content. As the *Columbia Journalism Review* noted, the latter ratings system "poses a serious financial threat to a network overloaded with violent and prurient shows—namely, Fox. " Murdoch's News Corp. owned *TV Guide,* as well as the salacious Fox TV network. This was clearly a conflict of interest, and the self-serving perspective was carried in the biggest single source of information for the general public on TV. Megamedia had struck again.

The best evidence of the impact of megamedia on regular television programs is in your living room: the weekly TV listings in your local newspaper or in *TV Guide.* Just run down the descriptions of the broadcast and cable TV shows and ask yourself what is the usual subject matter and patterns of behavior seen in these shows. Indeed, in 1996, a rigorous, comprehensive study of violence on television found that "'psychologically

harmful' violence is pervasive on broadcast and cable TV programs."
Another study in the 1990s found that "the average child will witness 8,000
made-for-TV murders before finishing elementary school." This pattern
from the megamedia corporations is why Congress insisted on the V-chip
provision in the Telecommunications Act so parents would be able to have
a mechanism to protect children from the worst of the video assault. Studies by communications scholar George Gerbner and colleagues have
shown a very distorted world on American network TV shows, with crime
"at least ten times as rampant as in the real world," highly distorted por-
trayals of various demographic groups, and so on; studies by Lichter and
colleagues have also shown such patterns. More ominously, from surveys
of citizens, Gerbner and colleagues found that heavy TV viewers from all
types of neighborhoods overestimate the general levels of crime and the
likelihood of being victims of crime. In fact, startlingly, another study
found little difference between the level of fear of crime among heavy TV
viewers among the elderly in St. Cloud, Minnesota, and in Miami.

Pulitzer Prize–winning television critic for the *Washington Post* Tom
Shales observed:

> I guess in any given year you say, "This is the worst it's ever been," and
> then the next year you say, "No, this is the worst it's ever been!" It
> seems like multiplying the number of channels has simply thinned out
> the available talent. It seems to have shrunk TV more toward the mid-
> dle line. Let's say the middle line on the oscilloscope is mediocrity;
> everything seems to be gravitating toward that line. . . .
>   The so-called narrowcasting [of cable and satellite TV] is really
> sort of camouflage for marketing. Even MTV will suddenly stop its pro-
> gramming and do a half an hour of selling Beavis and Butthead mer-
> chandise over the phone. The multiplicity of choices is turning out to be
> diversity in shopping channels.

Much of Shales's sentiment seems to be shared by the American public. In a fall 1997 national survey, Americans, by a large majority, said they
thought sex and violence on TV were getting worse.

The deleterious effects of megamedia corporate control on the
movies were most strikingly symbolized by the near shutout of the
major, conglomerate-owned movie studios in the 1997 Academy Awards
nominations. As movie and cultural critic David Anson pointed out, the
idea that a single movie could gross $100 million to $200 million or more
and much more in merchandising made the Hollywood studios attractive to the multinational corporations. Corporate giants from Time and
News Corp. to Sony and Seagrams have gobbled up the major film studios in the 1980s and 1990s. "It was the start of terrible times," lamented

Lawrence Kasdan, a leading script writer. "The quality of movies has steadily declined," he concluded. Now it was the marketing departments, not the filmmakers, that dictated the content of movies. Anson went on to point out that even executives in the major studios say the high costs of making movies and the eagerness of many studios to make "franchise films" to generate merchandise to sell at retail stores or exploit in theme parks has contributed to the decline of quality films. But it isn't the studios that are eager to make such franchise films, it is their conglomerate bosses.[18]

In the 1990s, especially after passage of the Cable Reregulation Act, cable TV systems began to drop the two channels of the Cable Satellite Public Affairs Network, better known as C-SPAN 1 and C-SPAN 2. The 1992 Act reestablished some requirements for cable TV in response to a tidal wave of outrage at the way local cable systems were exploiting their area monopolies by drastically raising prices and providing poor and arrogant service. Among those requirements was the "must carry" rule, which said that cable systems must carry local broadcast stations so that those sources of local news would not be lost—and disadvantaged—in the use of cable systems for delivery of television. But the cable system owners used the "must carry" rule as an excuse to eliminate C-SPAN. It had either been cut or eliminated entirely in some 9 million homes over three years in the early to mid-1990s, because, as a reporter in this subject area commented: "Cable operators will throw off C-SPAN if they can sell the same precious slot on the dial to a higher bidder." America's largest and most arrogant cable systems owner, TCI, was the biggest offender in these acts of irresponsibility. C-SPAN's respected chief, Brian Lamb, along with a good number of citizens in Citizens for C-SPAN, began a crusade over these C-SPAN ejections. Although Lamb misguidedly tried to assign a large part of the blame for these actions to the 1992 Act, most observers saw cable corporation greed and irresponsibility as the principal factor, given that there are forty or more channels on which to place C-SPAN. Eventually, after much negative publicity, a new president of TCI relented and pledged to return C-SPAN to the cable systems over the following three years. But, once again, eternal vigilance is necessary.

It is true, however, that in the cultural and entertainment realms, as opposed to news and public affairs, the technological expansion of channels on cable TV has given people some significant additional program options. To take my favorite example, there is a dramatic addition to the availability of music with MTV, VH-1, some of Bravo programming, and some material on other channels.

Two other developments illustrate the dangers of the spread of megamedia to alternative media outlets, however. In the Twin Cities, by September 1997, Chancellor/Capstar Broadcasting owned seven radio stations with about 30 percent of total listenership (37 percent of 18-to-34-year-old listeners), and Disney-ABC controlled five stations. This resulted in a station format shuffle over much of 1997. One noteworthy result was the loss of Rev 105, a progressive rock station. About the same time, the second alternative weekly newspaper in the metro area, the *Twin Cities Reader,* was lost through a buyout in the alternative weekly media market. (Things are consolidating even in that market.) As a Twin Cities music critic wrote, the result is that two of the area's "loudest voices outside the mainstream had been stilled."[19]

Public Broadcasting and a Question of Priorities. One final development must be discussed: the sad tale of the declining situation of public television systems in America. (The case of public radio is similar. The partly woeful, partly encouraging tale of public broadcasting in Europe is told in chapter 7.) The United States has never fully funded public television or radio, but the situation has gotten much worse in the 1980s and 1990s. As of 1981, funds from the federal government accounted for just under 30 percent of the public TV budget. However, owing to major cuts during the Reagan administration, federal support declined to about 16 percent of public TV funding by 1990. State governments added various additional amounts, in general providing about 30 percent of funding by the early 1990s. The reduction in government funding left public TV (and radio) constantly scrambling for funds and much more vulnerable to the influence of any entity that could offer lots of money. Regular citizens significantly stepped up their support for public TV over the years, but it was not enough. Especially after PBS, in its straitened condition, loosened restrictions on quasi advertisements, corporate America saw good opportunities for getting the word out further about their companies and enhancing their image. Corporations were increasingly relied on for public TV funding. The proportion of total public television income from business sources rose from 4 percent in 1973 to nearly 17 percent in 1990, and corporations provided 30 percent of all funding for national programming; and the proportion kept rising through the 1990s. This raises the specter of corporate influence on programming in what should be the last bastion of information and expression that is fundamentally independent of corporate special interests and the commercial calculus. The danger of such influence is highlighted by the fact that PBS began previewing its prime-time program schedule for the big New York ad agencies in the mid-1990s, rather like ABC, CBS, and NBC.[20]

Perspective, Priorities, and Democratic Responsibilities

Public Opinion on the News Media in the Megamedia Era

What is the public's conception of the primary purpose and responsibilities of the news media? A fall 1993 poll of the American public conducted for a study by the Freedom Forum First Amendment Center at Vanderbilt University found: "By an overwhelming majority, the public believes the first priority of the press is to find and publish important information on public issues (76%), over making a profit (6%) and giving readers and viewers what they ask for (18%)."

The Pew Research Center for the People and the Press has done extensive and astute public opinion polling on attitudes toward the media. Comparing results from polling in early 1997 and 1985, they reported: "The public's assessment of press performance has grown increasingly negative in recent years. A majority (56%) now say news stories . . . are often inaccurate, up more than 20 percentage points since 1985," which is roughly the beginning of the megamedia era. Several polls, as well as studies using focus groups and in-depth interviews, from 1992 through 1996 found that a large majority of Americans think the news media are much too fixated on sensationalism and less and less concerned with giving them the meaningful news they need. Indeed, several surveys have demonstrated that at the top of the public's criticisms of the news media is that, in pursuit of that sensationalism, news operations ignore and wantonly invade people's privacy; a major poll in 1997 for the Center for Media and Public Affairs showed this particularly well. Those trends were related to the increasing corporatization and money obsession of the big media organizations. One major study conducted during the 1992 presidential election found: "This theme, that the news media pander to the audience, recurred in in-depth interviews and focus groups throughout the campaign. People linked the media's taste for scandal and sensationalism to commercial motives that got in the way of useful information."

There was abundant sensationalism in newspapers in the "yellow journalism" era early in the century. But with higher levels of schooling and much public discussion of the role of the media in recent years, compared with the earlier era, the public today surely has decidedly higher expectations of the role the news media ought to play in a democratic society. The public certainly should have higher expectations, since we should expect progress in the operations of democracy. But clearly, the public does not think the news media are living up to these higher standards, andcorporate profit priorities, arrogance, and power are seen as a significant, if not central, part of the problem. Indeed, a July 1998 opinion poll for *Newsweek* found that 76 percent of the American public thought the media corporations, in "the competition for ratings and profits," had "gone too far in the direction of entertainment and away from traditional reporting" in their news operations; and the same percentage specifically cited pressure from "media owners and news executives" as being worse than in earlier years.

It is also vital to recognize the public's feelings about the concentration of business ownership in general and their corresponding power. A major poll repeatedly found in the late 1980s through the mid-1990s that over three-quarters of the American public agreed with the proposition that "there is too much power concentrated in the hands of a few big companies." And, while confidence in government in America has dropped drastically since the mid-1960s, confidence in major companies has also dropped sharply—from 55 percent in 1964 down to 21 percent by the 1990s.[21]

Perspective

The Canadians have wrestled thoughtfully with the role the broadcast media should play in society:

> Canada's policymakers have long subscribed to the view that broadcasting is more than just a business, that it had the potential to nurture and nourish national unity and Canadian culture. "Its potentialities are too great, its influence and significance too vast, to be left to the petty purposes of selling cakes of soap."

The code of ethics of the Society of Professional Journalists says: "The primary purpose of gathering and distributing news and opinion is to serve the general welfare by informing the people and enabling them to make judgments on the issues of the time," a responsibility the code calls "a public trust." The record under megamedia control indicates an increasing failure to fulfill those profound responsibilities. Although many journalists have their flaws, the primary fault here is not with the journalists themselves, as a rule. In fact, journalists are the first victims of the failure of big chains and megamedia conglomerates to invest fully in and generally support a vigorous, independent news process. Drawing on Gresham's famous "law" that "bad money drives out good money," political journalist R. W. "Johnny" Apple of the *New York Times* has commented: "I want to suggest Gresham's *second* law: 'Bad journalism drives out good journalism.' What we're seeing today is a tendency for the cheapest, most meretricious forms of journalism to eat the resources serious journalists need to do our jobs right."

There are, however, some admirable perspectives and practices from some media owners that can show the way. One such owner is C. K. McClatchy, head of the California-based newspaper chain of that name, whose major newspapers are generally praised for the quality of their journalism. As James Squires relates:

> C. K. McClatchy, a good businessman but an even better journalist-proprietor, once looked at his business manager . . . and said, "Do we really need to make this much?" McClatchy was a firm believer in the old hierarchy of priorities: the readers first, employees second and employers third. It was what kept both communities and employees convinced that the press was a special business.

McClatchy also said in the late 1980s: "There are many chains . . . that face great pressure to bolster the bottom line [and that face substantial debt]. These pressures fight against quality."

The high quality maintained by major family-owned newspapers with a strong tradition of stewardship, like the Ochs-Sultzbergers' *New York Times*, the Grahams' *Washington Post*, the Binghams' *Louisville Courier-Journal*, and others is testimony to what community-based owner-proprietors with a strong sense of public responsibility can mean to journalism.

But even relatively large multimedia corporations, if the commitment is institutionalized, can maintain some decent quality journalism. Journalist and journalistic reformer Tom Rosenstiel noted the case of A. H. Belo Corp., which owns the major Dallas newspaper, six other dailies, eight nondaily newspapers, and seventeen TV stations:

> Newspapers today also suggest quality and independence are good business. The A. H. Belo Corp., owner of the *Dallas Morning News*, has been carefully structured around certain values that are not strictly economic, including investing more in news and editorial independence than many regional newspaper companies.
>
> In the first six months of [1997], it has enjoyed a pretax operating profit margin of 25.1 percent, nearly five points higher than the industry average.

The quality question in news is increasingly critical, as suggested by public opinion data. If the megamedia-dominated news operations continue to lose the public's trust, at some point it gets very dangerous for democracy—and dicey for the news operations themselves. A member of a panel of citizens on a *PBS NewsHour* show in April 1997 expressed appreciation for the news media when they brought out significant issues people were not aware of. But "It has degenerated to the point where, when the media does that kind of a job, it's almost by accident—because they're so wrapped up in the . . . strategies and the one-upsmanship that they forget what people are really looking for in terms of news." A Louis Harris poll of American citizens from late 1996 conducted for the Center for Media and Public Affairs found that "Widespread support exists for drastic measures intended to improve the quality of reporting." Fully 85 percent "would like to see national and local news councils investigate complaints" about news coverage; 84 percent "support a government 'fairness doctrine' that would require equal coverage of all sides of a controversy"; 70 percent would "allow courts to impose fines for 'inaccurate or biased reporting'"; 53 percent would even require journalists "to obtain a license to practice their profession." Finally, half the public favored changing the libel laws "to make it easier for people to sue the news media."

Remember the observations of several notables, including people with press experience, regarding how the media are increasingly considered by the public compared with nonmedia businesses. As Richard Clurman from *Time*'s earlier era said, for the public "it was becoming harder and harder to think of the news media as different from any other business in free enterprise America"; and "the editors of daily newspapers have begun to behave more and more like the managers of any other corporate entity," Doug Underwood found.

If the perception that news media organizations operate no differently than any other money-maximizing business becomes truly generalized and ingrained, then the press's role in the democratic process is greatly endangered. Most critically, will the support be there for the special privileges the press requires to ferret out developments in government and other realms of society and report them so we can hold officials, corporations, and others accountable? The dean of the Columbia University School of Law has pointed out that the First Amendment protections for free press and speech are not automatically operative. Rather, they "depend on the spirit of tolerance in our society and the extent to which society as a whole understands the role of the press. Most important is the current social and political climate which is unfriendly to the press, viewing it as an uncaring, unresponsive big business." But in light of what we have discussed in these two chapters, perhaps (a) the public has good reason to view the media that way, and (b) perhaps it is really the megamedia executives who need a better understanding of the role of the press. Thus, former newspaper editor James Squires appears to have it right:

> Corporate America has been in the driver's seat as the press enters the new world of information. And it is this "corporate takeover" of journalism . . . that has weakened the press as an institution of democracy and destroyed its brand-name credibility.

New York Times editor Gene Roberts put it this way:

> It is time, high time, that newspaper corporations become subjects of debate and be held accountable for covering the communities they serve. Meanwhile, many are managing their newspapers like chain shoe stores, with no sense of being important community institutions with highly important responsibilities to the public.

The same goes for the broadcast news media.[22]

7

Megamedia and the World

···

This chapter examines the concentration of media control around the world at the end of the twentieth century. The cases of Japan and the societies in transition in Russia and Eastern Europe manifest three principal trends: in Japan, cross-media ownership; in Russia, the industrial-media conglomerate phenomenon; and in Eastern Europe, the struggle to develop media systems that genuinely serve their societies in the transition from state-socialist systems to more open, democratic economic and political systems. The situation in Great Britain, Germany, and France is also examined briefly. A truly comprehensive review of the structure of media ownership throughout the world is beyond the scope of this book, but some notes on some other significant areas provides a better sense of the widespread nature of the megamedia pattern at the end of the twentieth century.

Japanese Megamedia: A Cross-Media Ownership System

Geographically concentrated and densely populated Japan is also highly concentrated in ownership and control of the mass media. This concentration takes place within a general socioeconomic system that is very homogeneous and that has long embraced considerable central coordination and industrial collaboration (even while embracing competition). Japan is probably the most highly literate nation in the world and has the highest rate of newspaper circulation in the world.

A "big five" set of nationally distributed daily newspapers dominates newspaper publishing in Japan. As of 1995, the *Yomiuri Shimbun* had a circulation of over 14.5 million and the *Asahi Shimbun* had 12.7 million in circulation; the two are by far the largest-circulation newspapers in the world. The other three: the *Mainichi Shimbun* had a circulation of 6 million, the *Nihon Keizai Shimbun* had over 4.5 million, and the *Sankei Shimbun* had nearly 3 million in circulation. There are also many local newspapers.

On the television side of the media, the Japanese have the world's largest public broadcasting system, NHK. It broadcasts two channels (one for general programming, one for educational programming) and obtains its operating revenue from fees collected from television viewers throughout the nation. As of the early 1990s, the Japanese spent $18 per person on their public broadcasting system; the United States spent barely over $1 per person on public broadcasting.

There are four major commercial TV networks in Japan, all based in Tokyo and supported by advertising: NTV, Nippon Television, with twenty-seven local stations; FNN, Fuji Telecasting, with twenty-seven local stations; TBS (or JNN), Tokyo Broadcasting System, with twenty-five local stations; and ABC or ANN, Asahi National Broadcasting, with twenty local stations in its network. There is also a smaller TV network, Television Tokyo, with only four local stations in the network, all in large cities.

Each of the major national newspapers has both a financial investment in, and an organizational connection with, those TV networks. Thus, the Yomiuri organization has a major cross-media relationship with Nippon Television; the Asahi organization is connected with its namesake, Asahi National Broadcasting; the Mainichi organization is connected with Tokyo Broadcasting System; the Sankei organization is involved with Fuji Telecasting ("Fujisankei group"); and the Nihon Keizai organization has such a relationship with Television Tokyo. These connections exist despite the fact that Japanese regulations officially do not allow newspapers to control commercial television broadcasting. The connections are managed through "sister companies" and other means; and in reality, "the same person often simultaneously holds the chairmanship of the key broadcast station and the presidency of the newspaper enterprise."

These big media and connected operations are also involved in other major economic activities, giving them very sizable and wide-ranging "empires," as they are known in Japan. Those other areas include book and magazine publishing, real estate, music recording, travel, department stores, and even professional baseball teams and amusement parks (like a couple of American-based megamedia corporations). For example, there is the Yomiuri Giants pro baseball team, long the most dominant team in the Japanese league, and there is Yomiuriland amusement park. These organizations also have TV and radio production companies. The Fujisankei group controls about one hundred companies, including Nippon Broadcasting System, the leading radio network; the largest of the Japanese media conglomerates, it brought in $2.69 billion in revenue in 1996.[1]

These powerful media groups are also extensively interlocked with prime nonmedia big business through "extensive investments made by big business in the broadcasting industry." Thus, as a media scholar summarized in the early 1990s:

> Japan's five media conglomerates are, in effect, joint ventures between big business and the mass media industry. The financial interlocking between the two power groups, furthermore, has increased substantially since the advent of new media technologies as Japanese big business has joined the media conglomerates in dominating ownership patterns in such new media as . . . cable television and direct broadcast satellites.

In 1997 the ubiquitous Rupert Murdoch and News Corp. started a satellite TV operation over Japan, JSkyB. The operation fits the pattern just noted, as it is being done with partners Sony and big Japanese software company Softbank. Murdoch has worked on other investments in Japanese media as well.[2]

In summary, Japan has a strikingly concentrated pattern of megamedia conglomerates, with relatively few corporate chiefs in control of most of the main sources of information for the Japanese people. Japan's large, prominent, well-funded, and reasonably independent public broadcasting system (with an established source of funding not dependent on routine political appropriation) presumably helps break through such a media-conglomerate oligopoly to some extent. But the basic megamedia pattern is still the central reality in the Japanese world. That structure of control raises major questions about the democratic principles of diverse and alternative information and opinion sources for the Japanese general public. Indeed, a few years ago a mass communications scholar, after fourteen months of fieldwork in Japan, concluded that "the highly concentrated nature of the mass media in Japan is one of the major characteristics contributing to the media's collective power [among] the other traditionally recognized elite power groups" and has given them considerable power in affecting public policy on media.[3]

Russian Media and the Shadow of Industry and Politics

Historic Change and Transitions

The 1990s brought historic change to Russia, with the end of the Soviet-Communist regime. Thereafter, a new era of developing capitalism and struggle for democracy began. The transition has been a difficult and unsettled one not only in the political and economic realms but also for mass media, which are engaged in the struggle to establish and sustain free and independent journalism. In opening up the economy, the new era also opened up the media—and the effort to build democracy—to dangerous developments.

The dramatic changes in economic activity and their control that have rapidly developed in Russia should be noted. *Newsweek* captured the essence of these developments:

> In a so-called loans-for-shares swap, Menatep, a bank controlled by Mikhail Khodorkovsky, gave Boris Yeltsin's government $168 million to help plug its enormous budget deficit. In return, Menatep completed a deal giving it an 80 percent stake in a formerly state-owned oil company called Yukos. Under the arrangement, Yukos—a company that some analysts say could be worth $10 billion in five years—is supposed to give back to the state a percentage of any shares it resells at a profit.
>
> Khodorkovsky is part of a small group of capitalists who have, over the past two years, gained control over huge swaths of the post-Soviet economy. Rarely in history has so much wealth—both real and potential—fallen into so few hands so quickly. This elite crew of bankers and businessmen, the new owners of Russia's energy, mineral and media companies, inevitably have come to be known as the oligarchs.[4]

In an interview conducted for this book, noted veteran Russian journalist and author Melor Sturua said that "the 1992 Press Law for Russia completely guarantees press independence and free speech in Russia," although it, unlike the First Amendment in the United States, is so detailed it leaves open the possibility of nefarious government interpretations. In the Soviet era, TV, newspapers, and other major media were subsidized by the state, so they did not have to worry about how to sustain themselves financially, even if they had to worry about official censorship. But:

> After the disappearance of the Soviet state, the newspapers [and other media] became free and clear. However, newspapers and TV are very expensive to produce, and especially with newspapers in Russia, advertising does not yet come close to covering the costs, so they are not profitable by themselves. That means they have to be supported by some other source. And who has large amounts of money in Russia today? The huge banks and industrial corporations. They are buying newspapers and other media in a big way.
>
> A main reason is that those banks and industrial corporations need ways and means for [putting out their preferences in the public sphere and for] helping them in the final battles for the inheritance of the Communist Party and Soviet state—that is, the industrial and commercial assets. And they want the media to help them support their own political allies in the government.

In summary, there are several major financial and industrial groups who are buying newspapers [, etc.] and they're using them as their own political tools. This started at the beginning of the post-Soviet era, but it gained momentum during the last presidential election in 1996. [Yeltsin looked like he was in electoral trouble, and the Communist and Nationalist leaders were hostile to capitalism,] so the new capitalists joined forces and began to buy media. They played, I think, the decisive role in Mr. Yeltsin's election. This made them more fully realize how important it was to have media as a tool of their interests.

Ellen Mickiewicz, distinguished American scholar of Russian politics and media, has noted the enthusiasm among journalists for their new-found situation of free investigation during the initial phase after the collapse of the Soviet regime; but then, as she so aptly put it, "the economics of liberation did not, it seemed, match the intellectual euphoria." She has also drawn a parallel with the situation in the West: "The tension between efficiency of ownership strategies and assurance of multiple, especially unpopular, points of view remained for [Russia and the Eastern European] countries, as for media systems in the West, very serious."[5]

Three main groups of large banking and industrial interests have come to own all or significant parts of Russian media. The first is the group headed by Russia's most notable—or notorious—and richest new capitalist, Boris Berezovsky. Berezovsky heads LogoVAZ, a huge auto and computer conglomerate, as well as controlling oil giant Sibneft and having a significant piece of Aeroflot, Russia's principal airline. He and his allies now have a substantial investment in Channel 1 TV network, ORT (which is technically half public/governmental and half private, in terms of control). Further, Berezovsky is a prime backer of TV-6, one of two major ventures in national TV broadcasting beyond the traditional Russian Channels 1 and 2, which were the public/government networks during the Soviet regime. Berezovsky's group also owns *Nezavisimaya Gazeta* (Independent Gazette), which is one of the most influential of Russian print media; it is, roughly speaking, the organ of the highest strata of Russian society and of many intellectuals; and it owns *Ogonyok*, a prominent magazine. According to the estimate of *Forbes* magazine, Berezovsky is Russia's first billionaire, with a net worth of $3 billion.[6]

The second group is led by Vladimir Gusinsky, a former theatrical producer for the Communist Youth League, who heads the MOST banking empire. Gusinsky also owns Media MOST, a relatively new organization that includes the national TV network NTV and some newspapers. NTV is the second and more important of the two major newer ventures in national TV broadcasting. NTV airs much American material in its entertainment programming, and its news broadcasts have adopted more of an American style of news presentation: rather flashy stories, quick changes, and so on. NTV's prime news shows have become quite popular; their credibility was helped by strong and independent coverage of the military battle over separatism in Chechnya in 1994 and 1995. The most important of the newspapers owned by Gusinsky's group is *Segodnya* (Today). The most important related part of this group is Gazprom, the huge gas monopoly led by Rem Vyakhirev; Gazprom has a 30 percent stake in NTV and substantial stakes in twenty-nine regional newspapers, including two of the nation's largest, *Komsomolskaya Pravda* and *Trud*. Substantial resources from such organizations allowed NTV to build a national network, with arrangements with regional TV station affiliates; and it allowed NTV to design "an array of direct-broadcast satellite channels."

The third major banking and industrial group has as its two prime elements Uneximbank, one of the largest banks in Russia, and LUKoil, the country's largest oil company. The most notable of their media investments are: (1) 20 percent of *Komosomolskaya Pravda*, with a circulation of 1.25 million; and (2) in partnership with the paper's management, just over 50 percent of *Izvestia*, the most prominent of Russia's newspapers. LUKoil owns much of the rest of *Izvestia*.[7]

In summary, Sturua said, "almost every newspaper, these days, is controlled by one of those big banking-industrial groups. There are some small newspapers that belong to other groups, but they are relatively insignificant." These groups have substantial investment in TV broadcasting, as well. A couple of larger successful and independent newspapers are surviving on their own, but they are relatively low-grade tabloids.[8]

Concentrated Control and Its Consequences

These financial-industrial groups (called "FIGS" by some) have not been shy about using "their" media, especially their newspapers, as tools in their economic battles for control of business operations and resources, as well as tools in their political battles. Sturua noted that this intertwining of control of media and industry raises major conflict of interest issues. He said:

> This makes things difficult for journalists. . . . They [the financial-industrial groups] interfere, not only in the newspaper's official editorial expressions, but in everything. They send their representatives into the newspaper; they have offices in the newspaper's headquarters. And they, so to speak, "supervise" what's going on in editorial board meetings and anything else they are interested in. This is unacceptable for journalistic integrity.

Remember, during the Soviet era, we had official censors who read and censored what journalists wrote. . . . Now, instead of the government censors, we have representatives of the banks and big industrial corporations who do essentially the same thing. Of course they don't read everything, but still, they overrule the editors and editorial board whenever they feel like it.[9]

One case that raised this interference issue occurred at *Izvestia*, the prominent newspaper controlled by the group led by LUKoil and Uneximbank. There is some disagreement about precisely how strong a case of interference this is and how much some other factors make equivocal the corporate interference; but it certainly illustrates, to some significant degree, the actual and potential dangers involved in media control by big banks and industrial corporations.

Izvestia wanted to upgrade its operations but did not have the ad revenue or other resources to do it, so in late 1996 the newspaper entered an agreement with LUKoil to buy a significant stake in the paper and also commit to a $40 million investment in enhancing *Izvestia*'s capacities. But in April 1997, the foreign editor wrote about the increasing control of the news media by big banks and industries, saying: "In such circumstances, a free and independent press is doomed, but an unfree and dependent press can flourish." Also in April, the paper ran an article from French newspaper *Le Monde* saying that Russian prime minister Chernomyrdin "had amassed a fortune of $5 billion by taking a cut of Russian oil and gas exports." There was some other criticism of the government administration as well. The head of LUKoil was close to the prime minister, and LUKoil made its displeasure known and tried to get majority control of *Izvestia*, apparently with the intention of getting rid of the paper's top editors. *Izvestia*'s management then sought help from Uneximbank in keeping majority control out of LUKoil's hands. But, as a Moscow-based writer recorded it: "Like LUKoil, Uneximbank has a long history of close ties to the Yeltsin government. Within two months of bankrolling *Izvestia*'s defense against LUKoil, Uneximbank teamed up with the oil concern to oust the editor-in-chief, Igor Golembiovsky, and most other top editors, replacing them with lower-ranking *Izvestia* veterans."

One qualifier regarding this case, as a Moscow writer said, is the fact that "even detached observers thought it was irresponsible for *Izvestia* to reprint the *Le Monde* story rather than do its own reporting on such an incendiary issue"; the corporations also claimed the paper was plagued by poor management. But former editor Golembiovsky says they are just trying to remake the newspaper "into a mouthpiece for their interests." Some evidence to that effect was cited in the case of a controversial telecommunications acquisition by Uneximbank that was very belatedly covered in *Izvestia* compared with other media and with a spin favorable to the big bank.

Mickiewicz, however, cautions against too readily reaching conclusions about a high level of financial-industrial interference in media content itself. As a social scientist, she points out that the ideal way to determine definitively the levels of influence wielded by these ultimate owners of Russian news organizations would be to conduct systematic content analyses of actual news output, along with close observation of the news process. Additionally, from her observations and study in Russia, she suggests television does not manifest dramatic evidence of FIGS interference in content, notably in the case of NTV. Mickiewicz at least tentatively concludes that NTV's news operation is "still relatively independent," including the weekly news analysis show on the network. She also says the regional TV stations that have retained a fair amount of independence.

Still, Mickiewicz recognizes the danger inherent in the structure of the ownership situation and worries about the potential consequences for the democratic process in Russia. She also notes such questions have been raised in Russia. For example, regarding MOST's economic control of NTV: "As with many of the huge fortunes of the 'new Russians,' Vladimir Gusinsky's rise to prominence elicited suspicion and a flurry of conspiracy theories. NTV's spin in its news coverage was often ascribed to orders from Gusinsky."

A *Los Angeles Times* article summarized: "Media freedom in Russia, critics contend, has been steadily whittled away since the early 1990s. Now, much of Russia's media is owned by fewer than a dozen people."[10]

Russian journalist Sturua notes another danger of Russia's pattern of concentrated media control:

> It is *very* corruptive. It brings down the quality of the newspapers. Journalists have less opportunity to express the public opinion, and they can't really fight for public concerns. Journalists can't really act as the independent "Fourth Estate."
>
> And at the same time, because these banks and industrial groups are very closely intertwined with the government, through these groups, journalists experience the pressure of the government.
>
> *Question:* For example, Berezovsky?
>
> Yes. Berezovsky has, so to speak, two heads, since he is both head of the banking-industrial group, and he now [August 1997] is serving as Deputy Chief of Yeltsin's National Security Council. [Berezovsky is officially "on leave" from his corporation job.] In fact, almost *every* head of these big corporations has two heads: they are also either a member of Parliament or a member of the government administration or a former member or a member of some principal "advisory" panel.

Berezovsky has not been subtle about pronouncing the value of controlling major media: "By creating a powerful means of influencing society, we are supporting the continuation of economic policy . . . —a union of state and capital." Of course, that is economic policy that has benefited him immensely. And when *Ogonyok,* the respected public affairs magazine that he owns, published an article that embarrassed Prime Minister Chernomyrdin, Berezovsky sent an unmistakable message by simply cutting the journalists' pay.

As American Russian scholar Stephen Cohen summarizes: "Russia's market and its national television are not truly competitive or free but [are] substantially controlled by the same financial oligarchy whose representatives also now sit in the Kremlin as Yeltsin's chieftains." In November 1997, however, Berezovsky was ousted from his Security Council position in a battle with the reformist faction in Yeltsin's circle. First Deputy Prime Ministers Nemtsov and Chubais vowed "they would no longer tolerate the old rules of back-room deals and insider privatization of state companies in which the oligarchs often gained lucrative state-owned businesses at bargain prices." The power struggle rages as this book goes to print.[11]

Media, Megamedia, and Transitions in Eastern Europe

Eastern European nations have also been in a transition from Soviet-style systems to more democratic political processes and market economies. From Poland to Romania these nations have correspondingly been in the throes of profound changes in ownership and control of the mass media and have been struggling to reach collective decisions on acceptable policy regarding their media systems. The patterns of control of the media, especially regarding conglomerate ownership, are, over the whole of Eastern Europe, less extreme and more varied than in Russia. But the same basic forces are at work, and some of the same trends are evident. The situation is much less settled, however, and there are some countervailing forces in some areas.

There was a heady, idealistic, and brief initial postsocialist phase in most of Eastern Europe (as in Russia) that a European scholar calls the "participatory model":

> Proposals were introduced that aimed to block negative developments, such as overcommercialization of the media and concentration of ownership. The individual was seen as the owner of the right to freedom of expression, whom the media, free from governmental and commercial control, should serve. The "right to communicate," as an individual

and collective human right that guarantees access and participation for everybody, should become the backbone of a new democratized media system [many journalists, academics, and reformers in these nations argued].

That phase rather soon ran into the hard reality of three factors: declining or disappearing media subsidies from governmental sources; intense interest in the uses of the media by the new political leaders (more intensely asserted in some nations than in others); and especially the increasing intrusion of private economic organizations and the market economy. Because Eastern European governments in the socialist era had seen TV as a great instrument for propaganda and for maintaining their control, they had invested in basic broadcasting infrastructure and had assured widespread ownership of television sets. Thus, Eastern Europe after the fall of the Soviet-style systems was ready for a stepped-up effort at broadcast enterprise.[12]

Perhaps the most notable private media operator in the region is Central European Media Enterprises (CME). The company was started in 1991 by Americans Ronald Lauder, deep-pocketed son of cosmetics baroness Estée Lauder, and Mark Palmer, a former American ambassador to Hungary who had extensive knowledge of, and contacts around, the region. By 1997, CME, typically in some combination with local partners, controlled the leading national TV station in the Czech Republic, Nova TV, and national TV stations in Romania, Slovenia (the northern section of the former Yugoslavia), and Ukraine. They also operate regional TV stations in Poland and were launching a national station in fall 1997; and they operate regional stations in Germany.

There is an interesting point here about the megamedia giants of the world. As Lauder said regarding the Eastern European nations and their governmental broadcast authorities who were making decisions on licenses to operate broadcast stations: "Every other company came in and talked about how [media in] these countries would become part of a vast worldwide network. That was exactly the wrong story. What [the broadcast authorities] wanted was to be their own country and there [CME was] unique" because of its local partnerships and Palmer's experience in the region.

Much of the print media in the Czech Republic is controlled by German companies; they own the best weekly newsmagazine, have interests in the Prague dailies, and own virtually all the newspapers outside Prague. Those German companies are led by second-tier megamedia corporations like the Kirch Group and Axel Springer Verlag.

In the Czech Republic: "The question of cross ownership in media

. . . is not worked into present law. In the present legal order [as of 1996] there are no special conditions that restrict media conglomerates . . . except one which states that the Czech Council for Radio and Television Broadcasting (which grants broadcast licenses) must try to make sure while granting licenses that no subject [corporation] has received a dominant position."

In some nations, the government has vigorously asserted itself into controlling the media. Edward Baumeister, vice president of the Budapest-based Independent Journalism Foundation, notes that in several nations, "especially Romania, Slovakia, and the Yugoslav successor states, weak countries are run by strong leaders . . . and the model they use for running things is the most recent one they know, the one in place before 1989 [i.e., the Soviet-style approach]." In fact, it is not unusual, as in the state-socialist era, for it to be judged a crime for the media "to make 'insulting' comments about the government," and these governmental authorities have used various means to intimidate news operations. Further, Baumeister says:

> Control over television is easiest to maintain for those governments so inclined because in most countries [various] television organizations . . . remain state owned and their managements state appointed. Although changes in governments in this region are no longer followed by changes in the names of streets, . . . changes in government are likely to be followed by changes in the management of state broadcasting, most notably . . . in Hungary in 1993, but also in Slovakia in 1995.

Hungary, in fact, had what came to be called "the media wars," in which reformist radio and television leaders battled an intrusive government "that succeeded in withdrawing subsidies and substituting its loyalists for the more independently minded reformers." In 1995, the nation passed a general law on media regulation and ownership, but it was minutely detailed and most analysts thought it would be nothing but trouble to administer.

There is internal concentration among print media in Hungary. In the mid-1990s, "the state-controlled PostaBank has . . . put together a small media empire, controlling nine daily and weekly newspapers." On the other hand, there is still quite a bit of independent control of private media in parts of the region, perhaps in part because profitability of much of the commercial media was low or nonexistent through 1997.[13]

The East European nations are likely to increasingly become integrated with the full continent's economy and world economic currents, and the region's market economies and general economic forces are likely to impinge upon Eastern Europe. It is also likely that the megamedia giants will target Eastern European markets. Indeed, the process has already begun. In February 1997, a joint venture of second-tier megamedia corporation Seagrams-Universal and European megamedia company CLT-Ufa, of the Dominant Dozen Bertelsmann operation, established RTL-7 to broadcast programs via satellite and cable TV throughout Poland. Time Warner, through HBO, and France's big Canal Plus also have investments in cable and satellite in Central and Eastern Europe.

The transition from the state socialist system and from the early post-Soviet idealistic stage to predominantly commercial media systems in Eastern Europe and Russia is having an impact on journalism in both of those regions. As scholar Ellen Mickiewicz points out:

> The new competition for readers, viewers, and advertisers put a premium on dramatic revelations and speed of reporting. The whole definition of newsworthiness and standards of reporting had changed with great suddenness. Rumor and gossip were often reported without adequate verification, . . . and a whole new generation [of journalists] was learning on the job, and the job was often about sensationalism and tabloid values.

The Eastern European countries will be very interesting—and probably increasingly troubling—to watch as we move into the new millennium. The transition is still in an early stage and there is still the possibility that the nations can retain genuinely public, national control of their media and guide their uses for national and public purposes (with the probable exception of satellite TV). Then again, the power of the Dominant Dozen media conglomerates and other major media companies in the developed world and elsewhere will be very difficult to resist.[14]

Western Europe and Media Control Patterns

Public Broadcasting, Technology, the March of Commercial Media

Until well into the 1980s, the Western European nations had far more complete, well-funded, and well-respected public broadcasting systems than the United States. TV broadcasting tended to be either the exclusive responsibility of public systems or, as in the case of Great Britain, to have the public system, British Broadcasting Corporation (BBC), as the preeminent and amply funded system, along with the admixture of two carefully constructed and restricted commercial channels. The public networks tended to offer two or three channels with serious news and public affairs shows and significant cultural programs, as well as some standard entertainment shows, most produced within their nation. The broadcasting authority was governed not by the current political administration but by an independent board. The operation was, in most cases, in principle isolated from political meddling, although in some nations that principle was violated a fair amount in practice. The British, when they originally set up their system, felt that "to allow financing from advertisements would inevitably lower standards." There was a strong feeling that these systems genuinely contributed to people's capacity to be effective participants in the democratic process, as well as giving the public good exposure to the best of their cultures and creative achievements. (Newspapers have generally been in private hands, although Sweden, and to some extent Germany and France, have subsidized newspapers to keep them available throughout the nation and especially to retain competition between papers and to try to preserve a diversity of orientations.)

But then the European systems were affected by technological changes, including those like satellite TV that could supersede national boundaries, and they were assaulted by the megamedia, with their growing power. The results have been the privatization of various broadcast channels and the addition of new conventional channels. As of 1980, there were fewer than 50 TV channels in Western Europe; by 1997, there were about 150; by 1989, the private channels outnumbered the public ones for the first time. Cable and satellite modes of delivery created new media presences in these nations to varying degrees. Consequently, "private corporate control, with advertising as the financial base and with increasing competition for audience [ratings], is the new, dominant order of the day." Indeed, as two leading European media analysts have said, "injection of market forces into European television systems virtually ensures that . . . ratings will become an ever more salient currency of evaluation."[15]

Notes on Patterns of Concentration in Media Ownership in Europe

Great Britain. Concentration of media ownership is actually not a new phenomenon in Britain. Back in the 1930s, five companies (including those of Lords Northcliffe, Beaverbrook, and Kemsley) controlled 43 percent of all newspapers in the nation. (At one point early in the century, Northcliffe had an even larger piece of the national newspaper pie.) That concentration grew some in the postwar years. By the early 1990s, the concentration had grown further, and the ownership was no longer in exclusively British hands. Fully 60 percent of the national daily newspapers were controlled by just three media corporations, and nearly 40 percent of popular press circulation was controlled by Murdoch's News Corp. alone; he also controlled the greatest newspaper institution in Britain, the *Times.* The largest regional newspaper chain owner is the Thomson conglomerate, which is based in Canada; another preeminent newspaper chain owner, whose empire includes the major national paper the *Daily Telegraph,* is Conrad Black of Canada. (In Britain, there are newspapers distributed throughout the nation—ten, as of the later 1990s—and there are also local or regional papers; a distinction is also made between the popular press—typically tabloids aimed at the mass public—and the quality press, like the *Times.*) The local papers saw even more dramatic increases in concentration of ownership; by the end of the 1980s, the five largest owners controlled 54 percent of regional evening newspapers and 73 percent of regional morning newspapers.

In broadcast media, the privately held, for-profit Independent Television system (ITV) was established in the 1950s. Independent radio operations were established in 1971. The fact that big newspaper companies invested in the regional ITV station operations and then in private radio illustrates that a move to cross-media ownership has also taken place in Britain, as has increasing conglomerate ownership. Newspaper chains have merged with many of the major book publishing firms, and they have diversified well beyond media-related industries. For example, Pearsons, which is very big in book publishing and in regional newspapers, also owns Tussauds (the wax-figure museum and related enterprises), Alton Towers, and Chessington World of Adventures, among others. Other newspaper groups have bought into, or have been bought by, corporations involved in everything from oil and gas to air and road transport to furniture and plastics. Indeed, as British media scholar Kevin Williams comments, in a familiar refrain: "The old narrowly focused newspaper groups of [earlier years] are no longer. Today newspapers are simply small cogs in larger commercial enterprises." Especially with the growing control by non-British conglomerates, "British newspapers have increasingly found themselves outposts of large international business empires whose core interests lie elsewhere in the world." The consequence for newspapers and other media is an increasingly raw corporate profit orientation, with less and less commitment to public service responsibilities.[16]

Major changes in media law were made in 1990 and 1996, as a result of Murdoch's use of his newspapers to boost the Tory Party and his favorable treatment by Tory government leaders. In keeping with general trends, the control of private television became more concentrated and the orientation became more intensely commercial and ratings obsessed. As the Euromedia Research Group notes, ITV "became a more belligerently commercial network," and the network pressed hard to "reduce its already diminished public service obligations"—for example, seeking to move its main evening news to a lower rated time slot to take better ratings advantage of entertainment shows.

One quantifiable measure of the impact of concentration and commercialization on the news process is the fact that more than one hundred journalists left the *Sunday Times* in the paper's first five years under Murdoch's control. British author and analyst Anthony Sampson finds that the conglomeration and extreme commercialization have led almost to the "end of investigative journalism" in the print press; such reporting has been replaced by "an explosion of columns providing comment without facts, discussing friends, parties and other journalists." Scholar Kevin Williams found that trend in TV, as well: "The new competitive climate driven by ratings had made it more difficult to mount serious investigative journalism in prime time." Indeed, the head of the Carlton Corporation, one of the three companies that dominate ITV's broadcasting, said that if their show *World in Action* (a revealing title in itself) "were to uncover three more miscarriages of justice while delivering an audience of three, four, or five million, I would cut it. It isn't part of the ITV system to get people out of prison."

New rules resulted in three ownership groups becoming dominant within the regional broadcasting operations carrying ITV network programs and regional programs. Those three groups accounted for almost 70 percent of ad revenue in private broadcast television. Further, 1996 actions by the Majors government made new cross-media rules that allowed the press groups (except the two biggest, Murdoch's News Corp. and the Mirror Group) to buy into commercial broadcasting "on a substantial scale," and television and radio companies could buy into newspapers.

The Monopolies and Mergers Commission, especially under the Thatcher and Majors governments, seems to have operated largely in "a wink and a nod" mode. Two of the most notorious examples involve Murdoch. He was allowed to take over the *Times,* despite his already sizable control of newspapers in Britain. Murdoch also got his way on satellite operation. In 1990, Britain had two competing satellite systems, the official BSB, which was licensed by British regulators and "offered expensive programming with expensive technology," and Murdoch's Sky system, "using a Luxembourg-regulated Astra satellite and offering cheap programming and cheap technology." Both systems were losing money badly at the time. They initiated a merger, with Murdoch becoming the dominant force, "even though the merged BSkyB was radically at odds with the current 'official' policy of the Broadcasting Act of 1990," especially given that Murdoch controlled a large chunk of the newspaper world. But the Thatcher government simply waived Murdoch along on the merger. Because BSkyB had no public service responsibilities, unlike BBC and, to a lesser extent, the ITV system, the move "was making life very much harder for the BBC and ITV" with which BSkyB was competing for audience share.

In the 1980s, Murdoch used his control of the *Times* and the *Sunday Times* to support the Thatcher deregulation policies and to boost his television interests. Both in editorials and in regular news stories, the papers attacked the BBC and the public service broadcasting principle.

The push by the big media conglomerates to loosen up the media laws on concentration of ownership and public service responsibilities was spearheaded with a rationale that should sound familiar: "'Fundamental changes are taking place in the media industries throughout the world' and relaxation was necessary 'to enable British TV to compete effectively on an international stage with large multi-media organizations in the United States and Europe.'"[17]

Germany. Germany is a federal republic, and law and oversight regarding the media are variously divided between the national government and the Länder, or states. Like U.S. newspapers, German newspapers, on most matters, have long operated free of governmental oversight. Ownership of newspapers has become significantly more concentrated. By 1993, the ten largest publishing groups had 55.6 percent of total newspaper circulation in the territory of West Germany, and five of them controlled over 40 percent of circulation; second-tier megamedia corporation Axel Springer Group alone controlled about a quarter of newspaper circulation in the country. Springer is the largest newspaper publisher in all of Europe. Additionally in the print media realm, only four companies—two being Springer and Bertelsmann's Gruner & Jahr—control two-thirds of the magazine market.

With the disintegration of the Soviet-style regime in East Germany and subsequent reunification of Germany, newspapers in the eastern territory went through a good deal of upheaval. The giants and other large West German media empires invaded the print media in force. Bertelsmann got the main East Berlin paper and majority ownership of the Dresden paper, among others, and the Springer Group got the Leipzig paper and others, and so it went. Indeed, as the Euromedia Research Group notes: "The result is that practically all East German publishing rests in West German hands and the concentration rate is higher than in the West."[18]

In television, what had been an exclusively public service broadcasting system with channels ARD and ZDF was changed in the mid-1980s to permit commercial channels. By 1997, commercial TV in Germany was controlled primarily by two megamedia groups, demonstrating that here, too, cross-media ownership is advancing. Second-tier megamedia tycoon Leo Kirch and his son have primary control over Sat1, Pro7, DSF, Kabel 1; Kirch also has part ownership of the huge Springer empire. The other dominant TV group is led by Bertelsmann, which controls the CTL operations, including RTL, RTL2, and Vox. And Bertelsmann, Kirch, and the French Canal Plus jointly own the leading pay-TV company, Premiere. Further, in mid-1997, Bertelsmann's CLT-Ufa broadcasting company, the Kirch Group, and Germany's public telephone operation, Deutsche Telekom, agreed to a joint operation in providing digital pay-TV. The operation will be run under the umbrella of Premiere and will use Kirch decoder boxes and film rights and Deutsche Telekom cable connections for cable TV distribution.

In the late 1980s into the mid-1990s, German media scholar Horst Roper conducted detailed studies of the patterns of concentration. He reports that giants Bertelsmann, Kirch (which is the dominant owner of movies and movie rights in Europe), Springer, and Von Holtzbrinck held interests ranging from partial investments through total ownership in numerous operations in most or all media realms. In addition, Murdoch has shares in Vox TV channel, Berlusconi has shares in DSF TV channel, and Time-Warner and some other Dominant Dozen and second-tier megamedia have other investments in German media. As one researcher noted: "Obviously, this marked a very radical departure from the principle of a 'separation of media powers' that had hitherto characterized the mass media system" in Germany.

That, in turn, raises the question of German law on media. As in Britain, German national law on media ownership restrictions was changed, effective at the beginning of 1997, with the Dominant Dozen's Bertelsmann a force behind the change and a major beneficiary of it. A chief rationale Bertelsmann and others used for the need for the law was that it "allows us to finally compete on equal terms with the giants of North America." The limit on TV ownership that was left was "set so high that it is not reached by any broadcaster, including Kirch and Bertelsmann." Those loosened regulations led to the merger of Bertelsmann's Ufa broadcasting interests with the CLT/RTL broadcasting operation, which made it the largest TV force in Europe, controlling nineteen TV and twenty-three radio broadcasters.[19]

France. The pattern of concentration is repeated in France. In 1983, with concern about concentration of media ownership already at substantial levels, the French parliament had prominently on its agenda a press bill to limit media ownership—a bill widely seen as especially focused on the expansion (and arrogance) of Hersant's media empire. Then intense pressure came from the powerful press lords, and a year later: "[H]eavily amended, the 1984 press law fixed limits on the concentration of ownership that, in effect, did not force Hersant—or any other group—to divest itself of any of its titles." The official restrictions were that no press corporation was to control newspapers with a combined circulation of over 15 percent of national dailies, or 15 percent of regional dailies, or 10 percent of both. However, the law was not retroactive. And, "Hersant rode roughshod over it," acquiring more newspapers "irrespective of protests of government ministers and of the press transparency and pluralism commission." (The "transparency" part of the commission's name refers to its responsibility to assure that the full extent of a corporation's media holdings are known so the corporation can be held accountable.) In response to the official protests, Hersant said, with remarkable arrogance: "I am merely anticipating the next law." And, with the exertion of more power and the 1986 election of conservative forces and resulting Chirac government—with help from Hersant's media—a new press law was passed that greatly eased ownership restrictions. It also privatized the former public TV channel TF1. Further, in 1987, a new regulatory body for broadcast media set up by the 1986 law "awarded the franchise to operate the fifth terrestrial TV channel in France to a consortium in which a Hersant company, TVES, was the lead operator." The Hersant company was later replaced as leader of the consortium by Hachette, leaving the consortium squarely in the megamedia ranks.

By comparison with some other countries, concentration in newspapers and concentration of cross-media ownership are not quite as advanced in France. But, as the Euromedia Research Group notes, "the horizontal and vertical integration of leading communications groups increased" in the 1980s and 1990s, and "the structure of the French media market became more similar to that of other European countries" in the increasing concentration and conglomeration. Further, with the privatization of channel TF1; the partial use of ad revenue to sustain the other two public TV channels, Antenne 2 and FR3; and the intensified competition with purely commercial channels, media scholar Raymond Kuhn reports that by the mid-1990s, "Antenne 2 and FR3 were experiencing nothing short of a legitimacy crisis, as the values of the public service ethos in broadcasting became devalued and emptied of real substantive content."[20]

Europe-wide Institutions. The European Parliament has, on more than one occasion, expressed the need to deal with the megamedia threat in Western Europe; and twice the European Commissioner for the Internal Market has proposed a directive that would deal with the "merger mania" and put limits on the ownership of media. Through late 1997, however, the powerful megamedia and their political allies had repeatedly beaten back the establishment of any such rules.

The Stubborn Strength of Public TV News. Much evidence suggests a continuing decline in the public TV channels in Europe. There is indeed a fair amount of evidence of loss of audience for general shows on public TV channels in the major European nations. However, a study by economics and media analyst Richard Parker found that the prime newscasts of the main public TV stations retain strong viewership: "In those markets where new private channels have sprung up to challenge the traditional state broadcasters, what's striking is how many viewers continue to choose public broadcast news as their first choice over any of the new private broadcast alternatives. In Britain, the number one news program is on BBC 1, in France on TF1, in Germany on ARD 1, in Italy on RAI, in Spain on TV 1." He concludes that the "preference for established and recognizable news sources appears to be universal." This is in accord with the public desire for a significant news source that has real credibility. This also would seem to suggest a more general role for public TV in presenting important matters to the public—including perhaps a watchdog role regarding the commercial media.[21]

Some Megamedia Developments Elsewhere in the World

Global Expansion and Reach of Dominant Dozen Media Conglomerates

Richard Parker relates one of the most interesting examples of the penetrating reach of megamedia: "Filipino troops were able to surprise and capture a guerrilla mountain camp because its revolutionary inhabitants were too busy watching MTV," Viacom's musical messenger to the world. MTV is now available in over 250 million homes in many nations, including 38 European nations. MTV people use new digital technology to inexpensively customize programs for different nations and cultural and language populations; and in Asia, it has three different MTV channels in different languages. MTV is also a dominant force in the music industry. Its Nickelodeon companion in the Viacom conglomerate is the leading force worldwide in children's TV, offering its fare in several languages and in seventy nations beyond the United States.

The combination of big advertising money with the global reach of megamedia is also presenting noteworthy developments. Disney-ABC's ESPN and GE-NBC's international businesses are prime examples. ESPN is the leading force in international televised sports (along with Murdoch's satellite delivery and Fox Sports Net operations); ESPN International is broadcast in twenty-one languages to more than 160 nations. Herman and McChesney reported that by late 1996, ESPN was "offering global buys to advertisers utilizing all its channels and properties around the world, and giving these clients exclusive participation in ESPN programming." And, they reported, NBC and the big ad and PR agency Young & Rubicam were developing "an unprecedented partnership that would give all the agency's clients integrated marketing and promotional opportunities on all of NBC's global properties, while permitting the agency input on programming decisions." Time Warner, TCI, and some other Dominant Dozen megamedia have similar international operations and arrangements, some of which have been noted earlier.[22]

Notes on Megamedia Control in Other Nations

Australia and New Zealand. In Rupert Murdoch's land of origin, Australia, his News Corp. and one other media conglomerate overwhelmingly dominate mass media in general. Murdoch controls about 120 newspapers, or roughly two-thirds of all newspapers in the country, along with three TV stations, 50 percent of Foxtel satellite TV, and other media properties and investments. The other megamedia man in Australia is Kerry Packer, head of Publishing & Broadcasting Limited (PBL). PBL owns the leading commercial TV network and a numbers of magazines and has 17 percent of Fairfax, the second largest newspaper chain in the country. (Until 1998, Canadian second-tier megamedia mogul Conrad Black controlled 25 percent of Fairfax.)

The deregulatory zeal demonstrated in the United States, Britain, Germany, and France was echoed in similar strong actions in New Zealand. Laws passed in 1989 and 1991 opened up the nation's market to foreign ownership, and two public TV channels were made completely dependent on advertising and required to make profits a priority. The public telephone company, Telecom, was bought by regional U.S. Bell phone companies Bell Atlantic and Ameritech, which by December 1997 were talking about selling their interests. A new, third TV channel was given over to private control and came to be majority owned by a big

Canadian company. "Auction of UHF spectrum resulted in the acquisition of frequencies covering 80 percent of New Zealand for the three-channel pay-TV operation of Sky Network Television, owned by a consortium led by Time Warner, Ameritech, and Bell Atlantic." In the newspaper realm, two companies dominate. Newspapers of New Zealand–based Wilson and Horton and of a company called INL have 90 percent of metropolitan circulation and the majority of circulation elsewhere. INL is 40 percent owned by Murdoch. Further, TV has followed the corporatized pattern in the United States. Regional news programs have been cut back; American news consultants have been used for the same purposes they have been used in the United States; and a New Zealand political scientist has documented the shortened sound bites, heavy emphasis on crime, saturation of advertisements, and the like.[23]

Brazil and Mexico. Brazilian media are dominated by the Globo empire, with 1996 revenues of well over $2 billion, which is headed by Robert Marinho (estimated net worth: $3 billion). It is an empire with strong connections to U.S. megamedia. Back in the 1960s, Time-Life started putting money into Marinho's company, then led by the newspaper *O Globo,* the largest in Brazil. With help from the Time-Life money, Marinho's company got into TV. It also cultivated good connections with the military regime that ruled the country from 1964 to 1985 and in return received special treatment that allowed it to grow much larger. By the mid-1990s, the Globo empire dominated in newspapers, TV, and radio, as well as owning ad agencies, publishing companies, and so on; it received about 80 percent of all television ad revenue and 60 percent of all media advertising in Brazil. More recently, Marinho and O Globo have moved aggressively into cable and satellite TV—and even cellular phones. The satellite action is a joint venture with Murdoch's News Corp. and TCI, along with Mexican media giant Televisa.

Televisa is the dominant media presence in Mexico. Like O Globo, Televisa has benefited from close association with the dominant political force in the nation, in this case the PRI political party that ruled Mexico for decades into the mid-1990s. By 1993, more than 90 percent of Mexico's television audience watched one or another of Televisa's four channels; the company took in about three-quarters of all ad revenues in the nation. (Two public channels had a smallish audience.) In 1992, Televisa bought American Publishing Group, which made it the largest Spanish-language publisher of magazines in the world. Televisa also owns part of the American Hispanic channel, Univision; and, in a joint operation with the big Venezuelan network, Venevision, Televisa is a major supplier of Spanish-language programming around the world.[24]

On the Development of Democracy and Media in the 1990s

The rationale used by media giants around the world to justify changes in their nations' media laws to allow more concentration of ownership has consistently been that these nations must leave their megamedia alone in their quests to become even more gargantuan so as to enable them to compete with the giants of North America. Thus, the giant media corporations have been successfully playing one nation's government off against others, for the greater empire and power of megamedia. These developments are leading just where the head of Time Inc. predicted: "There will emerge on a world-wide basis, six, seven, or eight integrated media and entertainment conglomerates" that will dominate mass communications.[25] Meanwhile, genuine diversity of voices, a commitment to making major contributions to the democratic dialogue, and local control are clearly in serious retreat.

The disintegration of the communist or state-socialist regimes in Russia and Eastern Europe were the highlights of a more general trend toward democratization in many parts of the world. And the developments in media technology and organization that allowed global transmission of information and images played a significant part in loosening the grip of the nondemocratic regimes.

What a stunning development we have, then: During the very period when the world saw such dramatic moves toward democracy, the trend in media in both long-standing and newly emerging democracies was toward control of the central vehicles of public information and discussion by huge, largely unaccountable conglomerates that were using their captive mass media in ways that increasingly undermined those democracies. This suggests a need for some overarching perspective in considering those megamedia developments. Chapter 8 provides some of that perspective.

8

Megamedia and the Democratic Prospect

....

This book has told a tale of extraordinary developments in control of our societies' central vehicles of mass communication by a small number of giant "megamedia" corporations, control that spreads across the different mass media and across continents. Those mass media are centerpieces of the central nervous systems of our nations. They are also major sources (and resources) of social, economic, and political power. After all the details discussed in previous chapters on megamedia corporations and their impacts on economic competition and on news and creative outputs, it is important to take a step back and put these developments in more general perspective regarding the sociopolitical system.

As was noted earlier, in the 1930s President Franklin Roosevelt spoke of his concern about the "economic royalists" who ruled the great industrial empires, and he worried that economic developments "had enabled new tyrants to build kingdoms upon concentration of control over material things." In the 1970s, in the midst of congressional hearings on antitrust matters, U.S. Senator Philip Hart asked this concerned question:

> Have we now reached a point in our society where there has been permitted to develop a private concentration of power which, because of the enormity of their reach, makes impossible the application of public policy to them? We had better get an answer or the day will come when there will be private power . . . beyond reach.

By the 1990s a further dimension had been added to that concern. Not only are kingdoms of material things controlled by the barons of giant corporations, but also much of the central means of public communication in our societies and the public arenas of our democracies are ultimately controlled by a small number of megamedia moguls. This control of mass media constitutes a quantum leap in the danger to democratic society of concentrated private power. (This is not suggesting some big, dark, mysterious conspiracy; it is about the accumulation of structural circumstances

217

in our political economy and about the age-old impulse for individuals to seek wealth and power.)

In the late 1970s, in his widely praised masterwork *Politics and Markets: The World's Political-Economic Systems,* Yale professor Charles Lindblom summarized the basic workings of representative democracies in developed nations like the United States, which Lindblom calls "polyarchies":

> In . . . summary, polyarchal politics and government in market-oriented systems take on a distinctive structure. There exists a basic governmental mechanism [along with certain other key mechanisms]. . . . At any given time, that existing mechanism provides a system of controls for controlling authority. The system is a combination of market, privileged business controls in government, and polyarchal politics [i.e., parties, elections, etc.]. Who are the main leaders in the market? Businessmen. Who are the main leaders in the exercise of privileged business controls? Businessmen, of course. Who are the main leaders in polyarchal politics? Businessmen are influential in enormous proportion.

A prime illustration of the latter from the media realm is Rupert Murdoch, who was very influential in Britain during the Tory governments of Thatcher and Majors. In February 1998, an article in Britain's major newspaper the *Independent* captured several elements of the great power and extraordinary competitive business benefits Murdoch and his News Corp. have accumulated, and how that power had extended to the Labour Party leadership:

> A secret international task force of investigators has been set up to examine why Rupert Murdoch's News Corp pays virtually no tax . . . —a fraction of the taxes paid by his competitors. The unprecedented move against the Murdoch empire comes as ministers prepare to go into battle to defend the media baron's British interests. . . .
>
> Labour Prime Minister Tony Blair has ordered total retreat from any government confrontation with Mr. Murdoch over his aggressive pursuit of a price war in the newspaper industry.
>
> Reneging on pre-election pledges, Labour peers have been ordered to oppose an all-party attempt to curb Mr. Murdoch's power in a crucial House of Lords vote [upcoming].

The article included the text of the original resolution regarding Murdoch. The amendment to an existing law would have outlawed "any conduct on the part of one or more national newspaper undertakings . . . if it may reduce the diversity of the national newspaper press in the United Kingdom by reducing, retarding, injuring or eliminating competition." But by early 1998, even the Labour government leadership felt it had to bow to Murdoch's power and accept his mode of operations—to the point of violating election promises.

In the United States, Murdoch's large political contributions were virtually unreported in the news media, while vast atttention was paid to other, often less significant, political finance matters and alleged scandals. With the possible exception of Murdoch's media, for the most part this distorted perspective was not because of some right-wing bias in the media but because journalists were in frenzied scandal-chasing mode and lost perspective, as usual.[1]

In his 1996 State of the Union message, President Clinton declared that "the era of big government is over." But there was profound irony in that pronouncement. First, at the very point the president made that statement, the concentration of power in relatively few private economic organizations had expanded beyond the levels that had concerned Senator Hart in the late 1970s, and some of that private power had added the ominous dimension of control of major mass media. Second, President Clinton had actually helped make the situation worse by cooperating in making into law the Telecommunications Act of 1996. Further, the American system has been reducing and constraining the oversight authority of the national government and has been devolving various of its social programs and governmental authorities down to the state and local level. This is dangerous timing, if we believe in accountability and democracy. As Walter Russell Mead observed in fall 1997 (in a slightly different context): "The retreat of the state also raises troubling questions. For all their flaws, government institutions are at least partly controlled by democratically elected representatives. If power leaks away from these institutions to unaccountable private individudals [and corporations], or to an even less accountable global economy, the important decisions . . . might escape public control altogether. . . . Where does that leave democracy?" Good question.

The American Commission on Freedom of the Press noted at the midpoint of the twentieth century: "Our ancestors were justified in thinking that if they could prevent the government from interfering with the freedom of the press, that freedom would be effectively exercised." This has been the consistent focus of attention regarding the basic freedoms in the First Amendment. Now, however, there are megamedia empires with stupendous size and resources, national and international spread, and control across types of mass media; and they are led by captains of the conglomerates who have an appetite for power and a desire to dominate. Correspondingly, it is in those media empires where the greatest danger to freedom of the press and democracy and to genuinely free and diverse creative expression is to be found as we move into the new millennium. The preceding chapters have shown that "exhibit A" of that proposition includes Rupert Murdoch and his News Corp.–Fox empire, General Electric and chief executive Jack Welch and their captive NBC network, Disney-ABC and CEO Michael Eisner, Bill Gates and mighty Microsoft, S. I. Newhouse, the French media baron Hersant, and the other megamedia organizations and their moguls. As the twentieth century ends, Lord Acton's famous phrase, "power corrupts and absolute power corrupts absolutely," has a new area of application: conglomerate control of mass media.

The extent of public concern about the empire-building and power of these megamedia moguls was reflected in that prime forum of public interests and fears, the movies. In the late-1997 James Bond film *Tomorrow Never Dies,* the big villain is not a former Soviet agent or an underground overlord. Rather, the villain is a power-hungry and power-corrupted tycoon of an immense corporate empire of media and computer operations—basically an out-of-control cross between Rupert Murdoch and Bill Gates.

The highly successful American investor and financier George Soros, who experienced an authoritarian, closed society in his early years living in Soviet-dominated Hungary, had this troubling observation: "Although I have made a fortune in the financial markets, I now fear that the untrammeled intensification of laissez-faire capitalism and the spread of market values into all areas of life is endangering our open and democratic society." This is essentially the same conclusion economist Arthur Okun came to, as noted in chapter 5: "Some of our most cherished rights are auctioned off to the highest bidder." The extremely concentrated control over the media is the most crucial realm of that endangerment and of that auctioning of cherished rights.

In light of these concerns, it is worth noting that Fred Friendly passed away as this book was being completed (spring 1998). The passing of the partner of Edward R. Murrow and chief behind-the-scenes force producing the legendary *See It Now* and other CBS programs marked the end of an era in the powerful mass medium of television. Friendly himself, in an interview in his last years, provided the moral of the story: "There is no limit to the money you can make out of television. The only trouble is, you begin to take all of the integrity and all of the caring out of it, until you reach a point like we're in right now—where the only thing that matters is, will it make money?"[2]

The mentality and political reality of the endangerment of democratic society are reflected in the fact that general and genuine public purposes are missing in action in the formulation of the Telecommunications Act. The Telecom Act's supposed positive impact on "diversity of media voices, vigorous economic competition, technological advancement, and promotion of the public interest" is little in evidence. Indeed, the developments during and after passage of the Telecom Act seem to indicate that diversity of voices in the media is being steadily lessened, competition is being increasingly skewed and constrained, and the public interest and the democratic process are suffering. Given the language of the Act, the big benefits for private business activities, and other results, the Telecom Act seems to illustrate all too well Ambrose Bierce's cynical definition of politics: "The conduct of public affairs for private advantage."[3]

The democratic consequences of the megamedia's lobbying efforts and the lack of substantive news coverage have been conceptualized in political scientist E. E. Schattschneider's thoughts. Again, when an issue is kept out of the public arena and the "scope of conflict" about it is thus constricted, the insiders have a much freer hand in deciding policy—policy that will benefit the powerful organized interests.[4]

One other word is in order on the competition question and the media conglomerate buzzword of the 1990s, synergy. The media moguls repeatedly said that collecting a great variety of media and other programmatic and creative enterprises under one corporate umbrella would be a real boon for creative output—with cross-pollination and creative stimulation, wondrous new and exciting products and services would be forthcoming. Most observers have found little evidence for such benefits to creative output, however. But conglomerate synergy has been a significant factor in skewing economic competition in favor of megamedia conglomerates and is presenting troubling issues of conflicts of interest in and degradation of quality in news operations.

The fare that an increasingly corporatized and conglomeratized media are giving us, from news and newsmagazines to entertainment, increasingly treats its viewers and readers as purely atomized individuals-as-consumers. What seems lost is media material that meaningfully contributes to a recognition of common interests as members and citizens of our communities and general societies. Instead, media fare more and more seems to impoverish the realm of public discussion and interaction that is central to the democratic process. Robert Putnam's research on the high correlation between social capital and higher levels of public engagement in the democratic process reminds us of its importance in making democratic societies work. (Again, social capital is the well-developed and well-functioning social networks and social trust built through involvement in community organizations and activities.) Putnam found that TV is a prime factor in the deterioration of that social capital, and megamedia dominance of TV is steadily worsening the civicly destructive impact of television.

Professor Russell Neuman is a leading social science analyst in research on the nature and directions of media technology and their social functions. Especially in America, in assessing the "character of the commercial marketplace as a filtering mechanism," Neuman asks how well that commercial marketplace "serve[s] the goals of diversity and pluralism" in the mass media. The answer: "Not very well." Insightfully and a little startlingly, he points out: "The common-denominator pressures of the market render the flow of information and entertainment almost as homogeneous as that produced by the most attentive government-run media systems in single-party states [that is, nearly as homogeneous as the best of the former Soviet-style systems, although in different style]. It is a spectacular irony."

Speaking of the developing technologies of mass media and the actual and potential organizational and institutional arrangements for operating those media, Neuman also said:

> This process of change, although infused with conflicting vested political and economic interests, is still subject to our collective control. The key to controlling it is to understand the nature of those forces in tension. We stand at a historic threshold. A new electronic infrastructure is about to be built. How it is to be designed and used should be the subject of a self-conscious inquiry.

It is essential to have a "self-conscious," focused, and explicit inquiry and debate by the collective whole of the citizenry about the mass media and Internet system that is developing for the twenty-first century.[5]

Some have seen the Internet as a force to arrest the erosion of social capital, guarantee a diversity of sources of information and ideas, and enhance engagement and participation. But in cyberspace people essentially operate as isolated individuals. There is no shared physical space, no direct, face-to-face human interaction in the functions of a real community ("chat rooms" and on-line discussions are no substitute), no real-world walking, biking, and driving through neighborhoods and downtown areas where people actually live and work. Cyberspace surfers, with a simple click of a mouse or keyboard stroke, can electronically zoom off or zone out of any actual community problems, events, or developments. The Internet gives opportunities to enhance information-gathering and communications, but it is no substitute for geographically based, real community (and even national) media institutions. To borrow a Benjamin Barber concept, democracy based on the Internet must, of necessity, be a "thin" notion and practice of democracy; it can be a fine supplement, but it is no substitute for main mass media.

Daniel Yankelovich has long been a leading authority in the surveying and analysis of public opinion. In the early 1990s, he wrote a masterful book entitled *Coming to Public Judgment: Making Democracy Work in a Complex World*. The key point of the book was that public opinion, as captured in those many polls reported in the media, often does not represent genuine public judgment on major issues. What is all too often captured is mere mass opinion—people's off-the-top-of-the-head notion about an issue that they really have not had enough information, discussion, and time to ponder seriously. Public judgment, on the other hand, is the ultimate idea behind democracy. Public judgment is formed when there is a good deal of meaningful information and debate in the media and the public arena about the nature of public problems and alternative solutions to them. But, under increasing megamedia control, there is reason to conclude that the mass media's central role in this process has degenerated. Those structural developments and the impacts on democratic discussion need broad public debate.

This book has sought to present substantial evidence on the megamedia trend and its consequences for democracy and diverse, unconstrained creative expression. The intent of the book is to provoke much more discussion and debate among my fellow professionals and, more important, in the mass media and among the general public. Bill Gates, in the foreword to his book *The Road Ahead*, said about development of the Internet:

> During the next few years, governments, companies, and individuals will make major decisions about the network. It's crucial that broad groups of people—not just technologists or people who happen to be in the computer industry—participate in the debate about how this technology should be shaped and how it will in turn shape society.

Although Gates's apparent monopoly or near-monopoly behavior seems to belie that sentiment, we must apply it to public debate about directions in the control and use of mass media in general. The quality of our democratic processes and creative expression depends profoundly on having that broad, inclusive, societywide debate and the answers—and alternatives and actions—that are forthcoming.[6]

9

Accountability, Alternatives, and Action

....

Accountability and alternatives are the essence of democracy; and diversity and independence of mind and action in creative expression are vital for a vibrant and continually developing culture. This chapter discusses ways to enhance the independence of, and diversity in, the mass media and to improve the accountability of the existing structures of control of the main media, especially in the crucial news and opinion areas.

The most important concept in this discussion is that the mass media are a category of business and societal activity fundamentally different from other businesses. The First Amendment to the U.S. Constitution gives the media unique privileges and protections. The purpose of those protections is to facilitate the media's responsibilities in the democratic process and general creative expression. Correspondingly, the media and the organizations that control them require special mechanisms of oversight and accountability and, in certain respects, special financial allocations to assure that the media meet their unique societal responsibilities.

This chapter seeks to contribute to the general debate some suggested means of accountability, sorts of alternatives, and a series of possible actions. Some are less politically feasible than others (at least as things stand in 1998), but it is still important to add them to the debate, if we are to fully consider the possibilities. (It is appropriate to note that in 1996 and 1997 two successive Media and Democracy congresses were held to explore some of these issues. The congresses included a variety of alternative-media people, as well as some mainstream-media people for panel presentations, and they explored ways to enhance media and democracy. These congresses were completely ignored in the main media, however, even when the 1997 edition was held in New York City, the home of most of the prime national press.)[1]

225

Enhancing Quality and a Major Alternative Voice
in the Main Media

With the increasingly overwhelming control of most main media by megamedia and with their conglomerate dominance of public affairs and other programming, it is more critical than ever to have one or more significant, fully independent alternative outlets *within the main media channels* so that widespread public exposure to the alternative media material is achieved as a matter of "natural" accessing of media. It must not be stuck in the nether reaches of cable and satellite TV systems where more effort is required to gain access to it and far fewer citizens do so.

In America, there is already in place a basic set of alternative media organizations and offerings: public television and radio. Unfortunately, they have been more and more constrained and compromised by very inadequate funding and by being forced to go begging to big corporations—the very forces, along with the government, from which they most need absolute independence. One of the prime alternatives and actions needed is a substantial enhancement of the independence and capacities of public TV and radio. Especially compared with European nations and Japan, public TV and radio in the United States are severely underfunded.

One thing is fundamental: The increasing reliance on big corporate funding sources for public TV and radio and the inevitable corporate influence must be cut back or eliminated entirely. Besides being an increasingly prime source of funding for public radio and TV in general, big business has become an especially major source of program funding. To retain the integrity of the process, it is essential that there be *no direct connection* between program decisions and corporate financing.

As mentioned earlier, PBS executives are now previewing PBS programs for commercial ad people and corporate executives, as the commercial networks do. At a spring 1997 luncheon hosted by PBS executives to encourage big corporations to "invest" more advertising money in PBS, the first PBS speaker was the president of flagship public TV station WNET of New York. He said: "Welcome to the new PBS. Corporate messages on PBS get more creative every year. You can show products. You can use slogans." Additionally, in that corporate wooing context, he labeled PBS "user friendly," evidently meaning corporate-sponsor friendly. An executive from the big Young & Rubicam ad agency commented, "What we have here is the commercialization of PBS" (a positive development, as far as he was concerned). This clear and present danger of basic compromise of the independence of public television is a major loss to American democracy and society more generally.

The direct corporate sponsorship of programs—and the quasi ads for corporations that have been increasingly thrust onto the public TV airwaves—must be totally ended. If some corporations are responsible enough simply to support public TV and radio programming *in general* and would contribute to a *general unrestricted* program fund, that should be acceptable. The corporations would still be able to claim —more validly—in their own corporate PR that they were acting as responsible corporate citizens in contributing to genuine quality in media and to the independent, alternative voice of public TV.

Removing the creeping corporate influence (with assistance from the actions discussed below) would also enable public TV and radio to help hold the chain- and conglomerate-owned main media accountable. It should be a regular *feature function* of PBS, NPR, and their companion state and local organizations to do prominent reviews and critiques of what the main commercial media offer in the way of news, newmagazines, and other public affairs programs and articles, as well as entertainment programs. This should include review and critique of the general behavior of the parent corporations regarding their public responsibilities.

In the 1980s, Hodding Carter conducted an excellent PBS program focusing on review and critique of news operations; it was called *Inside Story*. But it could not find funding to sustain it, and its run was ended. Perhaps it was just coincidence, but the end came about the time of the notably increased reliance on corporate funding sources and lowered federal funding during the Reagan administration. (A minor bit of good news is that CNN now has a show called *Reliable Sources*, hosted by broadcast journalist Bernard Kalb and including *Washington Post* media critic Howard Kurtz and former journalists and news media analysts Ellen Hume and Martin Schram. Unfortunately, because of its obviously very limited budget, there is little in the way of independent investigation and full program presentations; it is basically just talk by the group.) The *Columbia Journalism Review* and *American Journalism Review* do a fine job and are important contributors to this crucial dialogue of democracy, and *Brill's Content* is a fine new addition to such efforts. But there is need of a well-funded and expertly staffed major media review effort presented in a main channel on the most powerful medium, television, as well as on radio.

Lawrence Grossman, former president of PBS, points out another significant element that has been missed because of substantial reliance on corporate sources for funding:

> During my years at PBS, public television could never raise enough underwriting money from independent sources to produce a single major television series devoted to labor and labor unions. It was a high

priority of mine, not only because of the subject's innate historic importance, but also because of the need to balance off PBS programs such as
Wall Street Week and *Adam Smith's Money World* [and *Nightly Business
Report*] that placed heavy emphasis on business and finance. . . . However, no corporate underwriting, station program funds, or endowment
money could be found to finance programs that dealt with labor's side
of the equation.

Clearly, such material is not going to be found on the networks (which no
longer do documentaries), and it is unlikely on Murdoch's Fox channels,
or on Time Warner, Disney-ABC, or Viacom broadcast or cable channels.
The result is that the American public continues to receive a very unbal-
anced view on that and other matters of significance to our society.

In general, it is nice that, beyond CNN, three or so cable channels like
Arts & Entertainment (A&E) channel, Discovery Channel, and the History Channel (which is not available on many cable systems) provide some
fairly meaty programs, some with significant public affairs material. The
public affairs material is on the latter three channels only occasionally,
however; it is not their primary focus. And since all the prime cable and
satellite channels, including A & E, Discovery, and the History Channel,
are totally or mostly owned by a half-dozen megamedia corporations,
they are not going to serve as fundamentally independent, alternative
sources of information and ideas. (In non-public-affairs material, those
three channels especially offer some fine programs that add dimensions
beyond the three traditional broadcast networks, though.)

The enhanced public TV and radio efforts must also be linked to a
substantial, top-quality Internet operation that is coordinated with the
offerings on TV and radio (as many public stations have already begun
doing). In light of the tendency for many in the public to turn to the low-
est common denominator fare that so dominates TV's commercial offerings, as Russell Neuman said, "the most effective strategy for reform of
the system is to work at the margin with new technologies to try to nur-
ture and broaden public tastes with innovative formats and designs."

Additionally, to assure independence, there needs to be more insulation from the political meddling by some presidents and forces in Congress that has been all too present at times. Currently, presidential
appointments are made (with Senate approval) to the Board of the Corporation for Public Broadcasting (CPB), which is the chief policymaker
regarding programming and related matters. Presidential political influence is evident through naming political comrades to the CPB Board. On
the congressional side, William Hoynes's study of public television spells
out a key element of the problem: "The Public Broadcasting Act . . . only
set up [the CPB], leaving the financing to the federal government's regu-

lar appropriations process. As a result, the funding of public broadcasting . . . has always been a politically charged issue." In 1992 and 1995, some congressional Republicans and related interest groups tried to increase government involvement in guiding program directions and to cut off all public funding of public TV and radio to privatize it. During that debate, public opinion polls showed strong public support for continued governmental funding and genuine independence for public radio and television. Two media activists put the funding matter in perspective in early 1995: "CPB disburses $286 million of federal money to public broadcasting for program production and local stations. The federal government . . . devotes almost $200 million yearly to military bands." In that light, it shows stunningly perverse priorities for anyone to maintain that the Corporation for Public Broadcasting "has been eating taxpayers' money," as Representative Newt Gingrich has said.[2]

Two ways are offered here to insulate public TV and radio from political—and corporate—meddling. One is establishing one or more independent, automatic revenue sources, rather than relying on politicized governmental processes and corporate money. This is discussed below. The second is restructuring the process of selection of the prime public TV and radio decision-makers. For illustrative purposes, I will focus on the Board of the Corporation for Public Broadcasting.

Quality Time, the report of the Twentieth Century Fund Task Force on Public Television, recommended that "the president select a nonpartisan committee of outstanding individuals to recommend qualified candidates" for seats on the CPB Board. Drawing on that idea but taking it a step further, I suggest that, since it is so easy for the selection to be politicized, the best solution is to find as respected, distinguished, and nonpartisan a set of people as possible to develop a short list from which the president must choose a nominee for Senate approval. Perhaps the two most respected and distinguished organizations in the realm of the mind and culture in America are the American Association for the Advancement of Science and the American Academy of Arts and Letters. These are, in effect, the ultimate "honor societies" in those realms. So, let us ask those organizations to establish a common selection committee, with half the membership from each body, which would select a slate of three candidates from which the president would nominate a new board member. The trio of recommendations should be offered in a public fashion, to discourage political game-playing or ideological ax-grinding. The great prestige of these recommenders should tend to dampen any political game-playing by legislators or others.

Given the elite reputation of those bodies and past claims that public broadcasting has been somewhat elitist in its programming and has paid inadequate attention to average citizens, it is surely incumbent upon public TV and radio to make more concerted efforts to involve a range of representatives of the general public in the process. Such efforts must include major attempts to fulfill the diversity demands of democracy that the main commercial media are so inadequately meeting—not only racial and gender diversity but also philosophical, artistic ,and other diversity. The marketplace of ideas does not mean whatever sells among the narrow range of material the megamedia offer in the rather distorted economic market. For society to progress, the democratic dialogue must include truly alternative voices and ideas that challenge the complacent status quo.

It is also fair, although some in the artistic community will complain about this, to request that public media pay due attention to matters of taste and respect for basic values of the American people. While the decisions must be kept out of the political and corporate arena, good judgment should be used. When some program might flagrantly and very offensively violate fundmental public values, there should be a mechanism for considering carefully whether the program should be supported and aired on the public media. If the material is very offensive but the program seems to have artistic merit, it should be incumbent on the decision-makers to try to find an alternative outlet. But, again, it is also a responsibility of the process to challenge the conventional wisdom. There is no simple formula or easy answer; only a painstaking decision process, independence, and good judgment will result in the right things being done, as a rule.

On the other hand, part of public media offerings *should be* elitist, in a sense. That is, they should offer the highest cultural fare in the visual and performing arts and so on. Under the megamedia dominance of TV, radio, and other media, for public TV and radio to provide high cultural fare is to offer another significant alternative to the standard commercial fare—not to mention helping sustain the best of human creativity, which enriches us all. The original Carnegie Commission report on public broadcasting in the late 1970s said: "The idea of broadcasting as a force in the public interest, a display case for the best of America's creative arts, a forum of public debate—advancing the democratic conversation and enhancing the public imagination—has receded before the inexorable force of audience maximization." Again, it is nice that some high cultural material occasionally appears on the Bravo and A & E cable channels, but more than half the public does not know they exist. Such is not the case for public TV.[3]

Finally, someone is needed to "watch the watchdog." The public TV and radio organizations should select a distinguished outsider to serve as ombudsman to monitor the performance of public TV and radio for diversity, balance of philosophical and political material, and so on, and to take and investigate complaints of bias, missing issues, and the like. The ombudsman should be given regular on-air time to discuss his or her findings. While the chief PBS administrator would (carefully) hire the ombudsman, only an extrordinary majority of the CPB Board should be able to fire him or her.

Obviously, the key question is, how are we to fund PBS, especially if we cut back on and constrain corporate program funding and at the same time enhance PBS's functions? The regular appropriations process in Congress is clearly a one-way ticket to more meddling and less independence, as is creeping corporate program sponsorship. For support of public broadcasting, and for other initiatives involving cable TV systems, satellite TV systems, and the Internet, which are discussed below, some specially designated *new taxes and fees* will be discussed. New taxes are not exactly politically popular in the late 1990s, to issue a major understatement. But keep in mind the following: First, we have noted the strong public support for public TV and radio. Second, we have also noted the public's concern that there is too much power in the hands of a few giant corporations, and their concern that megamedia are obsessed with money-making but care little about quality use of the media. Finally, other public opinion evidence suggests that people are more receptive to tax revenue-raising if it is *specifically targeted* to public-regarding purposes, rather than simply dumped into the general federal treasury, and will not be used and abused by big bureaucracies. Education, the environment, and public media appear to head the list of such purposes.

The place to start, in light of the great giveaway of the digital spectrum to the existing TV station owners, is to assess substantial "digital spectrum use fees" for TV station use of that spectrum. The digital use fees should be in two categories. First: A moderate fee should be assessed for use of the extra spectrum for digital broadcasting of the regular TV station programs. (As many critics have pointed out, it is about time we recapture some funds for public purposes from the hugely munificent gift to private corporations of licenses to use the public airwaves.) This should come with a graduated discount for the amount of broadcast time spent on genuine news and public affairs programming—in effect giving a tax break to those stations that are more sociopolitically responsible. Second, a substantial "alternative use of spectrum" tax should be imposed on economic activities not directly related to news operations and other regular TV. It is only fair and reasonable that a sizable amount of that extra enterprise—like using the extra spectrum for pagers, cellular phones, data services, etc.—be recaptured for public purposes. (Call this one a "tax" since it relates to pure economic opportunism, not First Amendment broadcasting.) These two revenue sources should provide tens of millions of dollars for the special fund I detail below.

Another revenue source has also been mentioned by Ben Bagdikian and one or two others. As leading histories of the media detail, advertising has increasingly come to dominate TV and radio. Further, TV ads are eating up more and more of the broadcast hour. A November 1996 survey by the Association of American Advertising Agencies reported that the time devoted to ads and promos *per hour* on the networks in prime time "totalled 15 minutes, 19 seconds on ABC; 14:53 on CBS; 15:19 on NBC; and 16:07 on Fox." And, the survey found, "In every case, with one exception, there were annual increases going back to our first survey in 1989." So, I recommend that a small tax on television and radio advertising be instituted; call it the "public purposes advertising tax." To protect small media and small businesses—a few TV and radio stations are still independently owned—the tax should only apply above a certain level, say, for all advertising buys from a given company in a given media outlet above the $5,000 level. (The levels suggested here are just illustrative; appropriate adjustments would be made in the actual debate to minimize any damage to small business and small media.) To make the tax a little progressive, perhaps there could be a 1 percent rate for buys of $5,000 to $25,000, and 2 percent above that. That would add only $50 to the cost of a $5,000 ad and would channel the money to the popularly supported public purpose of public TV and radio. This may not be politically feasible, but it is a very modest proposal. If political feasibility dictated lowering the assessment to 0.5 percent and 1 percent, respectively, the revenue would still be helpful in retrieving the independence and enhancing the excellence of public TV and radio. If polling asked the American people about this proposal, it is highly likely it would receive strong majority support.[4]

One final revenue possibility is to borrow from the British model and establish a small tax, say 1 percent, on each TV and radio set sold, above a floor cost level, say more than $40. On a $50 boom box, that is only an added 50 cents. For sales involving radios, the money would go to public radio; for TVs, the money would go to PBS. It seems likely that the public would support even this, if they knew the money would be exclusively channeled to public radio and TV and not used for anything else or waylaid by some bureaucracy. Call it the "supplemental public TV and radio tax."

Those fees and the other taxes and fees discussed below should be deposited in a *Democratic Diversity in Communications Fund (DDC Fund)* to be used for the augmented support of public TV and radio and to provide access to cable and satellite channels.

If all the revenue sources were instituted, the contribution of the spectrum use fees and taxes and the advertising tax could be divided 60-

40 between public TV and radio, on the one hand, and cable and satellite TV and the Internet, on the other. The TV and radio set tax revenue, as noted, should be devoted solely to the corresponding public media.

One final general note regarding public TV and radio: With such a major augmentation of funding, and in light of the British model of multiple public media channels, it should be an ultimate goal to have two full-scale public media channels, which should be in prime media positions (i.e., placed in the first thirteen channels on cable and satellite TV arrangements). This would dramatically enhance diversity, especially with the intensified commitment to such material by a newly well-funded and depoliticized PBS and NPR. (In a few areas, second channels already exist, especially on radio; but there is a constant struggle to maintain them.)

Cable and Satellite TV

The other prime use of the DDC Fund should be to enhance access to cable and satellite television. Cable TV, on the whole, has a rather sorry record in making contributions to the democratic process and community activities and community-building (C-SPAN and CNN being the national-level exceptions). Former FCC general gounsel and communications law expert Henry Geller said it simply: "Cable TV is a First Amendment horror story." Also, in policy matters, the American system has tended to regularly demand (or at least talk about demanding) that traditional networks and broadcast TV stations meet certain requirements, such as airing presidential and gubernatorial addresses and candidate debates and granting free time for candidates, and so on. But cable TV tends to escape such demands except for requirements for community-access channels. But even that minimal commitment is increasingly avoided by the local cable systems, and the access channels that exist have little or no funding.

A set of enhanced local-access channels should be a *federal requirement* for every system, since many municipal governments have failed in this responsibility. These reserved channels on local cable TV systems should come with studios, editing facilities, videocams (perhaps rentable at cost), and other means of facilitating alternative, community-based progam material. (Some American municipalities have required at least a modest version of this.) Financial support from the DDC Fund should be provided to defray organizing, personnel, and other program development costs. Community people, not people who work for the cable quasi monopoly, should be hired to administer the program in coordination with community nonprofit public service organizations. The funds would also help in setting up coordinated sites on the Internet. The democratic process and related community programs should also be coordinated with materials and programs at local public libraries. (Bill Gates has contributed a sizable sum to help get computers in public libraries, which also helps Microsoft over the long term. Perhaps he can be persuaded to make another significant contribution to help facilitate the library coordination effort.)

Satellite TV systems should also be required to include some channels—and not just relegated to the nether reaches of the 150-channel system—for public affairs and public access on a national level. Parallel provisions can be set in place.

With the exception of C-SPAN and CNN, these corporations have demonstrated their irresponsibility regarding media contributions to the democratic process and local or national community activities, and yet they are very ready to proclaim loudly their protection under the First Amendment. They should be required to make such contributions as part of their responsibilities under the First Amendment.[5]

Antitrust Enforcement

Antitrust law should be much more vigorously enforced, and the restriction of bases for action to narrow, "pure economic" matters should be rethought, especially given what has been done under the auspices and in the aftermath of the Telecommunications Act. The codirector of the Washington office of the Consumers' Union pointed out: "The [Telecommunications Act] is fundamentally flawed, because unless you have extremely aggressive antitrust enforcement, this law cannot and will not promote vibrant competition."

As Professors Gillmor, Barron, Simon, and Terry have written in their media law text: "When deregulation is based on assumptions about competitive benefits, antitrust laws—which protect that competitive environment—become surrogates for communications policy and increase in importance." The FCC itself gave us the most fundamental logic in a general statement of principle: "If our democratic society is to function, *nothing can be more important than insuring* that there is a free flow of information *from as many divergent sources as possible* " (emphasis added). That is the central point, and it is unfortunate that the FCC's actions have rarely matched those stirring words. Owen Fiss, Sterling Professor of Law at Yale University, points out that the First Amendment is meant not just as a "hands-off document" prohibiting government interference with free press and speech; it is also intended to be an affirmative encouragement to wide-ranging debate on public issues. Noting that the Fairness Doctrine rule applied to broadcast media to try to ensure that debate was presented from different viewpoints, Fiss continues:

> [T]he public debate rationale can be understood to have not just a quanititative but also a qualitative dimension. . . . the First Amendment can be viewed as a mechanism for protecting the robustness of public debate, for exposing the public to diverse and conflicting viewpoints on issues of public importance.
>
> But neither the FCC nor the President addressed the best and most plausible theory of the Fairness Doctrine, which identifies economics, not technology, as the constraining force on the press. The technological revolution now afoot in communications may present us with a large number of channels, but as long as they are all governed by the market, there remains a risk that coverage will be skewed.

The latter point understates the constraints of economics; the increasingly extreme concentration of chain and conglomerate control over outlets in each medium, across different media, and through all levels of the production and distribution system create a constant danger of skewed coverage—and of skewed economic competition.

Robert Pitofsky, chairman of the Federal Trade Commission, in his years as law professor, wrote a couple of law journal articles that contain very interesting explorations of reasonable legal and constitutional logic for broadening antitrust law. In one notable article, Pitofsky spoke to the increasing tendency, from the 1970s on, to use a narrow and exclusively economic basis for pursuing antitrust action. He responded:

> It is bad history, bad policy, and bad law to exclude certain political values in interpreting the antitrust laws. By "political values," I mean, first, a fear that excessive concentration of economic power will breed antidemocratic political pressures, and second, a desire to enhance individual and business freedom by reducing the range within which private discretion by a few in the economic sphere controls the welfare of all. A third and overriding political concern is that if the free-market sector of the economy is allowed to develop under antitrust rules that are blind to all but economic concerns, the likely result will be an economy so dominated by a few corporate giants that it will be impossible for the state [eventually] not to play a more instrusive role in economic affairs.

This is exactly what has happened using the tunnel-vision version of "pure" economic criteria in antitrust action as the operative rule (or inoperative rule). The greatest danger in the years since Pitofskty's article is that such private economic power will be beyond the reach of governmental intervention, as Senator Hart warned. Pitofksy went on to point out that even if a proposed mega-merger increased "efficiencies," in narrow economics measurement, and did not bring other purely economic dangers, "an antitrust challenge should incorporate some concern that the welfare of the country is being placed in the hands of a few economically powerful firms and individuals." That becomes a far greater concern when the powerful firms control most of the mass media. In an interview after Pitofsky became chairman of the Federal Trade Commission, he acknowledged that point: "You might take a tougher stance . . . in the media field because you are concerned that too much power in too few hands will impair freedom of expression." Further, in another law review article, Pitofsky pointed out that the guidelines put out in the later 1980s by the Department of Justice's Antitrust Division startlingly ignore the legislative purpose underlying Section 7 of the Clayton Antitrust Act: "This is nowhere more evident than in the failure to consider whether a merger would occur in a market that has recently experienced a *trend* toward increased concentration. The legislative history behind Section 7 leaves no doubt that Congress meant to apply more restrictive merger standards to such industries" to stop extreme and dangerous concentration *before it was accomplished*. Given the march of megamedia documented in this book, it is hard to understand how the media would not be subject to vigorous antitrust action in the late 1990s.

As of late 1997, Pitofsky's actions at FTC had not quite matched those words, but the strong logic is there. Professor John Busterna has provided a solid rationale for more vigorous application of antitrust laws to newspaper chains, as have others regarding media in general. Another First Amendment specialist, law professor Loftus Becker, noted: "Before we can decide what parts of the new Act are wise or unwise, we should decide what kind of telecommunications systems we want to develop. Before we can decide what kind of telecommunications system we want to develop, we need to decide what social functions we want it to serve." That is clear, basic logic, but it has been lost in the flurry of megamedia power politics and blind obeisance to a simplified notion of pure marketplace economics—which, in the real world of megamedia, as chapter 5 discusses, does not operate in pure marketplace fashion.[6]

Some Perspective by Way of a Humorous Aside

Finally, the tendency to seek control over a wide terrain and over anything that could possibly be claimed as the domain of a megamedia organization has now reached extreme levels. The basic inclination is not new, however. Consider the case of Warner Brothers movie corporation back in the 1940s when they found out that the zany Marx Brothers were coming out with a movie called *A Night in Casablanca*. As the producers of the legendary Humphrey Bogart–Ingrid Bergman movie *Casablanca*, they tried to force the Marx Brothers to take that name out of their comedy. Groucho Marx's reply to Jack Warner, rediscovered in fall 1997 in a Library of Congress collection, provides us with a humorous interlude and a little perspective on the control-everything mentality:

> Apparently there is more than one way of conquering a city and holding it as your own. For example, up to the time that we contemplated making a picture, I had no idea that the city of Casablanca belonged to Warner Brothers.
>
> However, it was only a few days after our announcement appeared that we received a long, ominous legal document warning us not to use the name "Casablanca."
>
> It seems that in 1471, Ferdinand Balboa Warner, the great-great grandfather of Harry and Jack, while looking for a shortcut to Burbank, had stumbled on the shores of Africa and, raising his alpenstock, which he later turned in for a hundred shares of common, he named it Casablanca.
>
> I just can't understand your attitude. . . . I am sure that the average movie fan could learn to distinguish between Ingrid Bergman and Harpo. I don't know whether I could, but I certainly would like to try.
>
> You claim you own Casablanca and that no one else can use that name without [your] permission. What about Warner Brothers?—do you own that, too? You probably have the right to use the name Warner, but what about Brothers? Professionally, we were brothers long before you were. . . .
>
> The younger Warner calls himself Jack. Does he claim that, too? It's not an original name—it was used long before he was born. Offhand, I can think of two Jacks—there was Jack of "Jack and the Beanstalk" and Jack the Ripper, who cut quite a figure in his day. . . .
>
> I have a hunch that this attempt to prevent us from using the title is the scheme of some ferret-faced shyster serving an apprenticeship in their legal department. I know the type—hot out of law school, hungry for success and too ambitious to follow the natural laws of promotion, this bar sinister probably needled Warners' attorneys, most of whom are fine fellows with curly hair, double-breasted suits etc. in attempting to enjoin us.
>
> Well, he won't get away with it! We'll fight him to the highest court! No pasty-faced legal adventurer is going to cause bad blood between the Warners and the Marxes. We are all brothers under the skin and we'll remain friends till the last reel of "A Night in Casablanca" goes tumbling over the spool.[7]

In fall 1997, a satirical news release captured the quintessential contemporary example of such impulses. Appropriately sent out over the Internet, it "announced" that the federal government had just become a wholly owned subsidiary of Microsoft and President Clinton would now report to Bill Gates. "It's a logical extension of our growth, it's a positive arrangement for everyone," "said" Gates. And closing the news conference, the mock Gates said American citizens "will be able to expect lower taxes, increases in government services, discounts on all Microsoft products, and the immediate arrest of all executives of Sun Microsystems and Netscape Corp." A little humor—sometimes of the witty ridicule sort—is a final weapon that can and should be used to hold accountable those pasty-faced adventurers of the megamedia empires.

It Can't Wait

Some have suggested that it is too early to reach a decisive conclusion about the Telecommunication Act's impact on democratic processes and diverse creative expression. But as Gene Kimmelman of the Consumers' Union has pointed out (with some understatement): "You had better get obligations up front that ensure you don't reach a concentrated level of a market; better to do it *before* they get any bigger [because,] as we've experienced in other areas, it can be very difficult to *come back* and reconfigure an industry that has grown beyond reasonable proportions."[8] In summary, if we wait, it will be too late, and we'll have sealed our fate.

Notes

Chapter 1

1. Royko quote: Nicholas Coleridge, *Paper Tigers: The Latest, Greatest Newspaper Tycoons* (New York: Birch Lane Press, 1993), 496. Moyers quote: "Taking CBS to Task," *Newsweek*, 15 September 1986, 53. Ted Turner quote: Mike Wallace interview for CBS *60 Minutes* show segment "Media Mogul," January 1997. Thomas Maier, *Newhouse* (New York: St. Martin's Press, 1995), 269, 300–301, 370. GE-NBC material: Ken Auletta, *Three Blind Mice: How the TV Networks Lost Their Way* (New York: Random House, 1991), 228, 569–70. E. L. Doctorow quote: Maier, *Newhouse*, 204.

2. Quoted in Erick Barnouw, *The Image Empire* (New York: Oxford University Press, 1970), 196.

3. G. Hunt, ed., *The Writings of James Madison* no. 9 (New York: Putnam's Sons, 1910), 103. Ethics code: Included in Louis A. Day, *Ethics in Media Communications* (Belmont, Calif.: Wadsworth, 1991), 351. For a good summary of agenda-setting research, see Maxwell E. McCombs and Donald L. Shaw, "The Evolution of Agenda-Setting Research: Twenty-Five Years in the Marketplace of Ideas," *Journal of Communication* 43, no. 2 (Spring 1993). Also see Dean Alger, *The Media and Politics*, 2d ed. (Fort Worth, Texas: Harcourt Brace College Publishing, 1996), chap. 2, 160–64, and chaps. 7, 8, 11, 13 and references therein; and see Marion R. Just et al., *Crosstalk: Citizens, Candidates, and the Media in a Presidential Campaign* (Chicago: University of Chicago Press, 1996). Robert D. Leigh, ed., *A Free and Responsible Press* (Chicago: University of Chicago Press, 1947), 3.

4. Sources on key information in this series of megamedia mergers and acquisitions: On the takeover of ABC, CBS, and NBC, see Auletta, *Three Blind Mice*. On Murdoch's Metromedia and Fox moves and on the buyouts of publishers, see William Shawcross, *Murdoch* (New York: Simon & Schuster, 1993), 241–48, 291; and see Maier, *Newhouse*, chap. 8. On Murdoch's control of the popular press in Britain: Ralph Negrine, *Politics and the Mass Media in Britain*, 2d ed. (London: Routledge, 1994), 62. On Westinghouse-CBS merger and Tisch profits: Associated Press, "CBS Accepts Westinghouse's $5.4 Billion Offer," *Star Tribune* of the Twin Cities, 2 August 1995, 1D.

5. On the Chancellor Media–Capstar radio chain figures: "Radio's New Order: Top 25 Radio Groups," *Broadcasting & Cable*, 23 June 1997, 26–28; Associated Press, "Foes Reed Elsevier, Wolters Kluwer Merge," *Star Tribune* of the Twin Cities, 14 October 1997, D1. "Dow Jones, NBC Join TV Forces," *Editor & Publisher*, 13 December 1997, 11.

6. Allan Sloan, "Landmark Legislation Ushering in the Old World of

Telecommunications," *Washington Post*, 3 June 1997, C3. Time executive quote: Shawcross, *Murdoch*, 354. Aulettta, *Three Blind Mice*, 86. Grossman quote: Warren K. Agee, Phillip H. Ault, and Edwin Emery, *Introduction to Mass Communications*, 11th ed. (New York: HarperCollins, 1994), 64. Murdoch quote: Shawcross, *Murdoch*, 231. Richard McCord, *The Chain Gang: One Newspaper versus the Gannett Empire* (Columbia: University of Missouri Press, 1996), 52, 142–43, 88–89, respectively. "TCI: Stick It to Customers and Blame Washington," *Grand Forks* (N.D.) *Herald*, 16 November 1993.

   7.   Auletta, *Three Blind Mice*, 327, and 226; revenue data on 78–79. Also see Dennis Mazzocco, *Networks of Power: Corporate TV's Threat to Democracy* (Boston: South End Press, 1994).

   8.   A. J. Liebling, *The Press* (New York: Pantheon, 1981).

Chapter 2

   1.   Robert A. Dahl, *Democracy and Its Critics* (New Haven, Conn.: Yale University Press, 1989), 109–12; Robert A. Dahl, *A Preface to Democratic Theory* (Chicago: University of Chicago Press, 1956), 3. Justice Black quote: cited in Donald M. Gillmor et al., *Mass Communications Law: Cases and Comment*, 5th ed. (St. Paul, Minn.: West Publishing, 1990), 546. Florida Supreme Court: cited in Lucas Powe Jr., *The Fourth Estate and the Constitution: Freedom of the Press in America* (Berkeley and Los Angeles: University of California Press, 1991), 269. E. E. Schattschneider, *The Semisovereign People* (New York: Holt, Rinehart & Winston, 1960), 3, 16–17.

   2.   Mann quoted in Michael J. Sandel, *Democracy's Discontent: America in Search of a Public Philosophy* (Cambridge: Harvard University Press, Belknap Press, 1995), 165. G. Gerbner, "Mass Media and Human Communication Theory," in *Sociology of Mass Communications*, ed. Denis McQuail (Harmondsworth, England: Penguin Books, 1972), 37–38. Plato quoted in Jean Bethke Elshtain, *Democracy on Trial* (New York: Basic Books, 1995), 99–100. Benjamin Barber, *Strong Democracy* (Berkeley and Los Angeles: University of California Press, 1984), 4. Other theorists: Sandel, *Democracy's Discontent*; Elshtain, *Democracy on Trial*; John Dewey, *The Public and Its Problems* (1927; repr. Denver, Colo.: Alan Swallow, 1954). John Keane, *The Media and Democracy* (Cambridge, England: Polity Press, 1991), 82–90, quote on 84.

   3.   Barber quote: Benjamin Barber, "The Tides in New Channels," *New York Times*, 24 June 1984, A27. On the movement among conservatives and liberals with respect to capitalism and values, see, e.g., Paul Starobin, "Rethinking Capitalism," *National Journal*, 18 January 1997, 106–9; see also Robert Kuttner, *Everything for Sale* (New York: Alfred A. Knopf, 1997).

   4.   Dean Alger, *The Media and Politics*, 2d ed. (Fort Worth, Texas: Harcourt Brace College Publishing, 1996), chap. 4; Neil Postman, *Amusing Ourselves to Death: Public Discourse in the Age of Show Business* (New York: Elisabeth Sifton Books/Penguin, 1985); George Comstock et al., *Television and Human Behavior* (New York: Columbia University Press, 1978), 10, 49–51, 70. Robert Putnam, "Tuning In, Tuning Out: The Strange Disappearance of Social Capital in America," *PS: Political Science & Politics* 28, no. 4 (December 1995): 664–83 (quotes from 664–65).

Dewey, *The Public and Its Problems*, 142. Elshtain, *Democracy on Trial*, 88. Pres. Roosevelt discussed and quoted in Sandel, *Democracy's Discontent*, 255–56.

Chapter 3

1. Edwin Emery and Michael Emery, *The Press and America*, 4th ed. (Englewood Cliffs, N.J.: Prentice Hall, 1978), 431 and passim. Emery and Emery, *The Press and America*, 221–24; W. A. Swanberg, *Pulitzer* (New York: Charles Scribner's Sons, 1967). W. A. Swanberg, *Citizen Hearst* (New York: Charles Scribner's Sons, 1961). On Scripps and other people's-champion owner-editors, see Emery and Emery, *The Press and America*, 266–70. William Allen White, *The Autobiography of William Allen White* (New York: Macmillan, 1964), 629. See also Sally Foreman Griffith, *Home Town News: William Allen White and the* Emporia Gazette (Baltimore, Md.: Johns Hopkins University Press, 1989).

2. Emery and Emery, *The Press and America*, 430. George Garneau, "Biggest Deal Yet," *Editor & Publisher*, 12 April 1997, 17; Newspaper Association of America, *Facts about Newspapers, '97*, Vienna, Va., 22.

3. Ben Bagdikian, *The Media Monopoly*, 1st and 5th eds. (Boston: Beacon Press, 1983, 1997), xiii (5th ed.).

4. Robert Horwitz, *The Irony of Regulatory Reform: The Deregulation of American Telecommunications* (New York: Oxford University Press, 1989), 113–21. Horwitz, *Irony of Regulatory Reform*, 169. Denis Mazzocco, *Networks of Power: Corporate TV's Threat to Democracy* (Boston: South End Press, 1994), 33.

5. Ken Auletta, *Three Blind Mice: How the TV Networks Lost Their Way* (New York: Random House, 1991), 33, and 36, 210, 291, respectively. Eisner salary package: Molly Ivins, "While CEO's Get Richer, the Workers Get Zapped," *Star Tribune* of the Twin Cities, 3 May 1994, 13A.

6. Information sources: Disney corporate Annual Report to Securities and Exchange Commission (Form 10-K) for fiscal year ending 30 September 1996; 1996 *Directory of Corporate Affiliations of U.S. Public Companies*, vol. 3, *U.S. Public Companies* (New Providence, N.J.: National Register Publishing, 1996), 527–31; "A Mighty Bucks Merger," *Star Tribune* of the Twin Cities, 1 August 1995, 1A; Edward S. Herman and Robert C. McChesney, *The Global Media* (London: Cassell, 1997), 81–83. Synergy statement: Disney Annual 10-K report to SEC; Disney Company Snapshot, 1998 Fortune 500, *Fortune* Web site, cgi.pathfinder.com/cgi-bin/fortune/fortune500/csnap.cgi?r96=51, downloaded 8 April 1998.

7. *Time* history: Emery and Emery, *The Press and America*, 383–84; and David Halberstam, *The Powers That Be* (New York: Alfred A. Knopf, 1979).

8. Porter Bibb, *It Ain't as Easy As It Looks: Ted Turner's Amazing Story* (New York: Crown Books, 1993), 73. Bibb, *Ted Turner's Amazing Story*, chaps. 4, 5, 7, 8; quote on 172. Bibb, *Ted Turner's Amazing Story*, chaps. 10–15; profit figure and global coverage on 342; Tinker quote on 394. Bibb, *Ted Turner's Amazing Story*, Malone quote on 318; Turner quote on 288. Turner wealth: "The Global Power Elite," *Forbes*, 28 July 1997, 135. "FTC Staff Raises Anti-Trust Concerns in Merger of Time Warner and Turner," *Star Tribune* of the Twin Cities, " 8 May 1996, D3.

9. Sources for material on Time Warner–Turner holdings: Lester Bernstein, "Time Inc. Means Business," *New York Times Magazine*, 26 February 1989; "Time Warner, Turner to Merge," *Star Tribune* of the Twin Cities, 23 September 1995, A1; "It's Time for Time Warner, Turner," *Star Tribune* of the Twin Cities, 23 September 1995, D1–D2; Walter Isaacson, "To Our Readers," *Time*, 21 October 1996, 20; "Cable Television's Top 10 MSO's," *Broadcasting & Cable*, 9 December 1996, 79; Alison Alexander, James Owers, and Rod Carveth, *Media Economics: Theory and Practice* (Hillsdale, N.J.: Lawrence Earlbaum, 1993), 66; Time Warner Company Snapshot, 1998 Fortune 500, *Fortune* Web site, cgi.pathfinder.com/cgi-bin/fortune/fortune500/csnap.cgi?r96=110&dep=113, downloaded 8 April 1998. Associated Press, "U.S. Reaches Pact to Allow Time-Turner Media Merger," *Star Tribune* of the Twin Cities, 18 July 1996, D1, D4; "Time Warner Purchase of Turner Broadcasting Approved 3-2 by FTC," *Star Tribune* of the Twin Cities, 13 September 1996, D1, D6; Herman and McChesney, *Global Media*, 78.

10. William Shawcross, *Murdoch* (New York: Simon & Schuster, 1992), 40–51; PBS *Frontline* show "Who's Afraid of Rupert Murdoch?" aired fall 1995. Shawcross, *Murdoch*, 68–72, quote on 68; *Frontline*, "Who's Afraid of Rupert Murdoch?" Shawcross, *Murdoch*, 240–52, quotes on 250, 248, respectively. William Shawcross, *Murdoch*, rev. ed. (New York: Simon & Schuster, 1997), 398–99.

11. Shawcross, *Murdoch* and *Murdoch*, rev. ed.; "News Corp's New Media World," *Broadcasting & Cable*, 22 July 1996, 7; Michael Meyer, "Rupert's New Road to the Internet," *Newsweek*, 22 May 1995, 62–63; "Murdoch Making Another Satellite TV Deal," *Star Tribune* of the Twin Cities, 28 May 1997, D1; Geraldine Fabrikant, "Murdoch Will Buy Cable Empire from Robertson for $1.98 Billion," *New York Times*, 12 June 1997, A1, C4; Seth Schiessel, "With a Sale, Murdoch Will End Direct-Broadcast Bid," *New York Times*, 12 June 1997, C4; John Lippman and Mark Rubichaux, "News Corp. Gains Entry to Cable Market," *Wall Street Journal*, 12 June 1997, A3; Associated Press, "Murdoch, TCI, Cablevision Teaming Up to Take On Top-Ranked ESPN on Cable," *Star Tribune* of the Twin Cities, 24 June 1997, D3; Johnnie L. Roberts, "Rupert's Team," *Newsweek*, 7 July 1997, 48–49. Murdoch wealth: "The Global Power Elite," *Forbes*, 28 July 1997, 103; Herman and McChesney, *Global Media*, 71–73.

12. Jeremy Tunstall and Michael Palmer, eds., *Media Moguls* (New York: Routledge, 1991), 192–94; Mary Williams Walsh, "Silent Giant: Few Are Untouched by Germany's Bertelsmann," *Los Angeles Times*, 19 November 1995, D1; Eric Hansen, "Debutant CLT-Ufa Aims High," *Hollywood Reporter*, 14 January 1997, from Internet; Patrick M. Reilly and Greg Steinmetz, "Bertelsmann to Buy Random House," *Wall Street Journal*, 24 March 1998, B1, B8; Jeff Giles and Ray Sawhill, "A Brand-New Chapter," *Newsweek*, 6 April 1998, 39.

13. Tunstall and Palmer, *Media Moguls*, 193–95; Walsh, "Silent Giant"; Herman and McChesney, *Global Media*, 87–88.

14. *Encyclopaedia Britannica*, 1976 ed., s.v. "Sarnoff, David." See also Reuven Frank, *Out of Thin Air: The Brief, Wonderful Life of Network News* (New York: Simon & Schuster, 1991); Frank, *Out of Thin Air*, quotes from 307–8, 362. Ken Auletta, *Three Blind Mice*, esp. 346, 410, 79. Welch compensation: Alan Sloan, "Reading the Fine Print," "Addendum," *Newsweek*, 24 March 1997, 90; General Electric Company Snapshot, 1998 Fortune 500, *Fortune* Web site, cgi.pathfinder.com/cgi-bin/for-

tune/fortune500/csnap.cgi?r96=5&dep=113, downloaded 8 April 1998.

15. "Fortune 500: America's Largest Corporations," *Fortune*, 28 April 1997, F1. Holdings information from General Electric corporate Annual Report to the Securities and Exchange Commission (Form 10-K) and from *1996 Directory of Corporate Affiliations*, vol. 5, *International Public and Private Companies* (New Providence, N.J.: National Register Publishing, 1996), 930–32; Herman and McChesney, *Global Media*, 94. NBC Europe: Erik Barnouw et al., *Conglomerates and the Media* (New York: New Press, 1997), 142.

16. See Halberstam, *The Powers That Be*; and Sally Bedell Smith, *In All His Glory: The Life and Times of William S. Paley* (New York: Simon & Schuster, 1990). Halberstam, *The Powers That Be*, quote on 38–39; Smith, *In All His Glory*. Kalb quote: Interview with the author, 30 July 1993. Auletta, *Three Blind Mice*; budget figures on 331, quotes from 249–53; Auletta, *Three Blind Mice*, 278–79. Associated Press, "CBS Accepts Westinghouse's $5.4 Billion Offer; Tisch Stands to Make $900 Million in Buyout," *Star Tribune* of the Twin Cities, 2 August 1995, 1D. "Federal Regulator Ready to OK $5.4 Billion CBS-Westinghouse Deal," *Fargo (N.D.) Forum*, 18 November 1995, D7; "Westinghouse Is Selling Its Defense Unit," *Star Tribune* of the Twin Cities, 4 January 1996, D1; "Westinghouse Splitting into Two," *Star Tribune* of the Twin Cities, 14 November 1996, D1, D2. "Radio Reordered: The Top 25 Radio Groups," *Broadcasting & Cable*, 1 July 1996, 25; "CBS Owner Westinghouse to Buy Infinity Broadcasting," *Star Tribune* of the Twin Cities, 21 June 1996, D1, D2; "FCC Clears Westinghouse Merger with Infinity," *Star Tribune* of the Twin Cities, 27 December 1996, D1, D8; "Radio's New Order: The Top 25 Radio Groups," *Broadcasting & Cable*, 23 June 1997, 26–28.

17. Sources: Westinghouse corporate Annual Report to the Securities and Exchange Commission (Form 10-K); *1996 Directory of Corporate Affiliations*, vol. 3, *U.S. Public Companies*, 1813–16; Herman and McChesney, *Global Media*, 96–97; CBS Company Snapshot, 1998 Fortune 500, *Fortune* Web site, cgi.pathfinder.com/cgi-bin/fortune/fortune500/csnap.cgi?r96=159&dep=113, dowloaded 8 April 1998.

18. Thomas Maier, *Newhouse* (New York: St. Martin's Press, 1994), 14. Maier, *Newhouse*, 18–25, quotes on 22, 25. Maier, *Newhouse*, esp. chap. 7, quotes on 352, 346, respectively. Newhouse brothers' wealth: "The Global Power Elite," 134.

19. Sources: Maier, *Newhouse*; *1997 Directory of Corporate Affiliations*, vol. 4, *U.S. Private Companies* (New Providence, N.J.: National Register Publishing, 1997), 19–21; Geraldine Fabrikant, "Time Warner and Newhouse Form a Joint Cable Operation," *New York Times*, 13 September 1994, D1; Geoffrey Foisie, "Time Warner Entertainment: A Big MSO Gets Bigger," *Broadcasting & Cable*, 19 September 1994, 12.

20. Associated Press, "11 Days before Deadline, Viacom Says It Will Buy Half of UPN for $160 Million," *Star Tribune* of the Twin Cities, 5 December 1996, D3; Viacom corporate Annual Report to the Security and Exchange Commission for 1996 (Form 10-K); Associated Press, "Viacom Is Selling Lion's Share of Simon & Schuster," *Star Tribune* of the Twin Cities, 15 January 1998, D2; "The Global Power Elite," 135; "Viacom Shareholders Blame Troubles on Redstone," *Star Tribune* of the Twin Cities, 30 May 1997, D2; Herman and McChesney, *Global Media*, 85–87; Herman and McChesney, *Global Media*, 85–87; Kevin Maney, *Megamedia Shakeout* (New York: John Wiley & Sons, 1995); Geraldine Fabrikant, "Simon &

Schuster in Sale to British," *New York Times,* 18 May 1998, A1, A16; Viacom Company Snapshot, 1998 Fortune 500, Fortune Web site, cgi.pathfinder.com/cgi-bin/fortune/fortune500/csnap.cgi?r96=103, downloaded 8 April 1998.

21. All sources in n. 20; Maney, *Megamedia Shakeout.*

22. John Higgins and Richard Tedesco, "PC/TV à la Bill Gates," *Broadcasting & Cable,* 16 June 1997, 7; "Microsoft Plans Deal with Cable Provider," *Star Tribune* of the Twin Cities, 10 June 1997, D1, D8; On Microsoft investment in Apple Computer: Steven Levy, "A Big Brother," *Newsweek,* 18 August 1997, 22–29; and on the antitrust insurance factor: Allan Sloan, "Bill Does What Is Good for Bill," *Newsweek,* 18 August 1997, 31. Steven Levy, "Microsoft Century," *Newsweek,* 2 December 1996, 57. Gates's wealth: Steven Levy, "Microsoft vs. the World," *Newsweek,* 9 March 1998, 40; Microsoft Company Snapshot, 1998 Fortune 500, *Fortune* Web site, cgi.pathfinder.com/cgi-bin/fortune/fortune500/csnap.cgi?r96=137, downloaded 8 April 1998.

23. Microsoft Company Snapshot; Higgins and Tedesco, "PC/TV"; Microsoft corporate Annual Report to the Securities and Exchange Commission (Form 10-K); *1997 Directory of Corporate Affiliations,* vol. 3, *U.S. Public Companies* (New Providence, N.J.: National Register Publishing, 1997), 1159–60.

24. Michael Palmer and Claude Sorbets, "France," in *The Media in Western Europe,* Euromedia Research Group (Newbury Park, Calif.: Sage Publications, 1992), 65; Tunstall and Palmer, *Media Moguls,* 137–39, 151–59.

25. Palmer and Sorbets, "France," 65; Tunstall and Palmer, *Media Moguls,* 137–39, 151–59; Keith J. Kelly, "Hachette Buying Spree Steams On," *Advertising Age,* 25 March 1996, 1, 46; *Business Week,* "Can *George* Cross An Ocean?: JFK Jr.'s New Toy Could Be the Next Magazine Hachette Clones," *Business Week,* 30 October 1995, 56; "Cautious Attitude Belies New Media Expertise of Franco-American Group," *New Media Age,* 8 February 1996, 13–14; Richard Cook, "French Media Empire Relies on Alliance of Odd Elements," *Campaign,* 40; Remi Bouton, "French Merger Is First Test for Media Ownership Laws; Hachette Will Merge with Filipacchi Medias," *Music & Media,* 10 May 1997, 3; *1997 Directory of Corporate Affiliations,* vol. 4, *International Public and Private Companies,* 795–99.

26. Ben Bagdikian, *The Media Monopoly,* 4th ed. (Boston: Beacon Press, 1992), chap. 4; Richard McCord, *The Chain Gang: One Newspaper versus the Gannett Empire* (Columbia: University of Missouri Press, 1996); James D. Squires, *Read All about It: The Corporate Takeover of America's Newspapers* (New York: Times Books, 1994), quote on 17–18; also 52–57.

27. Squires, *Read All about It;* Gannett corporate 1996 Annual Report to Securities and Exchange Commission (Form 10-K).

28. *TCI Profile,* report published by TCI, May 1993; "Cable Television's Top 10 MSOs," *Broadcasting & Cable,* 9 December 1996, 79; "Cable's Top 25 MSOs," *Broadcasting & Cable,* 16 June 1997, 36; "A Star War with 'Darth Vader'; Taking Aim at the Cable King," *Newsweek,* 4 October 1993, 89; Tele-Communications Company Snapshot, 1998 Fortune 500, *Fortune* Web site, cgi.pathfinder.com/cgi-bin/fortune/fortune500/csnap.cgi?r96=203, downloaded 8 April 1998.

29. "Star War," 89; Jolie Solomon, "Big Brother's Holding Company," *Newsweek,* 25 October 1993, 38–45; John M. Higgins, "TCI/Cablevision Numbers Puzzle Wall Street," *Broadcasting & Cable,* 16 June 1997, 54; *1997 Directory of Cor-*

porate Affiliations, vol. 3, *U.S. Public Companies*, 1651. Newspaper buy: Mark Fitzgerald, "Another Year Defying the Odds," *Editor & Publisher*, 3 January 1998, 9. International ventures: Herman and McChesney, *Global Media*, 71, 73–74, 89–91, 126.

30. Gianpietro Mazzoleni, "Media Moguls in Italy," in *Media Moguls*, ed. Tunstall and Palmer, esp. 166–73; Gianpietro Mazzoleni, "Italy," in *The Media in Western Europe*, Euromedia Research Group (Newbury Park, Calif.: Sage Publications, 1992), chap. 9; Richard Cook, "If Berlusconi Gets into Power, Can Fininvest Stay at the Top? " *Campaign*, 6 June 1997, 26. Personal wealth: "The Global Power Elite," 142.

31. "Cox Enterprises, Inc.," *International Directory of Company Histories* (Chicago: St. James Press, 1991), 595–97; "Cable's Top 25 MSOs," 37; Marc Rice, "Cox and Times Mirror Forming Giant Cable System," *Star Tribune* of the Twin Cities, 7 June 1994, 1D.

32. Tunstall and Palmer, *Media Moguls*, 136–53; quotes on 141, 144, respectively); Palmer and Sorbets, "France," 60–65.

33. Harrison E. Salisbury, *Without Fear or Favor: An Uncompromising Look at the* New York Times (New York: Times Books, 1980); Nicholas Coleridge, *Paper Tigers: The Latest, Greatest Newspaper Tycoons* (New York: Birch Lane Press, 1993), chap. 2; *1996 Directory of Corporate Affiliations* (New Providence, N.J.: National Register Publishing, 1996).

34. Maney, *Megamedia Shakeout*, esp. 324–28.

35. Halberstam, *The Powers That Be*; Coleridge, *Paper Tigers*, chap. 6; *1996 Directory of Corporate Affiliations*, 1690–92.

36. Emery and Emery, *The Press and America*, 159–60, 364–68, 488–90; Squires, *Read All about It!*; *1997 Directory of Corporate Affiliations*, 1691–92; Tribune Co. 1996 corporate Annual Report to the Securities and Exchange Commission (Form 10-K).

37. Halberstam, *The Powers That Be*; Coleridge, *Paper Tigers*, chap. 3; Washington Post Co., 1996 corporate Annual Report to the Securities and Exchange Commission (Form 10-K).

38. Herman and McChesney, *Global Media*, 91–98.

39. "FCC OKs US West Deal for Continental Cable," *Star Tribune* of the Twin Cities, 19 October 1996, D3; Dave Beal, "US West's New Line," *St. Paul Pioneer Press*, 12 August 1996, 1E; Jonathan Gaw, "US West to Be Split into Two Companies," *Star Tribune* of the Twin Cities, 28 October 1997, D1; Steve Alexander, "US West Doesn't Have to Sell Its Cable Operations," *Star Tribune* of the Twin Cities, 27 February 1998, D1, D2; Patrick Kennedy, "US West Offers New Internet Service, Local Information via USWest.net," *Star Tribune* of the Twin Cities, 26 February 1998, D3; Robert Frank and Matthew Rose, "A Massive Investment in British Cable TV Sours for U.S. Firms," *Wall Street Journal*, 17 December 1997, A1;

40. "British Telecom to Buy Out MCI in Largest-Ever Foreign Takeover," *Star Tribune* of the Twin Cities, 3 November 1996, A5; "MCI Accepts WorldCom's $37 Billion Takeover Bid," *Star Tribune* of the Twin Cities, 11 November 1997, D1; Michael Meyer, "Telecom: They Might Be Giants," *Newsweek*, 22 September 1997, 52.

41. "Baby Bell Merger Plan Assailed," *Star Tribune* of the Twin Cities, 23

April 1996, D1, D7; Brian Steinberg, "A New Bell Atlantic to Emerge," *Star Tribune* of the Twin Cities, 16 August 1997, D1; "Merger of Two Baby Bells OK'd," *Star Tribune* of the Twin Cities, 25 April 1997, D1, D4; Michael Hirsh, "But Nary a Trust to Bust," *Newsweek*, 2 June 1997, 44–45; Kirk Victor, "Reach Out and Crush Someone?" *National Journal*, 7 June 1997, 1132–33; Price Colman, "Ameritech Stays Its Wired Course," *Broadcasting & Cable*, 30 June 1997, 72; JMH, "SBC to Scrap Most Video Operations," *Broadcasting & Cable*, 23 June 1997, 11; "SBC Rings Up $56.6 Billion Deal for Ameritech," *Star Tribune* of the Twin Cities, 12 May 1998, D1, D2.

42.   Graeme Browning, "Busy Signal," *National Journal*, 2 August 1997, esp. 1553; John J. Kelley, "AT&T and SBC Are Holding Talks to Merge in Transaction Valued at More than $50 Billion," *Wall Street Journal*, 27 May 1997, A3, A13; Browning, "Busy Signal"; Kelley, "AT&T and SBC Holding Talks"; "AT&T-Unisource Enters Bid for French Network," *Star Tribune* of the Twin Cities, 6 November 1996, D3.

43.   John Dempsey, "Cable Ops Caught in the Nets," *Variety*, 17–23 February 1997, 1; Bagdikian, *Media Monopoly*, 4th ed., ix, 23; David Croteau and William Hoynes, *Media/Society* (Thousand Oaks, Calif.: Sage, 1997), 296; Herman and McChesney, *Global Media*, 20, 43.

Chapter 4

1.   Thomas G. Krattenmaker, "The Telecommunications Act of 1996," *Indiana University Law Journal* 49, no. 1.

2.   Quotes and political money data from: Jim Naureckis, "Info-Bandits," *In These Times*, 4 March 1996, 14–16; J. H. Snider and Benjamin I. Page, "The Political Power of TV Broadcasters: Covert Bias and Anticipated Reactions" (paper presented at the 1997 Annual Meeting of the American Political Science Association, Washington, D.C., 28–31 August), esp. 4–6. Naureckis, "Info-Bandits," 15. "CBS Owner Westinghouse to Buy Infinity Broadcasting," *Star Tribune* of the Twin Cities, 21 June 1997, D2; Westinghouse 1996 corporate Annual Report to the Securities and Exchange Commission (Form 10-K); *Broadcasting & Cable*, cover of 31 July 1995 issue. William Safire, "Media Giants Orchestrate Major Ripoff," *Fargo (N.D.) Forum*, 8 January 1996, A4; William Safire, "Broadcasters Strangely Silent on Digital Spectrum Heist," *Star Tribune* of the Twin Cities, 24 July 1997, A25. Dole letter: Snider and Page, "Political Power of TV Broadcasters," 25. McCain quote: Kirk Victor, "Here's a Train That Roared by Quietly," *National Journal*, 10 February 1996, 316.

3.   Michael I. Meyerson, "Ideas of the Marketplace: A Guide to the 1996 Telecommunications Act," *Indiana University Law Journal* 49, no. 2: 252.

4.   "AT&T Shying Away from Local Service," *Star Tribune* of the Twin Cities, 20 December 1997, D1. US West: "US West International Will Enter Dutch Market with Phone Joint Venture," *Star Tribune* of the Twin Cities, 1 July 1997, D3; "US West Media May Bid for Ailing Telewest, Accounts Say," *Star Tribune* of the Twin Cities, 9 December 1997, D1; "Consumer Coalition Claims US West Is

Attempting to Block Competition," *Star Tribune* of the Twin Cities, 29 May 1997, D3.

5. Safire, "Media Giants Orchestrate Ripoff." Radio concentration compiled from data in "Radio's New Order: Top 25 Radio Groups," *Broadcasting & Cable*, 23 June 1997, 27–28.

6. "Opened the door . . .": Warren K. Agee, Phillip H. Ault, and Edwin Emery, *Introduction to Mass Communications*, 11th ed. (New York: HarperCollins, 1994), 72.

7. Meyerson, "Ideas of the Marketplace," sec. 3.B. McCain quote from U.S. Senate Commerce Committee Hearing on Competition in the Cable TV Industry, 10 April 1997 (taped and transcribed from C-SPAN).

8. Meyerson, "Ideas of the Marketplace," sec. 3.A.

9. Jonathan Gaw, "US West to Be Split into Two Companies," *Star Tribune* of the Twin Cities, 28 October 1997, D1; JMH, "SBC to Scrap Most Video Operations," *Broadcasting & Cable*, 23 June 1997, 11; Jonathan Gaw, "US West's Move a Setback for Telecom Convergence," *Star Tribune* of the Twin Cities, 29 October 1997, D1.

10. Snider and Page, "Political Power of TV Broadcasters," quote on 13. Safire, "Broadcasters Strangely Silent," A25. Snider and Page, "Political Power of TV Broadcasters," quote on 11; Martin Gilens and Craig Hertzman, "Corporate Ownership and News Bias: Newspaper Coverage of the 1996 Telecommunications Act" (paper presented at the 1997 Annual Meeting of the American Political Science Association, Washington, D.C., 28–31 August), esp. 7–8.

11. Snider and Page, "Political Power of TV Broadcasters," 11.

12. Krattenmaker, "Telecommunications Act of 1996," sec. 6, "Evaluation." Denis McQuail, *Media Performance: Mass Communication and the Public Interest* (London: Sage, 1992), 103, 70, respectively.

Chapter 5

1. Michael I. Meyerson, "Ideas of the Marketplace: A Guide to the 1996 Telecommunications Act," *Indiana University Law Journal* 49, no. 2, introduction. All quotes: Paul A. Samuelson and William D. Nordhaus, *Economics*, 12th ed. (New York: McGraw-Hill, 1985), 46, 70, 522, respectively. John Kenneth Galbraith, *The New Industrial State*, 2d ed. (Boston: Houghton Mifflin, 1971), esp. chap. 18; Samuelson and Nordhaus, *Economics*, 532–33.

2. Donald M. Gillmor et al., *Mass Communications Law: Cases and Comment*, 5th ed. (St. Paul, Minn.: West Publishing, 1990), quotes on 542, 551–52, 547, respectively. On concentration in American economy in the late twentieth century, see Thomas R. Dye and Harmon Zeigler, *The Irony of Democracy*, 10th ed. (Belmont, Calif.: Wadsworth, 1996), chap. 4. Michael Hirsh, "But Nary a Trust to Bust," *Newsweek*, 2 June 1997, 44–45; Lucas A. Powe Jr., *The Fourth Estate and the Constitution* (Berkeley and Los Angeles: University of California Press, 1991), 220–21; Robert Kuttner, *Everything for Sale: The Virtues and Limits of Markets* (New York: Alfred A. Knopf, 1997), 278; Robert Pitofsky, "Antitrust in the Decade

Ahead: Some Predictions about Merger Enforcement," *Antitrust Law Journal* 57, no. 1 (January 1988): 65–73; Bryan Gruley, "Pitofsky Will Test Marketplace of Ideas Theory in FTC's Review of Time Warner–Turner Deal," *Wall Street Journal*, 9 October 1995, A14; FCC document from which quote is taken is a background paper on radio station ownership issues and radio "community contours" (undated and untitled, given to the author by an FCC official).

3.   Kalven quoted in Powe, *Fourth Estate*, 79; "Administration Urges FCC Not to Alter Local TV Rule," *Star Tribune* of the Twin Cities, 29 May 1997, A14.

4.   Quote sources: Porter Bibb, *It Ain't as Easy As It Looks: Ted Turner's Amazing Story* (New York: Crown Books, 1993), 288; Dorgan quote: Kirk Victor, "Media Monsters," *National Journal*, 2 March 1996, 484; Rode quote: Wendy Zellner, "A License to Print Money?" *Business Week*, 30 June 1997, 441.

5.   Concentration in local radio markets: compiled from data in "Radio's New Order: Top 25 Radio Groups," *Broadcasting & Cable*, 23 June 1997, 26–37; on Disney-ABC radio stations in Los Angeles: *PBS News Hour* segment "Media Mergers," aired 9 April 1997; cable concentration quote: "Out of the Many, Few," *Broadcasting & Cable*, 16 June 1997, 86; FCC waivers for Westinghouse-CBS: "FCC Clears Westinghouse Merger with Infinity," *Star Tribune* of the Twin Cities, 27 December 1996, D1; Representative Tauzin comment: Kirk Victor, "Sending Mixed Signals on Cable TV," *National Journal*, 4 October 1997, 1962–63.

6.   Alan B. Albarran and John Dimmick, "Concentration and Economies of Multiformity in the Communications Industries," *Journal of Media Economics* 9, no. 4 (Winter 1996): 46.

7.   "1993 Station Sales," *Broadcasting & Cable Yearbook 1994*, vol. 1 (New Providence, N.J.: R. R. Bowker), A-90; "The Big Deals Club" (Special Report), *Broadcasting & Cable*, 2 February 1998, 40; Changing Hands, *Broadcasting & Cable*, 5 January 1998, 37; Changing Hands, *Broadcasting & Cable*, 16 June 1997, 33; George Garneau, "Biggest Deal Yet," *Editor & Publisher*, 12 April 1997, 17; "Radio/TV Ownership: Telecommunications Act of 1996 Spurs Consolidation," *Broadcasting & Cable*, 9 April 1997, 43; Zellner, "A License to Print Money?" 41; George Garneau, "Chain Eats Chain," *Editor & Publisher*, 24 May 1997, 7; Renaissance Communications chairman quote: Douglas Gomery, "In TV, the Big Get Bigger," *American Journalism Review*, October 1996, 64.

8.   "Infinity Buyout Creates Radio Behemoth," *Electronic Media*, 24 June 1996, 42; Chuck Ross, "Justice Department Is Asking about CBS Radio Ad Rates," *Advertising Age*, 16 June 1997, 2; Mark Landler, "Westinghouse to Acquire 98 Radio Stations," *New York Times*, 20 September 1997, D1, D4; "CBS' Eye Looms Larger with ARS Deal," *MediaWeek*, 6 October 1997, 20; Thomas G. Krattenmaker, "The Telecommunications Act of 1996," *Indiana University Law Journal* 49, no. 1, "Measuring Competition" section; Richard Turner, "An Ear for the CBS Eye," *Newsweek*, 16 December 1996, 59.

9.   Kuttner, *Everything for Sale*, 246–49, 251.

10.   Krattenmaker, "Telecommunications Act," sec. 6, "Evaluation."

11.   Shales quoted in PBS *Frontline* program "Who's Afraid of Rupert Murdoch?" aired fall 1995. On Fox News: Neil Hickey, "Is Fox News Fair? " *Columbia Journalism Review*, March/April 1998, 31–33. Satellite information: Terry Fiedler,

"USSB to Drop Lifetime, Six Other Channels in Favor of More Movies, Pay TV," *Star Tribune* of the Twin Cities, 7 January 1998, D1, D5; James Derk, "New 18-inch Satellite Dishes Provide Competition for Cable," *Star Tribune* of the Twin Cities, 2 March 1997, D5; Kathryn Harris, "Falling Stars: Wall Street Has Soured on Direct-Satellite Stocks, and a Shakeout Is About to Begin," *Fortune*, 27 March 1997, 127–28.

12.   Newspaper chain concentration calculated from "Top Twelve Titans" listing in chap. 3; Thomson and Hollinger Canadian concentration: Edward Herman and Robert W. McChesney, *The Global Media* (London: Cassell, 1997), 95; Tim Jones, "That Old Black Magic," *Columbia Journalism Review*, March/April 1998, 40.

13.   Two examples of past ad rate studies: William Blankenburg, "A Newspaper Chain's Pricing Behavior," *Journalism Quarterly* 60, no. 2 (1983): 275–80; John C. Busterna, "Price Discrimination as Evidence of Newspaper Chain Market Power," *Journalism Quarterly* 68, nos. 1/2 (Spring/Summer 1991): 5–14, quotes on 5, 12. Richard McCord, *The Chain Gang: One Newspaper versus the Gannett Empire* (Columbia: University of Missouri Press, 1996), 170–71. McCord, *Chain Gang*, 21–22, 142, 251 (quoting from *Willamet Week*), 30, 68, 66, 22, respectively.

14.   Thomas Maier, *Newhouse* (New York: St. Martin's Press, 1994), 118–19. 132, 132–39, respectively.

15.   On book publishers, holdings, etc.: John Marks, "Publish and Don't Perish," *US News & World Report*, 12 January 1998, 38–40; Mark Crispin Miller, "The Publishing Industry," in *Conglomerates and the Media*, by Erik Barnouw et al. (New York: New Press, 1997); Ken Auletta, "The Impossible Business," *New Yorker*, 6 October 1997, 50–63; Herman and McChesney, *Global Media*, 43, chap. 3; Hearst entry in *1997 Directory of Corporate Affiliations*, vol. 4, *U.S. Private Companies* (New Providence, N.J.: National Register, 1997), 519–22; *1997 Directory of Corporate Affiliations*, vol. 5, *International Public and Private Companies* (New Providence, N.J.: National Register, 1997), 1476–79; Patrick M. Reilly and Greg Steinmetz, "Bertelsmann to Buy Random House," *Wall Street Journal*, 24 March 1998, B10; "German Firm Agrees to Buy Random House," *Star Tribune* of the Twin Cities, 24 March 1998, D1; Jeff Giles and Ray Sawhill, "A Brand-New Chapter," *Newsweek*, 6 April 1989, 39; bookstore material: Jeff Guinn, "Literary Lions: An Endangered Species," *Star Tribune* of the Twin Cities, 14 April 1997, E7; and Michael Skube, "Publishing or Packaging? It's Getting Harder to Tell," *Star Tribune* of the Twin Cities, 15 September 1997, E5; "Barnes & Noble, Microsoft Sign Deal," *Star Tribune* of the Twin Cities, 7 October 1997, D3. Barnes & Noble Internet-newspaper connections: David Noack, "E-Commerce and Online News," *mediainfor.com* from *Editor & Publisher*, November 1997, 19; Odegaard's: *PBS News Hour*, 20 August 1997; "Barnes & Noble, Borders Sued by Independents," *Star Tribune* of the Twin Cities, 19 March 1998, D1, D5; Doug Grow, "Bookstore Can't Buy an Ad, Let Alone a Break," *Star Tribune* of the Twin Cities, 17 June 1997, B2; $20 billion and book distributors: Miller, "The Publishing Industry," 107, 119.

16.   Associated Press, "America Online Exceeds 10 Million Subscribers," *Star Tribune* of the Twin Cities, 18 November 1997, D2; "Regulators Intensify Probe of MCI Merger," *Star Tribune* of the Twin Cities, 11 March 1998, D1. On Internet Explorer issue: *ABC World News Tonight* report aired on 30 September 1997 (with

acknowledgment of ABC's relationship with Netscape); Stephen Labaton, "Microsoft May Face Millions in Fines," *Star Tribune* of the Twin Cities, 21 October 1997, A1, A10; Associated Press, "Compaq Alleges Microsoft Threat over Browser Use," *Star Tribune* of the Twin Cities, 22 October 1997, D8. Senate hearing and Gates: "Gates Is Smart, Rich, and an Artful Dodger," Inside Washington, *National Journal*, 7 March 1998. Michael Hirsh, "The Feds' Case against Bill Gates," *Newsweek*, 9 March 1998, 43; William Powers, "Raising Caen," *New Republic*, 12 May 1997, 20, 22; research firm and Herman and McChesney quote: Herman and McChesney, *Global Media*, 124; Time Warner Web sites: Mark Landler, "From Gurus to Sitting Ducks: Media Executives Lose Their Edge," *New York Times*, 11 January 1998, sec. 3, p. 9; cable TV on-line material: "Time Warner, US West Media to Blend Online Cable Ventures," *Star Tribune* of the Twin Cities, 11 December 1997, D2; David Bank, "TCI Uses Hi-Tech 'Layer Cake' to Ward Off Microsoft," *Wall Street Journal*, 16 December 1997, B4; Nick Wingfield, "At Home and Unit of Time Warner Discuss Alliances," *Wall Street Journal*, 9 February 1998, B5; Michael Meyer, "It's a Windows World, after All," *Newsweek*, 26 January 1998, 45.

17.   Ozanich and Wirth cited in Albarran and Dimmick, "Concentration and Economics of Multiformity," 42; material on Brian Arthur and other economists: good summary in John Cassidy, "The Force of an Idea," *New Yorker*, 12 January 1998, 32–37 (most quotes from this source); another good summary, esp. on the QWERTY stimulus of the idea, is in Paul Krugman, *Peddling Prosperity* (New York: W. W. Norton, 1994), chap. 9; main source of Arthur's writings on this: Brian Arthur, *Increasing Returns and Path Dependence in the Economy* (Ann Arbor: University of Michigan Press, 1994), esp. preface, chaps. 1, 7, 9; other study mentioned: John Cubbin and Simon Domberger, "Advertising and Post-Entry Oligopoly Behavior," *Journal of Industrial Economics* 37, no. 2 (December 1988): 123–40.

18.   Hostetter: quote from "Cable Television's Top 10 MSO's," *Broadcasting & Cable*, 9 December 1996, 82;

19.   Synergism definition: *American Heritage Dictionary of the English Language* (Boston: Houghton Mifflin, 1981). ABC in Los Angeles: *PBS News Hour* segment "Media Mergers," aired 9 April 1997; ABC and Disney World: Richard Zoglin, "The News Wars," *Time*, 21 October 1996, 63; Westinghouse-CBS CEO quote: Turner, "Ear for the CBS Eye," 59. Seagrams: Herman and McChesney, *Global Media*, 55; Time Warner *Space Jam* quote: Richard Brown, "TBS Goes to the Movies with WB," *Broadcasting & Cable*, 20 January 1997, 47.

20.   NBC and Microsoft: *Columbia Journalism Review*, July/August 1997, 21. Time Warner production power: Johnnie L. Roberts, "The Friendly Giant: Is Time Warner Favoring Its Merger Partners?" *Newsweek*, 19 February 1996, 49. B. Erickson: Mike Meyers, "Experts Ponder: Merger of Peril or Promise? " *Star Tribune* of the Twin Cities, 1 August 1995, A10. Haeusler quote: B. J. Palermo, "Media Mergers Spark Conflict of Interest Lawsuits," *National Law Journal*, 31 March 1997, A9. Kirk Victor, "Sending Mixed Signals on Cable TV," *National Journal*, 4 October 1997, 1963. Hansen, "Debutant CLT-Ufa Aims High." Nicholas Johnson quote: Keith Conrad, "Media Mergers: First Step in a New Shift of Antitrust Analysis?" *Indiana University Law Journal* 49, no. 3: 31.

21.   Dorgan quote: Victor, "Media Monsters," 484. Polls: See Joseph S. Nye

Jr., Philip D. Zelikow, and David C. King, *Why People Don't Trust Government* (Cambridge: Harvard University Press, 1997), 1–2 and passim; Jason Vest, "Will Microsoft Squash the Alternative Press?" *U.S. News & World Report*, 28 July 1997, 49; Richard Tedesco, "Microsoft's Sidewalk Finds Montreal Streets Slippery," *Broadcasting & Cable*, 16 June 1997, 64; sidebar to "Microsoft Plans," *City Pages* of Minneapolis, 11 June 1997, 6. Hydra-like sprawl: Noack, "E-Commerce and Online News," 18.

22.   Skip Wollenberg, "It's Time for Time Warner, Turner," *Star Tribune* of the Twin Cities, 23 September 1995, D1. Susan Douglas and T. R. Durham, "Mergers, Word for Word," *Media Studies Journal* 10, nos. 2–3 (Spring/Summer 1996): 75; Kuttner, *Everything for Sale*, 266–67, 22, 66, and 35, respectively.

Chapter 6

1.   J. Apple quote: Joe Alex Morris Lecture, Kennedy School of Government, Harvard University, 18 April 1993; Lee C. Bollinger, *Images of a Free Press* (Chicago: University of Chicago Press, 1991), 26–27.

2.   James D. Squires, *Read All About It! The Corporate Takeover of America's Newspapers* (New York: Times Books, 1994), 218–19; Evans on Murdoch: PBS *Frontline* show, "Who's Afraid of Rupert Murdoch?" aired fall 1995; Westinghouse and News Corp. debt and Byron quote: *Slate* Internet magazine (on Microsoft Network) discussion of "Are Media Conglomerates Bad for Us?" 23 October 1996. Time Warner and Viacom debt: Associated Press, "Time Warner Seeking More Ways It Can Cut Costs," *Star Tribune* of the Twin Cities, 10 October 1996, D1; Associated Press, "Seagram Co. Is Buying Viacom's Half of USA Networks for $1.7 Billion," *Star Tribune* of the Twin Cities, 23 September 1997, D8; Ben Bagdikian, *The Media Monopoly*, 4th ed. (Boston: Beacon Press, 1992), 25; Robert G. Picard et al., eds., *Press Concentration and Monopoly* (Norwood, N.J.: Ablex, 1988), esp. James P. Winter, "Interlocking Directors and Economic Power," quotes on 109; Kyun-Tae Han, "Composition of Boards of Directors of Major Media Companies," *Journal of Media Economics* 1, no. 2 (Fall 1988): esp. 86, 94–95; Robert G. Picard, "Institutional Ownership of Publicly Traded U.S. Newspaper Companies," *Journal of Media Economics* 7, no. 4, quote on 57.

3.   Clurman quote in Richard Clurman, *Beyond Malice: The Media's Years of Reckoning*, rev. ed. (New York: New American Library, 1990), 253, 263; Goldensohn quote in Clurman, *Beyond Malice*, 281; Underwood quote in Doug Underwood, *When MBAs Rule the Newsroom* (New York: Columbia University Press, 1993), 15.

4.   Steve Johnson, "How Low Can TV News Go?" *Columbia Journalism Review*, July/August 1997, 24–29.

5.   On station profits and group owners' mentality: Ken Auletta, *Three Blind Mice: How the TV Networks Lost Their Way* (New York: Random House, 1991), 214, 367; John H. McManus, *Market-Driven Journalism* (Thousand Oaks, Calif.: Sage, 1994), 12. Gene Roberts, "Corporate Journalism and Community Service," *Media Studies Journal* 10, nos. 2–3 (Spring/Summer 1996): 104; Richard McCord, *The Chain Gang: One Newspaper versus the Gannett Empire* (Columbia: University of

Missouri Press, 1996), 142–43; Howard Kurtz comments: forum "The Real Dangers of Conglomerate Control," *Columbia Journalism Review*, March/April 1997, 50.

6. *Los Angeles Times* case: James Sterngold, "Visions Are Clashing at Los Angeles Times," *Star Tribune* of the Twin Cities, 14 October 1997, D1–D5; Richard Turner, "Snap, Crackle, Pop," *Newsweek*, 20 October 1997, 62–63; Tom Rosensteil, "Yet Another Peril for Journalistic Integrity," *Star Tribune* of the Twin Cities, 23 October 1997, A20. Doug Underwood, "It's Not Just in L.A.," *Columbia Journalism Review*, January/February 1998, 24–26; Thomson chain: M. L. Stein, "Get with the Program," *Editor & Publisher*, 17 May 1997, 16. Marquette survey: Bagdikian, *Media Monopoly*, 5th ed., xx. On advertiser pressure: Russ Baker, "The Squeeze: Some Advertisers Step Up the Pressure on Magazines to Alter Their Content," *Columbia Journalism Review*, September/October, 1997, 30–32; Fred Kaplan, "Stopping the Presses: With Threat of Pulling Ads, Big Accounts Have Their Say on Magazines' Content," *Boston Globe*, 15 July 1997, E1; M. Jordan speech on program previews: C-SPAN broadcast, 18 Nov. 1997; Thomas Maier, *Newhouse* (New York: St. Martin's Press, 1995), 145. Leo Bogart, *Commercial Culture: The Media System and the Public Interest* (New York: Oxford University Press, 1995), 108. Also, on local TV news and advertiser pressure, esp. regarding consumer reports, see Dean Alger, *The Media and Politics*, 2d ed. (Fort Worth, Texas: Harcourt Brace College Publishing, 1996), 141. Consumer reporting: *Newsweek*, "Consumer News Blues," 29 May 1991, 48; and see Tracy Lieberman, "What Ever Happened to Consumer Reporting?" *Columbia Journalism Review*, September/October 1994, 34–40. Howard Fineman, "Why Ted Gave It Away," *Newsweek*, 29 September 1997, 30. CNN reporters in films: Darts and Laurels, *Columbia Journalism Review*, September/October 1997, 28; "CNN to Review Appearances of Reporters in Recent Films," *Star Tribune* of the Twin Cities, 21 July 1997, E4; Marvin Kalb, "Movie about Search for Life Out There Distorts Reality Back Home," *Star Tribune* of the Twin Cities, 23 July 1997, A15. Starbucks-Trib: Darts and Laurels, *Columbia Journalism Review*, January/February 1998, 18; Disney-McDonald's: Edward S. Herman and Robert W. McChesney, *The Global Media* (London: Cassell, 1997), 55; Gannett case: Eric Black, "A New Tone of Voice?" *Star Tribune* of the Twin Cities, 28 September 1997, A22.

7. Isaacson quote from forum "Are Media Conglomerates Bad for Us?" in Microsoft *Slate* Internet magazine, 21 October 1996; and Walter Isaacson, "To Our Readers," *Time*, 21 October 1996, 20.

8. Time Warner budget and job losses and Squires quote about Madigan: James D. Squires, *Read All about It! The Corporate Takeover of America's Newspapers* (New York: Times Books, 1994), 100–101, 108; on GE quotes, see chap. 1 notes; James Fallows, *Breaking the News* (New York: Pantheon, 1996), 72–73. On CBS budget cut impacts: Robert Goldberg and Gerald Jay Goldberg, *Anchors: Brokaw, Jennings, Rather, and the Evening News* (New York: Birch Lane/Carol Publishing, 1990), 108. Grossman quote on GE: Lawrence K. Grossman, *The Electronic Republic* (New York: Alfred A. Knopf, 1995), 75; GE man, NBC president quote: Auletta, *Three Blind Mice*, 228. Frank Rich quote from *Columbia Journalism Review* forum "The Real Dangers of Conglomerate Control," March/April 1997, 50; Sig Gissler, "What Happens When Gannett Takes Over," *Columbia Journalism Review*, November/December 1997, 42–45. Goldberg and Goldberg, *Anchors*, 107; Eugene L.

Roberts, "Nothing Succeeds Like Substance," *AJR News Link* (*American Journalism Review* Web site, week of 10–16 February 1998).

9. Elizabeth Lesley, "Self-Censorship Is Still Censorship," *Business Week*, 16 December 1997, 78; Isaacson, "To Our Readers," 20. Turow study: Joseph Turow, "Organizational Tensions and Journalistic Norms: Dilemmas of News-work in the New Media System" (paper presented at the 1992 Annual Meeting of the International Communication Association), as reported in Richard Gershon, "International Deregulation and the Rise of Transnational Media Corporations," *Journal of Media Economics* 6, no. 2: 15. Corporate Control Alert case: "Synergy Watch: Playing Telephone at Time Warner," *Columbia Journalism Review*, September/October 1997, 22. On *Today* show and GE bolts story: see Goldberg and Goldberg, *Anchors*, 111. Firings by Eisner-Disney: Bagdikian, *Media Monopoly*, 5th ed., xxii; Maier's book and Newhouse press: Books section, "Fear and Favor," *Columbia Journalism Review*, May/June 1997, 77; and Mark Crispin Miller, "The Publishing Industry," in *Conglomerates and the Media*, ed. Erik Barnouw et al. (New York: New Press, 1997), 129–30.

10. Marvin Kalb quote is from an interview with the author on 30 July 1996.

11. On NBC News and Dan Rather comment: Andie Tucher, "You News," *Columbia Journalism Review*, May/June 1997, 26–31; Associated Press, "Koppel Raps Possible Network Budget Cuts," *Fargo (N.D.) Forum*, 25 September 1987, A12.

12. Center for Media and Public Affairs analysis: *Media Monitor* (Washington, D.C.: Center for Media and Public Affairs), July/August 1997. Reuven Frank and Andrew Lack comments and Dancy material: John Dancy, "Lights in a Box: Gotcha Journalism and Public Policy," *Harvard International Journal of Press/Politics* 2, no. 4 (Fall 1997): 106–13; trend in network newsmagazines quote: Jane Hall, "Interest, Economics Fuel Rise of TV News Magazines, *Star Tribune* of the Twin Cities, 6 October 1997, E8; Moyers quote: "Taking CBS News to Task," *Newsweek*, 15 September 1987; Howard Kurtz, "Tabloid Sensationalism Is Thriving on TV News," *Washington Post*, 4 July 1993, A1, A20; Catherine S. Manegold, "A Grim Wasteland on News at Six," *New York Times*, 14 June 1993, 41, 50; Rocky Mountain Media Watch analysis: Paul Klite, Robert A. Bardwell, and Jason Salzman, "Local TV News: Getting Away with Murder," *Harvard International Journal of Press/Politics* 2, no.2 (Spring 1997): 102–11; Michael Winerip, "Does Local TV News Have to Be So Bad?" *New York Times Magazine*, 11 January 1998, 38–39.

13. On local TV news coverage of state government, and for a thorough review of the studies and simpler reviews of the news in general, see 145 and 234–35 and chap. 6, chap. 8 on news coverage of the U.S. government, chap. 11 on news coverage of U.S. elections in Alger, *Media and Politics*. On British press: D. D. Guttenplan, "Dumb and Dumber? A Transatlantic Spat over the Quality of the 'Quality Press,'" *Columbia Journalism Review*, July/August 1997, 18–19; and for a partly contrary view of the British case, see Pippa Norris and Marvin Kalb, editorial, *Harvard International Journal of Press/Politics* 2, no. 4 (Fall 1997): 1–3; Herman and McChesney, *Global Media*; Carl Bernstein, "The Idiot Culture," *New Republic*, 6 June 1992; Goldberg and Goldberg, *Anchors*, 111.

14. John H. McManus, *Market-Driven Journalism* (Thousand Oaks, Calif.: Sage, 1994), especially 167–68.

15.   C. Edwin Baker, "Ownership of Newspapers: The View from Positivist Social Science," Research Paper R-12, Shorenstein Center, Kennedy School of Government, Harvard University, September 1994; Roya Akhavan-Majid, Anita Rife, and Sheila Gopinath, "Chain Ownership and Editorial Independence: A Case Study of Gannett Newspapers, *Journalism Quarterly* 68, no. 1/2 (Spring/Summer 1991): 59–66; David Pearce Demers, *The Menace of the Corporate Newspaper: Fact or Fiction?* (Ames: Iowa State University Press, 1996); Kimberley E. Fradgley and Walter E. Niebauer Jr., "London's 'Quality' Newspapers: Newspaper Ownership and Reporting Patterns," *Journalism & Mass Communication Quarterly* 72, no. 4 (Winter 1995): 902–12.

16.   Peter Phillips and Project Censored, *Censored 1997: The News That Didn't Make the News: The Year's Top Twenty-five Censored News Stories* (New York: Seven Stories Press, 1997).

17.   André Schiffrin, "The Corporatization of Publishing," *Nation*, 3 June 1996, 29–30. Murdoch-HarperCollins book case: Warren Hoge, "Murdoch Blames Staff for Embarrassment over Hong Kong Book," *New York Times*, 5 March 1998. A4; and Frank Rich, "Who's Biased Now? Take a Look at Citizen Murdoch," *Star Tribune* of the Twin Cities, 5 March 1998, A19. Viacom quote: Bagdikian, *Media Monopoly*, 5th ed., xxix. Borders' manager quote: Jeff Guin, "Literary Lions: An Endangered Species," *Star Tribune* of the Twin Cities, 14 April 1997, E7; Michael Skube, "Publishing or Packaging? It's Getting Harder to Tell" *Star Tribune* of the Twin Cities, 15 September 1997, E5.

18.   *TV Guide* case: Darts and Laurels, *Columbia Journalism Review*, March/April 1997, 21. For Gerbner studies, see, e.g., George Gerbner et al., "Charting the Mainstream: Television's Contributions to Political Orientations," *Journal of Communication* 32, no. 2 (1982); and George Gerbner et al., "Living With Television: The Dynamics of the Cultivation Process," in *Perspectives on Media Effects*, ed. Jennings Bryant and Dolf Zillman (Hillsdale, N.J.: Lawrence Earlbaum, 1986). Lichter studies: S. Robert Lichter, Linda S. Lichter, and Stanley Rothman, "From Lucy to Lacey: TV's Dream Girls," *Public Opinion* 9, no. 3 (September/October 1986); and S. Robert Lichter, Linda S. Lichter, and Stanley Rothman, *Watching America: What Television Tells Us about Our Lives* (New York: Prentice Hall, 1991). "'Psychologically Harmful' Violence Is Pervasive on TV, Study Says," *Star Tribune* of the Twin Cities, 6 February 1996, A8; Harry F. Waters, "Networks under the Gun," *Newsweek*, 12 July 1993, 65. Shales comments: "A Fan's Notes," *Broadcasting & Cable*, 26 September 1994, 35; "Poll: Americans Say TV Sex, Violence Are Getting Worse," *Star Tribune* of the Twin Cities, 21 September 1997, A10 (*Los Angeles Times* poll). Movies: David Anson, "The Dark Side of a Hit," *Newsweek*, 20 January 1997, 56; Bernard Weinraub, "Oscar Snub Shakes Big Studios," *Star Tribune* of the Twin Cities, 2 March 1997, F5.

19.   Frank Rich, "Venerable C-SPAN Is Losing Some Cable Slots to the Highest Bidder," *Star Tribune* of the Twin Cities, 6 February 1997, A21; Brian Lamb, "An Accidental Victim," *Washington Monthly*, March 1997, 20–22; Pat Aufderheide, "C-SPAN's Fight for Respect," *Columbia Journalism Review*, July/August 1997, 13–14. Jon Bream, "Revolution Radio Surrenders to Hard-Rock Format," *Star Tribune* of the Twin Cities, 12 March 1997, A1.

20.   See discussion in Alger, *Media and Politics*, 424–26; Elizabeth Jensen, "In

Funding Squeeze, PBS Cozies Up to Madison Avenue," *Wall Street Journal*, 3 July 1996, B1.

21. Beverly Kees and Bill Phillips, *Nothing Sacred: Journalism, Politics, and Public Trust in a Tell-All Age* (Nashville, Tenn.: Freedom Forum First Amendment Center, Vanderbilt University, 1994), quote on 4; Pew Research Center for the People and the Press, "Fewer Favor Media Scrutiny of Political Leaders," news release, Washington, D.C., 21 March 1997, 1; see also John W. Mashek, *Lethargy '96: How the Media Covered a Listless Campaign* (Nashville, Tenn.: Freedom Forum First Amendment Center, Vanderbilt University, 1997). "This theme . . ." study: Marion R. Just et al., *Crosstalk: Citizens, Candidates, and the Media in a Presidential Campaign* (Chicago: University of Chicago Press, 1996), 155; Evan Thomas and Gregory L. Vistica, "Fallout from a Media Fiasco," *Newsweek*, 20 July 1998, 26. Joseph S. Nye Jr., Philip D. Zelikow, and David C. King, *Why People Don't Trust Government* (Cambridge: Harvard University Press, 1997), 1.

22. William John Fox, "Junk News: Can Public Broadcasters Buck the Tabloid Tendencies of Market-Driven Journalism? A Canadian Experience," Discussion Paper D-26, Shorenstein Center, Kennedy School of Government, Harvard University, August 1997; Newspaper editors ethics code: reprinted in Louis A. Day, *Ethics in Media Communications: Cases and Controversies* (Belmont, Calif.: Wadsworth, 1991), 351; J. Apple, Joe Alex Morris Lecture, Kennedy School of Government, Harvard University, 8 April 1993; McClatchy: Squires, *Read All About It!* 82–83; Tom Rosensteil–Belo Corp.: "Yet Another Peril for Journalistic Integrity," *Star Tribune* of the Twin Cities, 23 October 1997, A20. *Media Monitor* (Washington, D.C.: Center for Media and Public Affairs), May/June 1997; Dean of Columbia University Law School quote: Clurman, *Beyond Malice*, 250–51; Squires, *Read All About It!* xv; Gene Roberts, "Corporate Journalism and Community Service," *Media Studies Journal* 10, no. 2–3 (Spring/Summer 1996): 107.

Chapter 7

1. Ofer Feldman, *Politics and the News Media in Japan* (Ann Arbor: University of Michigan Press, 1993), esp. 10–13; quote on newspapers' investment in TV networks on 13. Roya Akhavan-Majid, "The Press as an Elite Power Group in Japan," *Journalism Quarterly* 67, no. 4 (Winter 1990): 1008; Jon Herskovitz, "Fuji Television: New Digs, Deals Mark New Era," *Variety*, 15 September 1997, 43.

2. Herskovitz, "Fuji Television," 43; "Asahi Shimbun to Cooperate with Murdoch," Jiji Press Ticker Service, 5 September 1996, off Internet.; Akhavan-Majid, "Press as Power Group," 1009.

3. Akhavan-Majid, "Press as Power Group," 1007.

4. Bill Powell, "The Capitalist Czars," *Newsweek*, 17 March 1997, 30.

5. Melor Sturua, interview with author, 11 August 1997, Minneapolis. Ellen Mickiewicz, *Changing Channels: Television and the Struggle for Power in Russia* (New York: Oxford University Press, 1997); and Ellen Mickiewicz, "Transition and Democratization: The Role of Journalists in Eastern Europe and the Former Soviet Union," in *The Politics of News, The News of Politics*, ed. Doris A. Graber, Denis

McQuail, and Pippa Norris (Washington, D.C.: Congressional Quarterly Press, 1998).

6.   Mickiewicz, "Transition and Democratization"; "The Global Power Elite," *Forbes*, 28 July 1997, 102; Mickiewicz, *Changing Channels*, 222; Sturua, interview.

7.   Mickiewicz, *Changing Channels*, 222–23; Phil Reeves, "Russian Press Facing Threat to Free Speech," *Independent* (Britain), 18 April 1997, 14; "Big Stakes in Russian Media," *Baltimore Sun*, 4 July 1997, 18A. In a book and separate book chapter, Mickiewicz has discussed developments in media control during the transition period in Russia and in Eastern Europe and the general patterns of the media's role in Russia's political system in far more detail than is possible here. See Mickiewicz chapter in Doris Graber, Denis McQuail, and Pippa Norris, eds., *The Politics of News, The News of Politics* (Washington, D.C.: Congressional Quarterly Press, 1998); Mickiewicz, *Changing Channels*.

8.   Sturua, interview.

9.   Sturua, interview.

10.   Ellen Mickiewicz, personal communication to author, 15 November 1997; Vanora Bennett, "Troubling News for Izvestia Paper," *Los Angeles Times*, 18 July 1997, A5; Neela Banerjee, "Big Business Takes Over," *Columbia Journalism Review*, November/December 1997, 59–61; Mickiewicz, *Changing Channels*, 224. See also David Hoffman, "Russia's Robber Barons," *Washington Post National Weekly Edition*, 12 January 1998, 15.

11.   Reeves, "Russian Press Facing Threat "; Stephen F. Cohen, "The Truth of Russian 'Reform': Tragedy—Why Have U.S. Media Been So Silent? " *Star Tribune* of the Twin Cities, 9 January 1997, A18; Sturua, interview; "Yeltsin Ousts Billionaire from National Security Post," *Star Tribune* of the Twin Cities, 6 November 1997, A8.

12.   Edward Baumeister, vice president, Independent Journalism Foundation, Budapest, Hungary, personal communication to author. On "participatory model" and "proposals" and other matters: Wolfgang Kleinwaechter, "Broadcasting in Transition: Media Freedom between Political Freedom and Economic Pressures in Eastern and Central Europe," in *Democratizing Communication: Comparative Perspectives on Information and Power,* ed. Mashoed Bailie and Dwayne Winseck (Cresskill, N.J.: Hampton Press, 1997), 245.

13.   On CME holdings and operations: Louise McElvogue, "Must-See Euro-TV: Thanks to Early Foothold, CME is No.1 in Central Europe," *Los Angeles Times*, 13 February 1997, D4; Lisa Gubernick, "Chip Off the Old Block," *Forbes*, 24 February 1997, 103 (Lauder quote); Leslie Adler, "CME See TV Empire in Ex-Communist European States," *Reuters European Business Report*, 21 February 1997, off Internet. On print media in Czech Republic and other material: Baumeister, personal communication. Baumeister quote on government control efforts and internal concentration in Hungary: Edward J. Baumeister, "Opportunity Blown in Eastern Europe," *Harvard International Journal of Press/Politics* 2, no. 1 (Winter 1997): 104, 106. Quote on "media wars" in Hungary: Mickiewicz, "Transition and Democratization." On the question of cross-ownership in Czech media: Michele Legge, "A Bigger Slice of the Pie," *Prague Post*, 17 January 1996, off Internet.

14.   On two megamedia cases: "E.U. Clears Polish Venture," (news brief),

Cable & Satellite Express, 2, off Internet.; Louise McElvogue, "Must-See Euro-TV," D4. Mickiewicz quote: Mickiewicz, "Transition and Democratization."

15. Dean Alger, *The Media and Politics*, 2d ed. (Fort Worth, Texas: Harcourt Brace College Publishing, 1996), 99, 424–26; TV channels in Western Europe: Richard Parker, *Mixed Signals: The Prospects for Global Television News* (New York: Twentieth Century Fund Press, 1995), 30.

16. On early newspaper concentration: John Eldridge, Jenny Kitzinger, and Kevin Williams, *The Mass Media and Power in Modern Britain* (New York: Oxford University Press, 1997), 27; Colin Seymour-Ure, *The British Press and Broadcasting since 1945*, 2d ed. (Oxford: Blackwell), 118. On concentration in newspapers today: Kevin Williams, *Get Me a Murder a Day! A History of Mass Communication in Britain* (London: Arnold, 1998), 226; Ralph Negrine, *Politics and the Mass Media in Britain* (New York: Routledge, 1994), 62. On conglomerate control, etc.: Williams, *Murder a Day*, 228–29; and see Seymour-Ure, *British Press*, chap. 5.

17. ITV "belligerently commercial": Euromedia Research Group, ed. *The Media in Western Europe*, 2d ed. (Newbury Park, Calif.: Sage, 1997), 252. Impact on news: Williams, *Murder a Day*, 250–51. New ownership rules, actions by Majors government: Euromedia Research Group, *Media in Western Europe*, 2d ed., 252. BSkyB merger, etc.: Euromedia Research Group, *Media in Western Europe*, 247–48. Murdoch use of *Times* to support Thatcher, etc.: Gustaf von Dewell, "The Campaigns of the Media Barons," European Institute for the Media Web site, bulletin, April 1997. "Fundamental changes": Williams, *Murder a Day*, 242.

18. Largest newspaper groups: Euromedia Research Group, *Media in Western Europe*, 2d ed., 83; Hermann Meyn, *Mass Media in the Federal Republic of Germany* (Hamburg: Edition Colloquium, Volker Speiss, 1994), 64–70. Largest magazine groups: Meyn, *Media in Germany*, 64. Result, East German publishing: Euromedia Research Group, *Media in Western Europe*, 2d ed., 84.

19. German TV and multimedia control: Peter J. Humphreys, *Media and Media Policy in Germany*, 2d ed. (Oxford, England: Berg, 1994), 277–79. Digital TV consortium: "Media Business," European Institute for the Media Web site, December 1997; Mary Williams Walsh, "Kirch's Digital TV Efforts in Germany May Be Back on Track," *Los Angeles Times*, 26 July 1997, D1, D3. German law and impact, Bertelsmann: Euromedia Research Group, *Media in Western Europe*, 2d ed., 88.

20. Michael Palmer and Claude Sorbets, "France," in *The Media in Western Europe*, ed. Euromedia Research Group, 1st ed. (Newbury Park, Calif.: Sage, 1993), quotes on 63, 64. On increasing concentration, etc.: Euromedia Research Group, *Media in Western Europe*, 2d ed., 63. Public TV legitimacy crisis: Raymond Kuhn, *The Media in France* (London: Routledge, 1995), 198.

21. Eric Hansen, "Debutant CLT-Ufa Aims High," *Hollywood Reporter*, 14 January 1997, off Internet; Richard Gershon, "International Deregulation and the Rise of Transnational Media Corporations," *Journal of Media Economics* 6, no. 2: 13; Richard Parker, *Mixed Signals: The Prospects for Global Television News* (New York: Twentieth Century Fund Press, 1995), 82–83.

22. Filipino troops and MTV: Parker, *Mixed Signals*, 6. Nickelodeon worldwide: Edward Herman and Robert W. McChesney, *The Global Media* (London: Cassell, 1997), 65, 86–87. ESPN, NBC, and ads, etc.: Herman and McChesney, *Global Media*, 83, 63, respectively.

23.   Australia: Herman and McChesney, *Global Media*, 102; Colin Seymour-Ure, *British Press*, 129. New Zealand: Herman and McChesney, *Global Media*, 179–82; Stephanie Mehta, "Ameritech to Sell Stake in Overseas Carrier," *Wall Street Journal*, 23 December 1997, B5.

24.   Brazil: Herman and McChesney, *Global Media*, 163–66; Marinho wealth: "The Global Power Elite," *Forbes*, 28 July 1997, 126. Mexico: Tim Golden, "In Sale of TV Networks, Mexico Seeks to Create a Rival to Mighty Televisa," *New York Times*, 7 June 1993, A5.

25.   Quoted in Ken Auletta, *Three Blind Mice: How the TV Networks Lost Their Way* (New York: Random House, 1991), 86.

Chapter 8

1.   Roosevelt quote: Michael J. Sandel, *Democracy's Discontent* (Cambridge, Mass.: Harvard University Press, 1995), 255–56. Senator Hart quote: Anthony Sampson, *The Sovereign State of ITT* (New York: Stein & Day, 1973), 223. Charles E. Lindblom, *Politics and Markets* (New York: Basic Books, 1977), 199–200. Murdoch and Labour Party: Steve Boggan and Anthony Bevins, "Murdoch Faces Global Tax Inquiry, but Blair Backs Him," *Independent*, 4 February 1998, 1. On Murdoch political money: Charles R. Babcock and Ruth Marcus, "RNC Gave $2 Million to Tax-Reform Group; Media Tycoon Murdoch Donated $1 Million to California GOP," *Washington Post*, 29 October 1996, A9; and see Federal Election Commission reports.

2.   Walter Russell Mead, "Private Pursuits," *Los Angeles Times*, 28 September 1997, M1. Commission on Freedom of the Press quote: Robert D. Leigh, *A Free and Responsible Press* (Chicago: University of Chicago Press, 1947), 14. George Soros, "The Capitalist Threat," *Atlantic Monthly*, February 1997, 45. Okun quote: Robert Kuttner, *Everything for Sale: The Virtues and Limits of Markets* (New York: Alfred A. Knopf, 1996), 35.

3.   Bierce quote: Benjamin Barber, *Strong Democracy* (Berkeley and Los Angeles: University of California Press, 1984). E. E. Schattschneider, *The Semisovereign People* (New York: Holt, Rinehart & Winston, 1960).

4.   W. Russell Neuman, *The Future of the Mass Audience* (New York: Cambridge University Press, 1991), 137–38 and 165, respectively.

5.   Daniel Yankelovich, *Coming to Public Judgment* (Syracuse, New York: University of Syracuse Press, 1991). Bill Gates, *The Road Ahead*, rev. ed. (New York: Penguin Books, 1996), xiv.

Chapter 9

1.   See Web site: www.mediademocracy.org. And for the Institute for Alternative Journalism: www.alternet.org; phone: (415) 284-1420.

2.   "Privatized Broadcasting Service," *Extra!* July/August 1997, 4. Lawrence K. Grossman, *The Electronic Republic: Reshaping Democracy in the Infor-*

mation Age (New York: Viking Press, 1995), 183; William Hoynes, *Public Television for Sale* (Boulder, Colo.: Westview Press, 1994), 2; Jeff Cohen and Norman Soloman, "Both Sides in Broadcast Flap Overstate Case," *Star Tribune* of the Twin Cities, 22 January 1995, 21A.

3. *Quality Time?* (New York: Twentieth Century Fund Press, 1993), 6; *A Public Trust: Report of the Carnegie Commission on the Future of Public Broadcasting* (New York: Bantam Books, 1977), 22.

4. David Walstad, "More and More TV Ads Mean Less and Less Show," *Star Tribune* of the Twin Cities, 12 October 1997, F3.

5. Geller quoted in Lawrence K. Grossman, "Bullies on the Block," *Columbia Journalism Review*, January/February 1997, 19.

6. Consumers' Union quote: Kirk Victor, "Reach Out and Crush Someone?" *National Journal*, 7 June 1997, 1132. Donald M. Gillmor et al., *Mass Communication Law: Cases and Comment*, 5th ed. (St. Paul, Minn.: West Publishing, 1990), 541. FCC statement of principle quoted in Lucas A. Powe Jr., *The Fourth Estate and the Constitution: Freedom of the Press in America* (Berkeley and Los Angeles: University of California Press, 1991), 204. Owen M. Fiss, *The Irony of Free Speech* (Cambridge, Mass.: Harvard University Press, 1996), 37, 59. Robert Pitofsky, "The Political Content of Antitrust," *University of Pennsylvania Law Review* 127, no. 1 (January 1979): 1051, 1957. Pitofsky "tougher stance" quote, etc.: Brian Gruly, "Pitofsky Will Test Marketplace of Ideas Theory in FTC's Review of Time Warner–Turner Deal," *Wall Street Journal*, 9 October 1995, A14; Robert Pitofsky, "Antitrust in the Decade Ahead: Some Predictions about Merger Enforcement," *Antitrust Law Journal* 57, no. 1 (January 1988): 71. John C. Busterna, "Daily Newspaper Chains and the Antitrust Laws," *Journalism Monographs*, no. 110 (March 1989). Keith Conrad, "Media Mergers: First Step in a New Shift of Antitrust Analysis?" *Indiana University Law Journal* 49, no. 3. Loftus E. Becker Jr., "Comments on 'The Telecommunications Act of 1996,' by Thomas G. Krattenmaker," *Connecticut Law Review* 28, no. 1 (Fall 1996): 175.

7. "Groucho Marx's Letter on 'Casablanca' Tickles the Library of Congress," *Star Tribune* of the Twin Cities, 12 October 1997, A10.

8. Kimmelman quote: testimony in Senate Commerce Committe Hearing on Competition in the Cable TV Industry, 10 April 1997.

Index

About the Author

Dean Alger received his Ph.D. in political science from the University of California, Riverside, and has taught college in Minnesota, North Dakota, Iowa, and California. He has been a fellow in the Joan Shorenstein Center on the Press, Politics and Public Policy in Harvard University's John F. Kennedy School of Government, where he codirected the study *Crosstalk: Citizens, Candidates, and the Media in a Presidential Campaign.* He is also author of *The Media and Politics* (2d ed.) and has written widely on the media's role in public affairs. He has served as an analyst for commercial and public television and radio and for newspapers. A resident of Minneapolis, he is active in election-reform initiatives in Minnesota, including the Minnesota Compact. For the 1998 election, he served as director of the Citizens' Campaign Advertising Code.